Designed and created by
Berkeley Publishers Ltd.
9 Warwick Court
London WC1R 5DJ

Text: Angela Thompson

Editor: Gaynor Cauter
Design: Keith Worthington and
   David Moore
Consultant: Sally Baker
Photography: Chris Ridley
Illustrations: Ray and Corinne
   Burrows

**Photographs, samples and
   equipment supplied by:**
Bellinky Linking Machine, Belna
   Corporation
Bernina, Bogod Machine Company
   Limited
Elna Sewing Machines (GB)
   Limited
Frister & Rossman Sewing
   Machines Limited
Viking, Husqvarna Limited
Jones & Brother Sewing Machine
   Company
Necchi (Great Britain) Ltd
New Home Sewing Machine
   Company Ltd
Pfaff (Britain) Limited
Riccar (U.K.) Ltd
Singer Company (U.K.) Ltd
Vigorelli (U.K.) Limited

Samples contributed by:
Silvia Amner
Stella Bird
Ina Buckland
Gaynor Cauter
Joan Appleton Fisher
Lorna Langton
Eve Petty
Jill Purchall
Angela Thompson
Jane Thompson

Note: All measurements and
conversions are approximate
unless otherwise stated.

*Jacket illustration: The latest in
sewing machine technology – the
Memory 7 by New Home.*

The Complete Book of the
Sewing Machine

Angela Thompson

HAMLYN
London · New York · Sydney · Toronto

Sewing Machines
Contents

Sewing machines

Mastering the miracle of the sewing machine

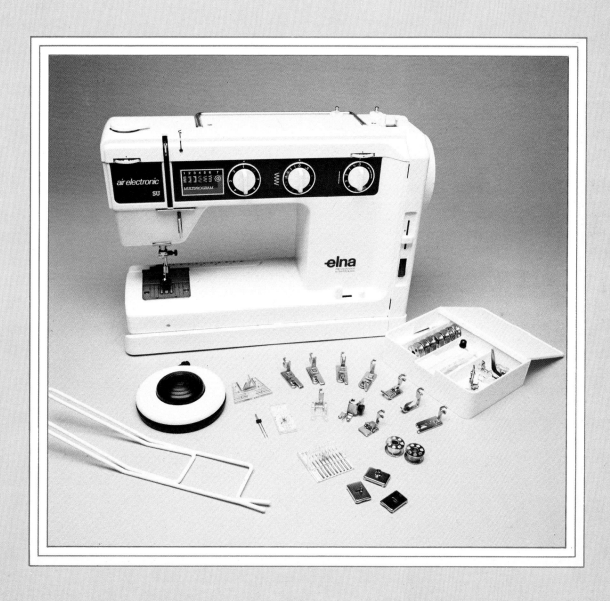

Choosing your machine

A sewing machine of one kind or another can be found in the vast majority of homes. Many of these machines are never used to their full extent, and some are not used at all. This book is intended to help you to understand and use your sewing machine to the best possible advantage. It will help you to choose alternative methods and discover new ways of making things. Manufacturers of modern machines have simplified many machine processes during the last few years. However, in doing so, their machines have either been made to look more complicated or have been streamlined into shapes bearing little resemblance to familiar traditional machines.

An instruction book is essential to every machine. If your machine is old and the book has been lost, try writing to the makers or place an advertisement for one in the paper. Many instruction books tend to assume the user has a prior knowledge of how to operate a sewing machine. Others are loosely translated from some foreign language. This book does not take the place of your machine instruction book, but is intended to be used in conjunction with it. The aim is to give an understanding of machines generally rather than of one specific model or make.

A good sewing machine can cost a considerable sum of money, but a well-made machine will last a lifetime. Many venerable machines are still in constant use today. If you are considering buying a new machine, buy as good a model as you can possibly afford. Go to a reputable dealer who will undertake after-sales service. It is no use buying a machine cheaply from a store or a mail order firm unless the after-sales service is guaranteed. Some dealers do not like servicing machines which were not bought from their own establishment.

Before buying a machine, decide what type of sewing you wish to do and where you are going to do it. A simple-to-operate zig-zag machine with a free arm, an automatic buttonhole and choice of stretch and overlock stitches will be more than adequate for all simple dressmaking. A heavier type of machine, with full needle penetration power and slow stitch control, will be better for heavy fabrics and tailoring processes. If you make things to sell, for charity stalls, or just love decorative effects, then choose a machine with plenty of automatic patterns. For those who like gadgets, there are many attachments to help in all kinds of machine processes, both decorative and practical.

If space is limited and your sewing is done on one end of the kitchen or dining room table, then you will need a portable, lightweight machine which can easily be packed away. A machine that is constantly put away tends to stay put away. If it is at all possible to have a permanent place for your machine, do so. There is a choice of folding cabinets on the market and this is a good compromise. The ideal arrangement is to have a sewing corner or a sewing room. A spare bedroom or a guest room can do double duty if care-

A Bernina Record free-arm machine and a Jones 641 flat-bed (behind).

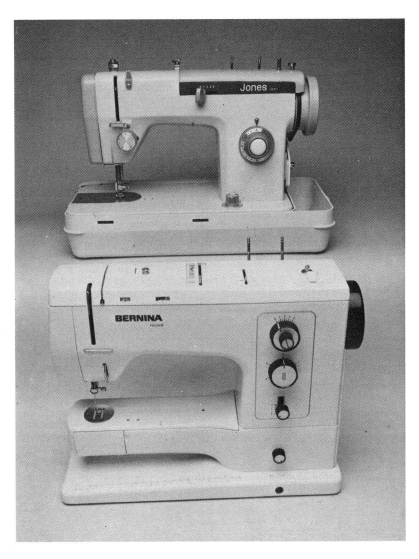

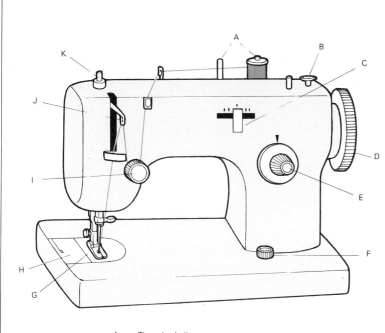

A	Thread spindles
B	Bobbin winding position
C	Stitch width control
D	Balance wheel
E	Stitch length control including reverse
F	Drop feed control
G	Needle plate and feed teeth
H	Bobbin location
I	Tension control
J	Take-up lever
K	Presser bar pressure control
L	Pattern selector
M	Buttonhole control

fully planned. Understandably, some sort of compromise is necessary if you want to sew heavy fabrics but have no permanent place for sewing. Make sure you can lift the machine by yourself, easily, without strain.

Plan your sewing area so that everything you need is to hand. An old desk with drawers divided into compartments for cottons, needles and machine tools makes a good sewing table if you have no cabinet. If you work in a room that is also used for other purposes, fit out a cupboard with pull-out, compartmented boxes that can be slid back into place when you finish sewing. Always sew in a good light. As well as the machine light you will need an adjustable lamp and, where possible, daylight from a window. A chair at the right height will make your sewing position and posture better, saving backache and strain. Use a dish or a pincushion for pins and always have a small pair of scissors at hand.

If you are buying a new machine, do your own market research first. Try out as many different makes as you can, using scraps of your own material – not the material used by the demonstrator which will show all the stitches to advantage. Use the material swatches double and machine from the fold towards you. This will show any tendency of the machine to sew unevenly and the fabric to 'creep'. Ask the demonstrator to show you the stretch stitches and those designed for neatening edges. Don't make up your mind at once, but go home and have a think about it.

When you get your machine home, read the instruction book carefully from cover to cover. Have the machine in front of you and name all the parts. Identify the attachments

1 (Left) An automatic free-arm machine with concealed tension threading; (above) a flat-bed zigzag machine with exposed threading.

and special feet, one by one. Become familiar with your machine, take care of it, and it will serve you well. Use it whenever you can, for whatever you can. You bought your machine at expense, to save money and to give you that greatest of pleasures – making something yourself, that is yours and therefore completely unique.

It is almost impossible for us to conceive, in this era of mass produced clothing, that before Queen Victoria's reign, virtually all sewing was done by hand.

Up until the end of the 18th century nearly all clothing, for both men and women, was sewn by tailors; the garments being 'built-up' on the customer. As dresses became lighter and simpler, dressmakers took over. Sometimes, the dresses which can be seen in our museums, are beautifully sewn with neat, strong backstitches and carefully inserted pipings and trimmings. Others are almost thrown together, hurried running stitches telling their own sad story.

The early lock stitch machines were either too heavy or too light for effective domestic sewing and the chain stitch machines unreliable. One ladies' magazine urged its readers to sew each seam twice, from opposite ends, in case the chain stitches should inadvertently unravel. It was not until the late 1860s that sewing machines took over and became part of the domestic scene. Dressmakers, whether professional or amateur, took to the new invention and delighted in covering their clothes with masses of frills and trimmings, ruching, piping and braiding. The machine manufacturers soon found they could boost their sales with the addition of special attachments.

Although the mechanical principles of those early machines remain basically the same today, the Victorian dressmaker would hardly recognise the modern machine, and would find its capabilities un-

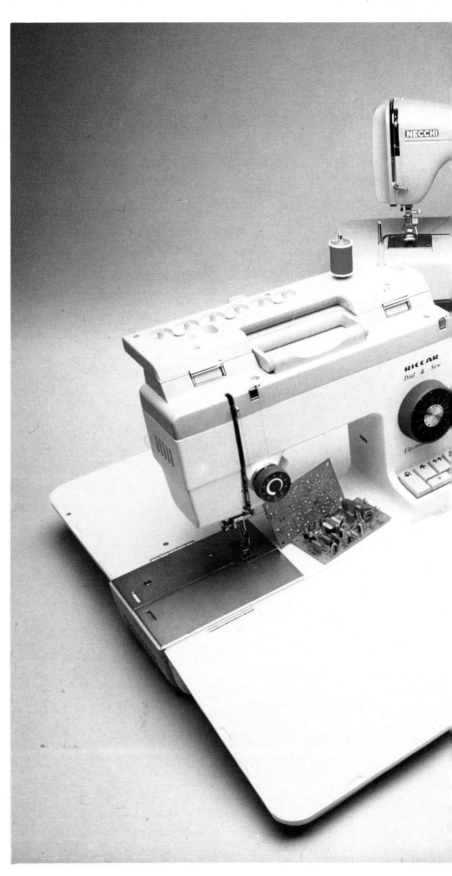

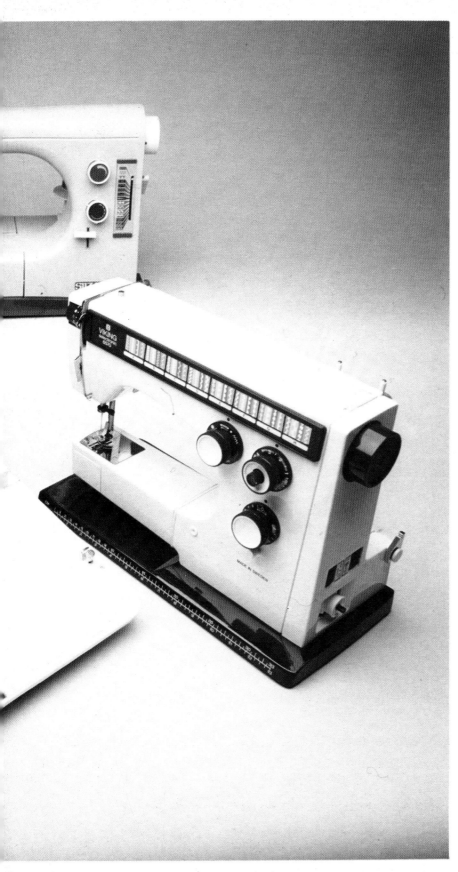

believable. Every few years there is a revolution in domestic machine design. The first innovation was the substitution of electrical power for hand- or treadle-operated machines. The next was the introduction of the domestic *swing needle*, or *zig-zag*, machine with a narrow *free arm* for easy garment sewing. Soon the manufacturers had added *pattern cams* which could control the swing needle to form *automatic patterns*. Later, *fully automatic* machines were introduced with an automatic reverse feed, which meant that buttonholes could be stitched without turning the cloth and patterns and stretch stitches could be sewn in *trimotion*. This combined the side to side motion of the needle with the backwards and forwards motion of the feed.

The latest development is the *electronic* machine. The integrated circuit allows full needle penetration power, even when sewing at slow speeds. The minute microprocesser, or miniature computer, has already become the brain of some new sewing machines, allowing touch button control and pattern memory.

With the variety of patterns available becoming almost limitless, manufacturers are now turning to ways of making the actual sewing processes easier, giving skill to the sewer of lesser experience. These new machines require a radical change in attitude by the machine user. At the moment the inventive expertise of the manufacturer has far outstripped the user's grasp of the potentials of these machines. Old ways may die hard, but with these new ideas, exciting developments in sewing and the allied crafts are just around the corner. Whether these machines remain a manufacturer's gimmick, electronic playthings, or become the path to new experiments in design interpretation is up to us.

(Clockwise) Riccar, Necchi and Viking sewing machines.

History of the sewing machine

The story of the sewing machine is not only one of brilliant innovation; it is also a story of bitter rivalries, persecution and legal process.

At first the inventors tried to imitate the motions of hand sewing – especially the popular chain stitch embroidery, or tambour work, so-called from the circular frame in which the fabric was stretched.

Aristocratic ladies passed their time creating delicate designs, using the slender, hooked needle to draw the thread from beneath in a series of chain stitches. In industry, thousands of poor women and girls worked very long hours at oblong frames that stretched the fine muslin dress fabric, which was so fashionable at the time. As the demand increased, manual labour alone could no longer cope, and the sewing machine was born.

1750 Karl Weisenthal, a German, invented a machine with an eye in the middle of the needle and a point at both ends capable of sewing a single thread running stitch.

1790 Thomas Saint, an Englishman, patented a design for a machine to sew leather. This machine made a chain stitch with a tambour-type needle to produce a mechanical crochet or chain stitch. It is doubtful whether it actually worked.

1810 Baltasar Krems of Mayern, Germany, made a chain stitch machine for sewing night caps. This had a crank-operated needle and a continuous material feed, but its greatest innovation was a needle with an eye in the tip.

1814-1830 Josef Madersperger, an Austrian tailor, used two of these eye-pointed needles in a machine producing a stitch resembling a lock-stitch. He was awarded a bronze medal, but afterwards faced a life of prejudice and died in an almshouse.

1830 Barthelemy Thimonnier, a French tailor, produced the first commercially viable sewing machine. Worked by foot treadle, a barbed tambour-like needle pierced the cloth and drew up thread from below, through the upper loop, to form a chain stitch. The fabric was fed through the machine manually by the operator since there was no mechanical 'feed'. By 1831 he had 80 machines at work making Army uniforms. But jealous French tailors, fearing for the livelihood, destroyed his workshop, Thimonnier fled and managed to save one machine, which he exhibited at country fairs.

1832-1834 Walter Hunt, an American, invented the first lock-stitch machine for sewing corsets. An eye-pointed needle carrying one thread, combined with a shuttle carrying a second thread. Hunt's daughter, Caroline, a good Quaker, persuaded him not to patent the machine, because it would put poor seamstresses out of work.

1846 Elias Howe Jr, an American, patented a machine with an eye-pointed, curved needle that stitched a loop through which a shuttle thread passed, so forming a lock stitch. The feed had to be reset every six inches and was awkward to use. Meeting indifference in America, he sold the British patent rights to William Thomas in England but returned penniless, four years later.

Late 1840s Allen B. Wilson, an American, invented a shuttle, pointed at both ends, which made an improved lock-stitch.

1848 Thimonnier went to England and in 1850 was granted an American patent.

1849 John Bachelor, an American, invented a feed device that moved the cloth horizontally, not in the vertical plane.

1850 S. C. Blodgett and J. A. Lerow, Americans, introduced a shuttle with a circular movement and a thread tension control. These machines were manufactured by Orson C. Phelps of Boston.

1850-1851 Isaac Merrit Singer, who came from a poor German immigrant family and had already invented a wood-carving machine, felt he could improve the Blodgett machine. With the help of Phelps and a borrowed 40 dollars, he worked 18 hours a day for 11 days, but the newly invented machine would not work. He nearly abandoned the project but then remembered a certain thread adjustment, returned to the shop after midnight and finally triumphed. This was the first practical sewing machine. It had an overhanging arm, a vertical needle, a yielding presser foot, a serrated wheel to 'feed' the cloth, a horizontal shuttle moving to-and-fro beneath, and foot treadle operation. This heavy duty machine, known as the No 1, was more suited to industry than domestic sewing. The patent was granted in August 1851.

1851 Elias Howe returned from England to find his original ideas had been incorporated in the improved machines. This was the start of the 'sewing machine war'. A court case followed, Howe suing Singer and two other manufacturers. Singer was joined by Edward Clarke, a lawyer, and they became equal partners in the Singer Company, which was founded in 1851. Elias Howe

(Below) An early 19th century Singer machine.
(Right) One of the latest machines from the Singer range.

won his first court battle, but when he himself set up as a manufacturer his machines would only work with the improvements made by the other companies.

1851 A. B. Wilson, an American, patented a rotary hook and in 1852 a 'floating' disc bobbin. A rotating hook caught the needle thread which was carried round, interlocking with the bobbin thread, ready to be slipped off and drawn up to form the next stitch. In partnership with **Nathaniel Wheeler,** he produced a beautifully made, lightweight machine.

1854 Wilson brought out an improved version of this machine. A four-motion feed automatically moved the cloth under the needle, producing even stitches. This was the forerunner of the modern lockstitch machine.

1855 James Gibbs, a Virginian, invented a revolving hook for a chain stitching machine. **Charles Willcox** helped with improvements.

1856 The Sewing Machine Combination was formed when four sewing machine companies finally agreed to pool all their patents.

1856 Clarke, Singer's lawyer-partner, introduced a method of hiring out his costly machines while the purchaser payed by instalments. The revolutionary idea of hire purchase had an even greater impact on modern civilization than the machines it helped to sell. Singer's other innovation was to build splendidly furnished showrooms in which to sell his machines.

1857 Willcox and Gibbs, on opposite sides during the American Civil War, reunited to perfect their chain stitch machine.

1858 Singer, faced with strong competition, brought out the 'family machine', a lighter version of his No 1. In 1859 the 'new family' was an improvement and was in production until 1865 when another version was introduced. All these machines had vibrating shuttles. This system was used in many machines up till 1939.

1859 William Jones, an Englishman, owned an engineering firm specializing in small steam engines. He decided to manufacture sewing machines, developing and improving upon Elias Howe's long shuttle. He was always anxious to improve design and production methods. His first factory was built at Guide Bridge, Manchester.

1862 Pfaff introduced their first sewing machine. This is now in the Deutches Museum in Munich.

1864 Frister Rossmann star-

ted to manufacture sewing machines at their original factory in Berlin.

1869 Singer Co. first manufactured in Glasgow and later at Kilbowie, Clydebank. Singer added the letter K (Kilbowie) to their identification. These machines were known as the **K** class.

1869 William Jones took out his first sewing machine patent, and in 1870 built a new factory at Guide Bridge. Machines produced for export to the tropics had heavy metal plating on unpainted parts to prevent rust.

1872 Huskvarna (Viking), of Sweden, who made rifles, started producing sewing machines after a slump in the munitions industry. Their first model was nicknamed the 'catback' because of its arched shape.

1872 Positive take-up was invented. Machines were fitted with a take-up lever which helped control the tightness of the loop of thread made when the needle pierced the cloth.

1878 Max Gritzner invented the rotary hook with integrated bobbin movement.

1879 Singer introduced machines fitted with an oscillating hook and a round bobbin placed horizontally.

1882 John Kayer, a German, invented the first zig-zag machine.

1883 Huskvarna (Viking) introduced the Freja model, capable of sewing stitches in a neat line, driven by gears and all mechanical parts enclosed. The Triumph followed in 1885.

1884 Wheeler Wilson brought out patents for automatic buttonhole sewing obtained by a switch cam mechanism, and in 1885 patented a device for twin-needle sewing. Two needles mounted on a single needlebar sewed parallel seams connected by a single underthread.

1886 Friedrich Gegauf (later Bernina Co.) of Steckburn, Switzerland, founded a mechanical workshop in the buildings of a former Cistercian monastery. He invented and produced monogram embroidery machines. In 1893 he built

the world's first hemstitching machines. This process became known as 'gegaufing'.

1900 Frister Rossmann machines were imported into England.

1902 Singer produced the first domestic machine with a horizontal oscillating hook, concealed needlebar and a link take-up.

1903 Viking Huskvarna introduced the central bobbin (CB) system with an oscillating hook. This dominated the world market for more than 50 years.

1919 Vickers Ltd introduced reversible feed.

1920 Alfa was a company started by a small group of Basque workers from the northern Spanish town of Eibar. At first, they made revolvers but in 1925 they turned to making sewing machines. These were strongly made, simple to operate and were exported to countries all over the world.

1920 Necchi, iron founders, established in Italy in 1835, produced straight-stitch sewing machines.

1921 Singer introduced a portable, electric, domestic sewing machine, and in 1931 one that stitched forwards and backwards and had exact stitch-length control.

1932 Bernina produced a new machine. The introduction of artificial silk, which was unsuitable for hemstitching, forced F. Gegauf to turn to the production of a sturdy, high-quality domestic machine.

1934-1939 Yasui, a Japanese, who produced machines for the manufacture of straw hats, became the founder of the Brother Sewing Machine Co.

Mid 30s Arnaldo Vigorelli of Pavia, Italy, chief engineer for a sewing machine company, decided to start his own family business.

1938 Necchi were the first to design, produce and market a zig-zag machine for domestic use.

1940 Ramon Casas, whose mother worked an industrial free arm machine, invented a portable domestic model made from strong, light metal alloy. It had a built in sewing light, an electric motor and a carrying case that could be converted to a sewing table. Later, this was manufactured by a Swiss firm, under the name of Elna.

1943 Bernina brought out the first portable free-arm zig-zag sewing machine.

1948 Riccar Co. began to manufacture sewing machines in Tokyo.

1952 Elna produced the first domestic machine with automatic utility and ornamental stitches.

Late 1950s Vigorelli developed the first domestic machine with an oscillating needleplate to give a stitch patterning width of 12 mm ($\frac{1}{2}$ in).

1961 Viking Huskvarna used automatic feed for stretch stitches and colour-coded pattern setting.

1965 Frister Rossmann machines, manufactured in Japan, were made to British design by Kenneth Grange, RDI, FSIA.

1965 Necchi introduced a compact machine incorporating a single pattern selector. This machine was later awarded Place of Honour for Industrial Design, Museum of Modern Art, New York.

1966-1967 Viking Huskvarna were the first to adapt a sewing machine for the use of the blind, with knobs and controls marked in braille, and special guides and needles with slotted threading. Adaptions for the handicapped included extensions for the controls, tongs for taking the bobbin in and out and elbow-worked speed controllers. Newer models could be adapted.

1968 Elna Lotus produced the first compact machine incorporating the carrying case which opened out to form a work surface.

1968 Jones Sewing Machine Co. joined with Brother International.

An early Weir chain-stitch machine and some items of Victoriana.

1969 Pfaff made the first domestic machine to have built-in dual feed, and the first to incorporate an electronic circuit to control the motor for slow-speed running and full-needle penetration power.

1969 Newhome, a subsidiary of Janome Sewing Machine Co., Japan, were established at Stockport, Cheshire.

1971 Viking Huskvarna brought out the first self-oiling machine.

1976 Riccar made an electronic machine, the first in Japan, with push-button control and without a foot pedal.

1976 Singer brought out the futura, the first fully electronic machine with a microprocesser.

1978 Elna's Air Electronic had the first air pressure foot control.

1979 Newhome produced the first electronic machine with programmed pattern memory.

Machines and their functions

The choice of sewing machines available on the market today appears completely bewildering at first. The number of firms who manufacture these machines is limited. Each has a range of machines which varies from the simple to the sophisticated and these generally correspond to those of competitive manufacturers. Each firm has certain design elements or patented features that are unique to their own machines. These design features can often be traced back to the early machines, having evolved gradually over the years.

Although the manufacturers are constantly bringing out new models, they still continue producing those which have been popular during the past years and which continue to fulfil a need. However, there is a limit to how many types of machine they can continue to produce

and from time to time, certain models have to be dropped. A few firms still produce a plain straight-stitch machine, but in general, the simpler models are now zig-zag machines with buttonhole facility and a number of stretch and utility stitches. Presumably there must eventually be a limit to what can be achieved with a sewing machine. Even now the sophistication of some new machines, while making sewing processes much easier, tends to deny the operator complete freedom of control. For some people this is not necessary, but we need a choice.

Price, quality and performance

Different manufacturers cater for different markets. The more expensive machines, precision-made to last a lifetime, are quiet-running with perfect stitching. Their very reliability means that the manufacturers only need a few models within that range. In the mid- to lower-market range there is far more choice. New models come out more frequently with more varied design features and there is a greater variety within any one manufacturer's range.

What you want to sew and where you are going to sew it will decide the type of machine you need. The next consideration is price. Decide how much you can afford and buy the best machine in that price range. Alternatively, if the machine does all you want of it, choose a cheaper model in the upper price range. It is worth remembering that no single machine will do everything.

Straight-stitch flat bed machines

These are the simplest types of machine available. They can be hand- or treadle-operated, or have an electric motor. These machines sew straight-stitch forward and reverse. Num-

bered tension threading is on the outside of the machine and the stitch length adjusted by a vertical lever in a slot with graded markings. The bobbin thread is wound externally at the front, not on the top as in later machines. The bobbin itself is located below and to the left of the needle, fitting vertically into the bobbin housing on some machines or sitting horizontally on others. Some old machines have a long shuttle instead of the round bobbin. The needle threads from left to right or from right to left. It is impossible to use a twin needle on this type of machine. There is a pressure selector for different thicknesses of material and a drop feed or a cover plate for working free embroidery or darning. A lever control gives reverse stitching.

Before the advent of the domestic zig-zag, all sewing machines for home use were of this type. With a variety of feet for special processes and various attachments, they performed all simple sewing functions. Because the mechanism is simple and the machine only sews in one plane backwards and forwards, it is extremely reliable. This is proved by the number of early sewing machines still in good running order.

These machines all have a flat bed – a flat working surface beneath the machine arm and the needle, to support the sewing. Some models have an extension table that clips on to the left of the machine base to increase the area of the working surface.

Simple zig-zag or swing-needle machines

The introduction of the zig-zag or swing-needle for domestic machines was the liberating factor that made possible all the pattern and utility stitches we now take for granted. A reciprocating arm, located inside the top of the machine, allows side to side movement of the needle. This, in conjunction with the forward movement created by the feed teeth moving the cloth, results in a zig-zag stitch. When the stitch-length is closed up, satin stitch is formed.

In addition to the stitch-length control, these machines have a stitch-width control. This control can take the form of a knob or a lever worked horizontally from side to side. These controls have graded markings. Extra calibrations on the stitch-length control, whether knob or lever, indicate the shortened stitch area suitable for satin stitch. Some machines with a vertical slot lever have a *fine stitch control* adjustment for perfect satin stitch. These machines are often fitted with a self-releasing push-button reverse knob. The reverse action works only so long as the knob is held pushed in. The zig-zag stitch was used both as a decoration and for neatening edges. A zig-zag stitch with small stitch-width and length settings, became the first stretch stitch for seams on jersey type fabrics.

At first these very simple zig-zag machines had no automatic patterns. Buttonholes could only be worked manually. After one side had been sewn, the operator had to turn the cloth before sewing down the opposite side. It was also necessary to alter the width controls to form the bar tacks at either end. It is possible for the skilled operator to work swing-needle patterns by the movement of the stitch-width control. However, this needs a lot of practice to achieve an even and symmetrical effect.

These simple machines were sold as flat bed models. Later some were brought out as *free arm* machines. This narrow arm was introduced to help in sewing narrow areas or openings such as cuffs, trouser legs, set-in sleeves, which on a flat bed tend to get screwed up and difficult to sew. An extension table converts these machines for flat bed sewing. On simple machines the table slides on. Later models have various systems of conversion including flaps or raising part of the machine up to the bed. Some models have a see-through panel above the bobbin changing area.

Sometimes the tool and attachment box is located under the extension. Other machines have a space in the top or in the carrying case. Nowadays, many machines have a built-in carrying handle.

Semi-automatic machines

The manufacturers soon realised the potential of the zig-zag machine and made improvements. These machines can be flat bed or free arm. Like the simple zig-zag machines, they have both straight-stitch and zig-zag facilities, push button reverse and stitch-length and width controls. In addition they have pattern *cams* to alter the width control automatically. These produce simple patterns similar to those achieved by hand manipulation of the stitch-width lever.

On the semi-automatic machines, pattern cams take the place of the operator's hand on the width lever. At first these cams were separate items fitted into position in the top of the machine. They mechanically transferred the pattern movements to the reciprocating arm controlling the needle. A later development involved sets of these pattern cams, threaded on to a bar, permanently situated inside the top of the machine. These could be selected by a knob or lever on the outside. The patterns were first based on geometric or curved shapes, or combinations of both. They could be sewn on a close satin stitch setting or opened up with the stitch-length lever.

These machines have a manually operated semi-automatic buttonhole. Those that thread from left to right, with the bobbin case to the left of the needle, cannot take twin needles. Later machines of this type have additional utility stitches and a blind hem stitch.

Automatic machines

An automatic machine is one that has a built-in automatic buttonhole, which can be sewn without pivoting or turning the cloth. This is the commonly agreed definition of this type of machine. The buttonholes can be two-step, four-step or five-step. The machine operator still has to alter the control settings for the various steps and gauge the length. True automatic buttonholes require an attachment for the foot.

Machine design categories vary and those with an automatic buttonhole may have a good range of utility stitches, but few or no automatic patterns. Others have an automatic buttonhole, three-needle position and a large selection of removable cams instead of automatic dialling or push-button.

As designs became more complicated, the word *automatic*, first used to describe a pattern process, was not enough to cover the new improvements. Sometimes the title *fully automatic* is used to describe a machine that has a no-turn buttonhole, dialled or push button automatic patterns, some stretch and utility stitches and three-needle position to give twin-needle decorative sewing.

All these machines have a centrally placed bobbin. This is located below, either in front of the needle in a vertical position or sitting horizontally, in front of or behind the needle. All these machines have a full rotary hook and the needle threads from front to back. Variable needle positions give greater width range and allow further diversity of pattern and multiple-needle sewing. Some have concealed tension discs and one-step threading.

The bobbin is wound from a position on top of the machine. On some models an automatic clutch disengages the motor. Other, newer machines wind the bobbin through the needle doing away with the necessity to unthread the machine.

Even the title *fully automatic* was not enough to describe the next innovation – the automatic reverse feed used in conjunction with the swing-needle mechanism to give trimotion stitches. The cloth is moved backwards and forwards beneath the needle automatically by the feed teeth while the needle bar moves from side to side. This dual movement, directed by the reciprocal arm inside the machine, is controlled by double cams, whether slotted-in or chosen by push button or dialling system. The result is stitching in a circular or concentric motion. This gives all the stretch stitches, overlock and flexi-stitches.

The only term that can cover all these capabilities is *super automatic*.

Electronic machines

The word *electronic* refers to an integrated circuit, located either in the machine or in the foot control. Some machines use both methods. These electronic machines still have the internal pattern cams which direct the movement of the reciprocating arm. This pattern mechanism is not electronically controlled. Sometimes the pattern indicators are lit up by light-emitting diodes. These are tiny lights that show which stitch is in the *on* position.

These machines are not the same as the *fully electronic* machines which are controlled by a miniature computer containing silicon chip memories and a microprocessor. The stitches are called up from the memory by pressing the appropriate pre-programmed selector buttons. You can only get out of the machine what has been programmed in.

There is no particular mystique about electronics, whether in the form of integrated circuits or silicon chips. These are merely sophisticated electrical circuits increasingly used to control and replace former mechanical functions.

Electronic foot control
The electronic foot control not only regulates the speed of the motor, but also ensures full needle penetration power at very slow speeds or when sewing thick material. It allows more sensitive control, the ability to stop and start immediately, and to sew stitch-by-stitch.

Stitch completion device
As well as the slow stitch-by-stitch sewing made possible by the electronic foot control, there is also an electronic stitch completion device. This allows the machine to stop with the needle down in the cloth for pivoting on corners or up for threading and fabric removal. Automatic cut-off can allow a single stitch to be made. This device is located in the machine and is sometimes used in conjunction with the electronic foot control. The most favoured name is *Stopmatic*.

Fast/slow speed control
As well as the electronic foot control and the stitch completion device, other slow speed methods are used. Sometimes this is in the form of a slow speed reduction gear. This can be used alone or in conjunction with other methods. Some machines have a two-speed switch on the machine. One manufacturer has a fast/slow control switch on some foot pedals. This is for use by beginners or in schools.

Machines without a foot control
Some electronic models feature a push button unit on the machine to control both stitch completion and a variety of sewing speeds. These machines dispense with the foot control altogether. Push buttons are operated manually to start and stop the machine and to sew in reverse. A choice of three speeds can be varied on one machine by selecting a combination of buttons.

Alternating the use of the Stopmatic buttons (needle up and needle down) produces a very slow speed sewing. One model features a lever above the needle area to control functions such as reverse sewing and automatic seam finishing. The machine can be stopped immediately by pushing this lever up with the back of the hand.

The first reaction to these machines is a feeling of doubt at the omission of the foot control. This is overcome surprisingly quickly and they are very easy machines to work. The user will be bound by the manufacturers' set choice of speeds. Anyone unable to use a foot control would find these machines invaluable. One manufacturer gives the option of a knee-operated speed control.

Fully electronic machines
There are no mechanically operated pattern cams in this type of machine. The pattern movements are stored in the silicon chip memory of the miniature computer. These electrical signals are transformed into mechanical movements to form the stitch patterns.

The stitch patterns are chosen by touch-button switches. Stitch-width and length can be altered on dials. Any number of different patterns can be sewn before reverting to the original alteration by re-touching the width and length dials.

Stitch-by-stitch sewing, a one-step buttonhole, stitch completion and speed basting are all controlled electronically. In addition, an electronic foot control makes for easier operation.

Super electronic machines
This latest development is even more sophisticated than the fully electronic machine. It can contain more than one microprocessor and it has full pattern memory. A pattern sequence can be chosen and dialled into the machine. This sequence will be repeated exactly as it is programmed in. It is also possible to alter set pattern motifs. They can be elongated

or shortened without losing stitch density. They can be inverted or sewn in mirror image.

Single motifs can be sewn and repeated at intervals. In fact, the pattern potentialities are almost endless. A built-in one-step buttonholer can be dialled for different length buttonholes which will be repeated exactly. These machines also contain the stitch control devices used in the other electronic machines.

Controls and knobs

Individual machine instruction books give a diagram showing the machine and naming its parts. The time may come when you are faced with a strange machine or have to choose between various models when buying a new one. It helps to know exactly what the different controls are for and how they vary from machine to machine.

Basically, all controls are the same. They may look different or be placed in a variety of positions, but their primary function is unaltered. A sewing machine requires a continuous thread to be fed to the needle at the correct tension and another tensioned thread on the bobbin below. These two threads form the lock stitch. The thread spindle, located on top of the machine, holds the reel, enabling it to unwind easily. Some machines have more than one of these spindles to carry reels for twin- and triple-needle work.

Tension discs
The thread is guided to the tension discs. These can be situated on the front of the machine or semi-concealed within the top. They act like tiny disc brakes and control the rate at which the thread runs to the needle. The tension is altered by a numbered dial or set by a plus and minus indicator. There may be an additional disc for twin-needle sewing.

Take-up lever and thread guides
The thread passes through the eye in the take-up lever and down to the needle. In newer machines the take-up lever is slotted, as well as all the thread guides, to give simple one-step threading.

Presser bar
This supports the machine foot. The pressure can be adjusted for sewing different thicknesses of material. Newer machines have an automatic pressure control, but even this needs some adjustment. A thread cutter is sometimes located to the rear of the presser bar.

Machine feet
All new machines are provided with two basic feet, one for straight-stitch and one for swing-needle sewing. They are hinged to accommodate varying thicknesses in the cloth. A selection of special-purpose feet is provided. Originally all machine feet screwed on. This is a firm method of holding the foot. The first machine to have an easily removable foot has the foot and shank fitting up on to a spike at the base of the presser bar.

It was some time before other manufacturers were able to devise alternative methods for a detachable foot. The most popular is a removable foot that snaps or clips on to a shank which itself is screwed on to the presser bar. In some machines these feet are held on to the shank by a retaining lug which can be released by a push button or lever. Another machine has the foot and shank fitting inside, instead of up and over, the presser bar.

Presser bar lifter
This lever, situated at the rear, raises and lowers the foot. The tension is only engaged when the foot and presser bar lever are lowered. One machine has the only domestic knee operated lift lever. This leaves both hands free for certain embroidery techniques.

Another machine has the lever placed to the right. This also activates the Stopmatic mechanism. Some machines are fitted with a double lift presser foot lever. This makes it easier to insert layers of thick material.

Needle
This is held by a screw into the needle bar. It has one, and sometimes two, thread guides, the latter for twin-needle sewing. Some machines have the needle set at a slant towards the worker.

Feed teeth and stitch length control
The length of stitch is determined by the rate at which the feed dog teeth, situated beneath the needle, push the cloth.

Some machines have a vertical stitch-length lever with graded markings 0-20. For reverse feed motion this lever is pushed to the top of the slot. Others have a dial control marked 1-4 and a push button for self release reverse.

It is possible to drop the feed on most machines by a lever, knob or screw control. This puts the stitch-length control out of action. On machines where it is impossible to drop the teeth, a separate cover plate is provided. This control is used for darning or when working free embroidery.

Even feed
One machine has a *dual feed* system built into the machine. This device can be put out of action for normal sewing. It has a row of feed teeth that push the top of the material in conjunction with the feed teeth below and ensures that both layers of material pass through at an even speed. It is used for matching stripes or when sewing velvet or slippery materials.

In addition, some manufacturers produce a screw-on foot called a *walking foot* or an *even feed foot*, which performs a similar function with slippery or other difficult fabrics.

Needleplate

This plate, surrounding the feed teeth, has a round hole for straight stitching and a transverse slot for zig-zag sewing. Both types can be on one change-around needleplate, otherwise separate plates are provided. Two makes have systems for an automatic-change needleplate. The action of setting the machine for straight stitching works a lever to close up the slot to form a round hole.

Plates can be removed by unscrewing. Others are held magnetically or simply clip or slot in. All have cloth guide markings to aid straight sewing, some on the right hand only, others on both sides.

Press-button controls on the Pfaff Tipmatic machine.

Bobbins and bobbin cases

Circular bobbins or spools vary in size and fit the machine they are designed for. The drop-in type fit into a fixed bobbin case. This is encircled by the shuttle race with its hook.

The centre front bobbin cases are removable. In some models a little lug, attached to a hinged bar on the front of the case, fits into the spool and prevents it from falling out when the case is removed. On some, a projecting arm on the bobbin case fits into the encircling shuttle race, which is itself fitted into the bobbin housing. A small hole on certain models is threaded for increased buttonhole tension.

The bobbin thread passes through a tension spring on the bobbin case. It is possible to adjust this when necessary to obtain the correct tension.

Lock stitch

After the threaded needle pierces the cloth it hesitates on its upward journey and a small loop forms below the cloth. This loop is caught and expanded by the race hook which carries it over and round the bobbin to interlock with the bobbin thread. The feed teeth move the cloth forward, the slack thread is pulled up by the take-up lever and a stitch is made.

Balance wheel and bobbin winding mechanism

The machine is activated by turning a balance wheel which is driven by hand, treadle or electric power. This wheel can be turned by hand for making a single stitch or to raise or lower the needle.

The balance wheel can be disconnected from the sewing mechanism in order to wind the bobbin. Some machines have an inner fly wheel that unscrews. Others have a push-in clutch or touch control, or an automatic de-clutch.

The bobbin winding position varies, but the thread always passes through some sort of tension control. Nearly all have an automatic cut-off when the bobbin is full. One machine features an indicator that lights up when only 10cm (4in) of thread is left on the bobbin.

Certain machines wind the bobbin through the needle. On some models the drop-in bobbin is wound through the needle while still in the sewing position.

Foot pedal controls

These can be electric, electronic or worked by air pressure control. Whatever the type, make sure the plug fits firmly in the socket and the cable is in good condition.

One machine has a cable and foot control that retracts into the machine base, and another a retracting cable and plug.

Machine light

This is normally situated over the needle area, although sometimes it is above the sewing area. Old machines

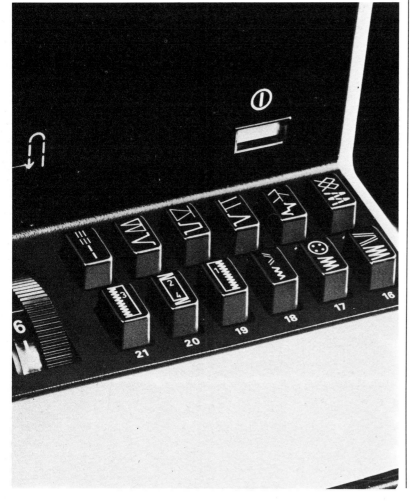

may have a separate bulb fixed behind the machine arm. All light bulbs should have a protective guard as they get hot.

Some lights have an independent switch, while others share the main on/off switch. This is included as a safety factor. The light always shows when the machine is on – useful when children are around.

To prevent accidents, the machine should always be switched off when the needle and foot are changed.

Controls on zig-zag and automatic machines

Width

All swing-needle and automatic machines have a width control. It may take the form of a lever in a numbered, transverse slot, which sometimes has a device to limit the swing. Other machines have a numbered dial. The normal width of throw is 4 mm ($\frac{5}{16}$ in) but some machines have 5 mm ($\frac{3}{16}$ in), and 7 mm ($\frac{1}{4}$ in).

By using an oscillating needleplate in conjunction with the width control one machine has attained a width of 12mm ($\frac{1}{2}$ in), the widest for a domestic machine. The greater width increases the scope of twin- and triple-needle sewing and gives a wider satin stitch.

2 How the lockstitch is formed by the needle and shuttle race.

Some swing-needle machines have a three-needle position control lever, placed above the sewing area and marked L M R (left, middle and right). This can take the form of a knob which also controls the no-turn buttonhole. On a machine using drop-in cams this knob is sometimes used to engage the cam mechanism. However many functions this knob controls, they are all connected with needle position.

Length

All these machines have a stitch-length lever or dial, positioned towards the right.

Pattern stitches

If there are only a few patterns or utility stitches, these can be located on the stitch-width dial. This is frequently marked with the pattern symbols, including straight-stitch and zig-zag of different widths. The chosen symbol is set to a marker.

Fully automatic machines have a pattern panel with a control that moves a selector pointer, or a lever on the top of the machine that clicks into position. Sometimes this includes the automatic buttonhole.

Normally, all simple automatic pattern stitches are worked at the widest width setting and a very short stitch-length to give a close setting.

The trimotion or stretch stitches are worked at the widest width setting, but a longer stitch-length. On some machines this alteration of the stitch-length in relation to the

width is selected automatically. On others it needs to be set by the operator. To help in this, many manufacturers have a colour code uniting the type of stitch with the appropriate stitch-width and length settings. This makes things much easier.

Some machines have a control to maintain the density when a pattern is elongated, while others have an indicator to show the start and end of a pattern motif. Some manufacturers have sought to simplify the look of the machine by reducing the number of control knobs. To do this they combine the stitch-width and length control as two dials, one within the other.

The automatic buttonhole either has a control of its own or can be combined with the length or the width dial. There may be an even balance control to keep both sides of the buttonhole the same.

As a safety precaution, on certain machines it is impossible to move the stitch-width control when the machine is set to straight-stitch. This prevents the needle damaging the needleplate.

Fully electronic machines

All machine functions are chosen by touch control, either singly or in conjunction with another control. Stitch-width and length can still be altered by dialling wheels. These can be re-activated by touch.

Stop, start, reverse, stitch pattern and buttonhole symbols are all displayed on a selector panel. A tiny light shows when the chosen symbol is touched and activated. It is possible to limit sewing to one motif or repeat a pattern sequence.

Needles

The modern machine needle has a rounded shank, flattened on one side; older ones may be round. Always thread a mach-

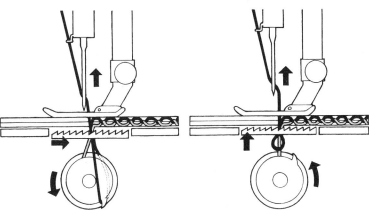

ine needle from the grooved side. Never use a blunt or bent needle, it could damage the machine. Some machine manufacturers recommend their own needle system.

Different sized needles are made to take a variety of thread thicknesses. In addition, different needles are designed for specific sewing purposes.

Ball pointed needles do not damage the threads in fine jersey fabrics. The needle passes in between the looped stitches.

Basting needles have two eyes, the bottom for normal sewing, the top for machine basting.

Leather needles have a sharp, spear-type point to cut cleanly.

Open needles have a slit eye as an aid to easy threading.

Perfect stitch needles have an elongated indentation, or scarfe, round the eye. This aids the stitch mechanism when used on fine, synthetic fabrics.

Twin or triple needles are multiple needles used for double or triple line sewing.

Wing or hemstitching needles have a wing or flange on one or both sides to make a larger hole in decorative sewing.

Twin wing needles have one straight and one wing needle.

Needle threaders

One machine has a built-in needle threader which pushes a tiny hook through the needle eye to catch the thread and pull it through. Some manufacturers make separate hand operated needle threaders that work on a similar principle. Others feature a contrasting white patch behind the needle eye. The very simple type of needle threader sold for hand sewing can also be used.

Fabrics, needles and threads
The type of needle is chosen according to the kind of fabric used. The thread will determine the size of needle used. Where there is a three-needle position, on certain fabrics it may be necessary to sew

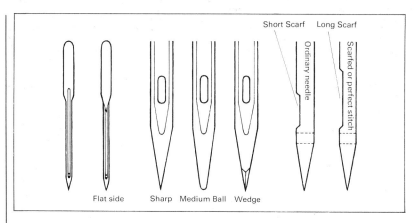

3 Types of needle point.

straight-stitch with the needle to the left. This results in better stitching. Use the style or needle system recommended by your machine manufacturer. Some have a colour coding system for different types of needle.

Caring for your machine

A machine that is well cleaned and oiled will last much longer, give better service and need less professional attention. When the machine is not in use, keep it covered and dust free. Wipe the machine with a damp cloth and keep the surrounding work area clean. Never leave a sewing machine connected to the power source when not in use. Switch off and disconnect it even if you are leaving the machine for a short period. Always switch off when changing the foot or the needle.

It is no economy to continue using a blunt needle. This causes badly made or missed stitches. A bent or deformed needle can damage the sewing mechanism. If you are in any doubt, hold the needle up to the light against a flat surface. The needle needs to be changed after every other sewing project, and twice as often if you are using synthetic fabrics which tend to blunt the needle.

Clean the machine before oiling. First disconnect the power, then remove the needle and the foot. It is essential to keep the sewing mechanism

free from fabric lint and fluff. Each time the needle pierces the cloth, tiny fragments are torn off which build up under the feed teeth and inside the shuttle mechanism. A lint brush is indispensible for this.

Remove the needleplate and use the brush to clean around and under the teeth which are now exposed. Next, follow your machine instruction book and clean the shuttle mechanism. The fixed type needs to be brushed well, but the removable type should be taken apart. Sometimes the shuttle race ring is screwed in, but it is more likely to be held on by clasps.

The bobbin case is removed first, then the shuttle race ring and next the shuttle hook. Turn the balance wheel by hand towards you while cleaning the inside of the race. Hard little wads of lint form at the base of the race mechanism and can be the cause of poor stitching or a noisy machine. These areas need cleaning after every sewing project or if the machine is in constant use, a couple of times a week.

The area inside the face plate and the tension discs need cleaning less often. Feed thin cotton material between the tension discs, lower the presser bar lever to engage the tension and draw the fabric through in the same direction the sewing thread passes. If yours is a flat bed machine, keep the inside of the base free from fluff and pins.

Oiling the machine

To ensure that the machine is kept in perfect running order the moving parts should be covered with a thin film of oil. Use the best quality machine oil as a coarse oil could damage the parts.

If the machine is in constant use, it will need oiling every 8 – 10 sewing hours. If used infrequently, then oil before use. The machine should not be over-oiled. Only a tiny drop is necessary in all the points marked in your instruction book. After oiling, run the machine for a few minutes to allow the oil to penetrate. Leave the machine with a piece of cloth under the foot to absorb any excess. Always put the machine away with the foot down and the needle lowered into the cloth.

Some machines have a sealed oil system and should not be oiled. Some are made of sin-tered steel which is impregnated with a special lubricant. Heat from the working parts helps the oil to seep from within the metal to lubricate the bearings. When cool, the oil returns to the metal core.

All machines need a drop of oil in the shuttle mechanism after cleaning.

Threading up and starting to sew

Even if the machine is clean, oiled and ready, a little preparation of the work area beforehand will make sewing easier and more pleasant.

Machine tools, needles in assorted sizes, pins and sewing tools should be to hand, but not so near that they clutter up the immediate sewing area.

Always try to sew in a relaxed atmosphere, even when you are in a hurry. Make sure you are comfortable; a swivel chair is an excellent method of adjusting height. The machine should be 10 – 12 cm (4 – 5 in) from the edge of the table so that you can rest your elbows.

If you have never used a sewing machine before, or have never used one with an electric foot control, you may prefer to do some practice sewing before the machine is threaded up. Use a striped cotton fabric rather than paper as you need to get the feel of guiding a fabric.

Insert a needle up into the needlebar and secure by tightening the needle clamp with a screwdriver. If the machine threads from front to back, the flat side of the needle will be towards the back and the groove to the front. If it threads from the left, the flat side will be to the left. Conversely, if the machine threads from the right, it will be towards the right.

Switch on the machine. Turn the balance wheel towards you by hand, raising the take-up lever to its highest position. Next, raise the lever to lift the presser foot. Choose one of the stripes on the fabric and try to centre it beneath the slit in the middle of the foot.

Turn the balance wheel until the needle is in the cloth. Lower the foot. Never start the machine with the needle out of the cloth. This makes a whirring noise in the motor and causes the drive band to stretch.

Press gently on the foot control and the machine will start to sew. The needle will move up and down and the feed teeth will push the cloth away from you. Left to itself the machine will sew straight. It is up to the operator to guide the cloth. Any kind of pressure on the cloth will cause the fabric to pull sideways or sew in a wavy line.

Try to guide the cloth so that the needle pierces the line. When you come to the end, stop with the needle out of the cloth, lift the foot, move the cloth and start again.

There are various methods of guiding the machine. You can use either of the two outer, or

4 Cleaning the feed teeth (left) and shuttle race (right).

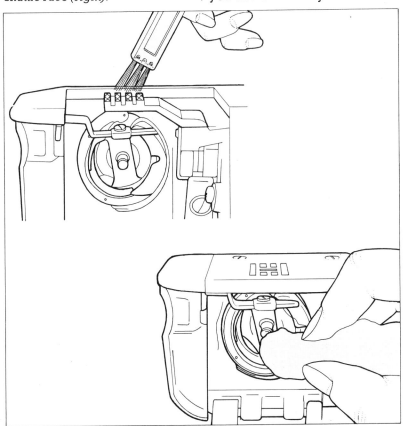

the two inner edges of the presser foot held against your guide lines. This will result in rows of stitch holes at varying widths apart.

The needleplate has a series of guide lines marked on it. Put the edge of the material against a guide line and machine once more. Try to gain control of the machine. Stop and start it when you want to and do not let it run on. A machine with an electronic foot control will stop immediately pressure is released. Once you have got the feel of it, it is time to thread up and start sewing.

Winding the bobbin

If your machine has the bobbin wound externally on the machine, this must be done first. If it is wound in the sewing position or through the needle, the top is threaded first.

The external winding position is on the top of the machine. The bobbin or spool is located on a spindle, placed horizontally on old machines, upright in newer ones. There is a hole in the top of some bobbins which marries with a lug on the winding mechanism. Often there is a second thread spindle to take the thread reel for bobbin winding. The reel thread is passed through a tension device and if this is missed out, the bobbin winds unevenly. The end of the thread is wound round the empty bobbin a few times or secured through a hole in the top.

The winding mechanism can be activated in a variety of ways. Either the bobbin on its spindle is clicked into position, which engages the winding mechanism automatically, or the sewing mechanism has to be disengaged. To do this the inner wheel or knob inside the balance wheel must be unscrewed in an anti-clockwise direction. Hold the balance wheel steady in your left hand. Other machines have a push-pull clutch knob in the same position or a touch button. Depress the foot control and let the thread wind until the automatic

cut-off works or the bobbin is nearly full. If the bobbin winds unevenly, there may be an adjuster on the tension device. Consult your instruction book. Try to keep an even speed with the foot control and do not allow it to wind too fast.

Top threading

Use a colour to contrast with the bobbin thread and place the reel in position on the spindle, making sure the thread does not snag. Some plastic reels have a pronounced slit for the thread end. If the unwinding thread catches on this, turn the reel upside down.

Lead the thread through the guides until you come to the tension discs. Whether these are of the semi-concealed type, recessed into the machine head, or exposed on the front of the machine, the threading procedure is basically the same. The thread must go through the discs. If there is an additional disc for twin-needle sewing, the single thread can go either between the first and second, or the second and third disc.

The thread is pulled through the discs and caught under a spring or a tension hook. Sometimes this is called the slack thread regulator. It controls the amount of thread drawn by the take-up lever to make a single stitch.

The thread then passes through the eye or slot of the take-up lever and down the guides to the needle. As a general rule the needle is threaded

from the side that the final thread guide is on. If there is a second thread guide for twin-needle sewing, and you are in any doubt consult the booklet.

The needle is always threaded from the grooved side. When the needle is in the cloth, the thread is pressed into this groove. It is very important to have the right needle for the chosen thread. Too thick a thread in a fine needle will fray and break.

There are several needle threading devices on the market and the white patch behind the needle on some machines is a help. One of the best ways to thread a machine needle is by feel. This is easier with a natural fibre. If the end is cut to a slant with a sharp pair of scissors and twisted to a nice point, it can be poked through the eye. Unfortunately the synthetic threads in general use tend to unravel when cut and splay out.

If you have any difficulty, do use a needle threader. They work extremely well. The hook on the little hand-held ones can be pushed through the eye by feel and the thread passed across the front of the hook. The hook is withdrawn from behind, pulling the thread through. The mechanical kind works in a similar manner, but the little hook fits into place automatically.

5 How to place the bobbin in the bobbin case, winding the bobbin in a clockwise direction. Pull the thread through the slot as shown until it is caught in position.

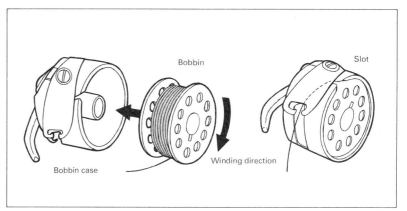

Bobbin

Slot

Bobbin case

Winding direction

Bobbin winding through the needle eye

On some machines the bobbin is wound in the sewing position with a continuous thread from the needle.

Raise the presser bar lever to lift the foot and disengage the top tension, making sure that the needle is centered and the stitch-width control at 0. With an empty bobbin in position, move the small button or lever to the left to activate the winding mechanism. Draw the needle thread out and wrap the end round the presser foot screw. Hold on to this end while you depress the foot control to activate the machine. Let the thread wind until it fills up to the limit marked on the see-through bobbin. There is an automatic cut-off but by this time the bobbin may be too full.

There is a continuous thread between the needle and the bobbin. Raise the needle, pull the double thread to the back and cut. The act of closing the sliding cover plate releases the bobbin winding lever automatically.

Other machines wind through the needle on to a bobbin placed in a winding position at the right side of the machine. This is activated in the usual manner.

Starting to sew

Place the wound bobbin in position inside the bobbin case so that the thread unwinds in an anti-clockwise direction. Bring the thread up through the slit in the outside of the bobbin case and pull it under the tension spring. It should click into position. A few machines thread the opposite way round. Consult your booklet.

Draw the end of the thread

Secure straight stitching with a few back stitches (viewed from behind under the machine foot).

through. Leave 2-3cm (1 in) protruding from the open slide cover if the bobbin case is fixed. Insert the removable type into position. If this has a protruding arm or finger, it should point upwards. Close the cover.

Bringing up the thread

Hold the needle thread towards you with your left hand and turn the balance wheel towards you with your right hand. When the take-up lever reaches its highest position, the needle should pull a bottom thread loop through. Draw this loop out and towards the back.

Pull the needle thread down

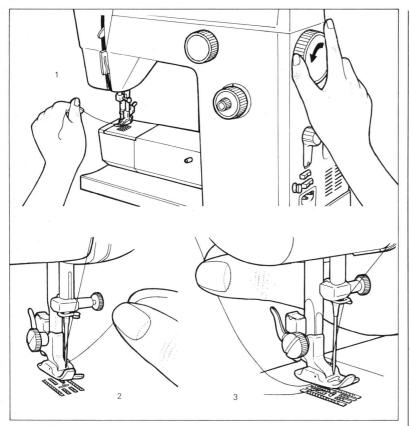

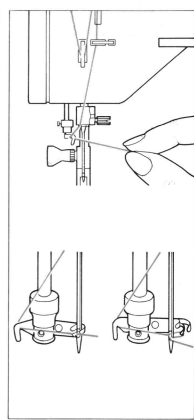

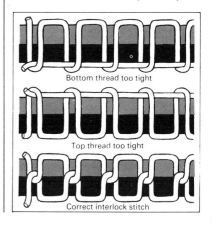

6 (Above) Pulling up the lower thread turning the balance wheel in an anti-clockwise direction by hand.

7 (Above right) Using the built-in needle threader on the Pfaff machine.

between the slit in the presser foot and out behind the machine for about 5cm (2in) together with the bobbin thread. Place some double fabric beneath the raised foot. Lower the needle into the cloth, turning the balance wheel towards you by hand. Lower the presser foot. Depress the foot control and start to sew.

When you stop, lift the foot, raise the needle out of the cloth, with the take-up lever at its highest point, and pull the two threads towards the rear. Keep the top one in the presser foot groove. This prevents strain on the needle. Cut the threads with the thread cutter and remove the fabric.

Have a look at the stitches. They should interlock evenly in the middle of the two fabric layers. If the top tension is too tight, the bottom colour thread will show through and the top thread will be stretched tight. Loosen the top tension control anti-clockwise. The higher the number, the tighter the tension. The lower the number, the looser it is. If the top colour thread shows through to the bottom and the bottom thread is stretched too tight, tighten up the top tension, clockwise. Some tension controls are set to a plus and minus sign.

The bobbin tension should be set for the machine. Sometimes a slight adjustment is necessary. It can be altered by turning the screw on the tension spring a quarter turn at a time: clockwise to tighten, anti-clockwise to loosen. Normally this only needs to be done when using thick threads wound round the bobbin. It is a good idea to have a separate, removable bobbin case for this work.

Experiment until you have the tension exactly right on your first piece of material. Next try altering the stitch-length control. Too small a stitch distorts the cloth. Too long a stitch will not hold firmly. Try out various stitch-length settings and tension experi-

(Right) Pure wools, lining fabrics, polyesters and sheer pure silks.

8 (Below) Tension for interlocking of threads; bottom thread too tight (top); top thread too tight (centre); correct interlock stitch (bottom).

Bottom thread too tight

Top thread too tight

Correct interlock stitch

ments on different types of material. The machine needs a slight adjustment for each kind and thickness.

Next try out the reverse lever or button. This enables the machine to sew backwards and is used at the beginning and end of seams as a means of securing the stitches before cutting off the threads. Just a few stitches in reverse are sufficient. Do not use the quick-reverse for more than a few stitches.

Fabrics and threads

The choice of fabric will influence the kind of thread you use and the type and size of needle.

Fabrics

These can be divided into categories according to their fibre content. A fabric may contain more than one fibre type to form a blend.
Natural fibres Cotton; linen; silk; wool.
Man-made fibres Rayon; acetate and tri-acetate rayon derived from cellulose.
Synthetic fibres Acrylic; nylon; polyester derived from chemicals.

Fabrics are produced in two ways, either woven or non-woven. The non-woven fabrics include jersey or knitted as well as bonded fabrics, plastic-coated fabrics and interfacings. Leather and suede come into a category of their own.

The appropriate needle type is chosen to match the fabric. The composition of the cloth will determine the needle size. Thin, light materials are all sewn with a fine needle. A heavyweight, woven cotton or silk will need a thicker needle. Very closely woven fabrics will sew more easily with a fine needle to pierce the cloth. There is a needle type and size for every fabric. (See needle size table).

Threads and natural fibres

Cotton thread

Most cotton sold for machine sewing is mercerized The fibres have been treated to give a smoother, more lustrous appearance. This process was invented by John Mercer in the 19th century.

Chain, or unmercerized cotton should not be confused with tacking cotton which is a very soft thread and designed to break easily. These threads come in various thicknesses. The higher the number, the finer the thread.

Silk thread

Threads for machine sewing are available in two thicknesses. The thicker thread is very effective for topstitching. Silk is sometimes used for sewing fine woollen fabrics, as well as being used to sew all silk fabrics. The slight elasticity of the silk thread matches the springiness of the wool fibres. Buttonhole silk can be used for top stitching and for sewing leather.

Synthetic threads

These are made from spun polyester and can be used for types of fabric other than synthetic, including plastic, suede or leather. They come in two thicknesses, fine for general purpose sewing and heavier for topstitching. They are excellent for all synthetic fabrics, particularly synthetic jersey as the thread contains a slight elasticity. The fibres of these threads are inert and they should be cut and not broken. Do not use a natural thread with synthetic fabrics.

Nylon is a monofilament thread. It can be useful for sewing plastics but it is not sympathetic to handle. Some synthetic threads tend to shred little wisps that get caught in the tension discs and shuttle mechanism. Clean the machine more often when using this type of thread.

A thread with a cotton-wrapped polyester core helps solve this problem.

Machine embroidery threads

Machine embroidery thread is designed to give a lustrous appearance and to lay evenly when stitched into a close satin stitch. It can be obtained in a variety of colours and comes in two thicknesses, no. 50 (thin) and no. 30 (thicker). Reels of shaded thread come in no. 30. No. 50 can be used to sew buttonholes and no. 30 is good for top-stitching.

Flat lurex and metallic cord are used for decorative sewing. The flat lurex requires a special bobbin winding technique as it is essential not to twist the flat metal thread. Slip the reel of thread on to a skewer and hold this parallel to the bobbin winding position. Fix the end on to the bobbin as usual. Do not thread through the tension device. Tension is controlled by the operator as the reel unwinds on the skewer. Keep the winding speed even.

Metallic threads are wrapped round a nylon core and any friction will cause this outer layer to wear away, so wind on to the bobbin by hand. A very fine metallic cord will work on the top of the machine threaded through the needle eye. Use a looser top tension than usual.

Sewing

A fine material will require not only a fine needle and thread, but a correspondingly shorter stitch-length. A heavy material will require thicker thread, a strong needle and a longer stitch-length. Before you start any sewing project make a test on a double piece of the fabric in question using matching thread. Experiment until you have a satisfactory stitch length for the fabric type and an even tension top and bottom.

Adjusting the pressure bar

The other control that may need adjustment is the pressure on the presser bar. On many machines this is controlled automatically, according to the thickness of the material fed through beneath the presser foot, but even these will need a fine adjustment from time to time.

Old machines have a screw on top of the presser bar. Turning it clockwise tightens and anticlockwise reduces the pressure. Some machines have an indicator knob which can be turned for various fabric types, from fine to heavyweight. Other machines have a regulator ring which encircles the top of the presser bar. This ring is pushed down to release the pressure. For a light pressure, when sewing thin cloth, push the top of the bar down lightly. When sewing thicker cloth, push the bar down further to increase the pressure. Some machines have a regulator control inside the faceplate.

To test the pressure, use an oblong piece of the material you intend to sew and fold it in half keeping the raw edges level. Place a row of pins against the fold and another row against the raw edges. Machine from the fold towards the raw edges. If the pressure is too tight, the top layer will pucker. Loosen the pressure. If it is too loose the fabric will move sideways. The two layers of fabric should pass evenly beneath the foot. Avoid too heavy a pressure on fine fabric as the feed teeth may damage the material.

Firm, but not too closely woven, fabrics are the easiest to practice on. Find as many different types as possible to get the feel of the sewing.

Straight stitch on different materials

Use the perfect stitch needle for synthetic and fine fabrics. When working with synthetic thread use a slightly longer stitch-length and adjust the tension carefully.

Woollen fabrics need to be handled a little more gently, even the thick ones. Let the machine do the work for you,

never be tempted to help the work along.

Jersey fabrics need even more careful handling. On no account must they be stretched or the sewing will be wavy and distorted.

Always support the fabric on the left hand side, either on the extension table, sewing cabinet or work table. Keep this area clear so that the material does not pull from under the foot. Up until now you will have been sewing small items; sewing heavy garments or curtains is a very different matter. The right hand lightly guides the work forwards while the left hand prevents the cloth from moving sideways. If the machine is set correctly, there should be no effort on your part.

Leather, velvet, plastic, net or slippery fabrics all have their special problems and these can be solved more easily by using special feet or stitch techniques.

Using the stitch-width control

Once the technique of sewing straight-stitch has been mastered it is time to use the stitch-width control and enjoy a whole rane of new sewing opportunities. First change the straight-stitch presser foot for the wide slotted zig-zag foot. If your machine has a stitch-width lever or a control knob which moves with a continuous motion, you will be able to alter the stitch-width while you are sewing. This type of control is essential for anyone wishing to work free embroidery.

The other type of width control has a series of stops, set to various widths increasing from straight-stitch to widest zig-zag. Sometimes these controls are marked with symbols showing the various widths. Some machines combine the width control with the stitch-length control. Thus the symbols will show zig-zag stitches, not only of different widths but of various different densities as well.

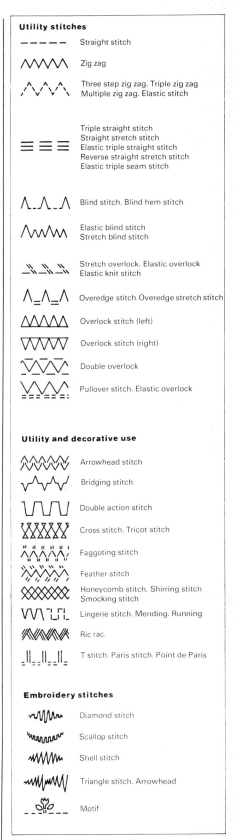

Utility stitches

----- Straight stitch

Zig zag

Three step zig zag. Triple zig zag. Multiple zig zag. Elastic stitch

Triple straight stitch
Straight stretch stitch
Elastic triple straight stitch
Reverse straight stretch stitch
Elastic triple seam stitch

Blind stitch. Blind hem stitch

Elastic blind stitch
Stretch blind stitch

Stretch overlock. Elastic overlock
Elastic knit stitch

Overedge stitch. Overedge stretch stitch

Overlock stitch (left)

Overlock stitch (right)

Double overlock

Pullover stitch. Elastic overlock

Utility and decorative use

Arrowhead stitch

Bridging stitch

Double action stitch

Cross stitch. Tricot stitch

Faggoting stitch

Feather stitch

Honeycomb stitch. Shirring stitch Smocking stitch

Lingerie stitch. Mending. Running

Ric rac.

T stitch. Paris stitch. Point de Paris

Embroidery stitches

Diamond stitch

Scallop stitch

Shell stitch

Triangle stitch. Arrowhead

Motif

Different machine stitches.

It is easier to understand the relationship between the stitch-width and stitch-length controls on the simpler type of zig-zag machine. Set your stitch-length control to half-way and the stitch-width control to 0. Sew a few stitches and open up the width control slowly while you are sewing. The line of straight stitches will have opened up to form a wide zig-zag stitch.

The next stage is to alter the stitch-length control. If it is opened right up to the longest stitch-length, the row of zig-zag stitches will open out until they become distorted. Close the stitch-length lever gradually and the zig-zag stitches will close up until a thick bar of close, wide stitches is formed. This is called satin stitch.

Too close or too small a stitch-length will result in the stitches piling up on top of each other, causing a nasty lump underneath and probably a broken needle. To avoid this, many controls are marked with a colour coding to indicate the area most suitable for satin stitch.

Vertical slot levers are more critical to set as the point is soon reached where the lever passes 0 and goes into reverse. To overcome this some machines have a fine stitch control.

Tension for zig-zag stitch

The tension settings need to be altered when working zig-zag or satin stitch. Set both the stitch-length and width levers to half way and sew a test sample using a contrasting thread in the needle and in the bobbin.

If the bobbin thread comes to the top of the material and shows more than a tiny bead of colour at the start and end of each stitch, the top tension is too tight. Loosen it.

Automatic stitches using oscillating needleplate to give 12-mm pattern width on the Vigorelli machine.

If nearly all of the top thread is taken through to the underneath, and the bobbin thread is distorted into a wavy line instead of a zig-zag, the top tension is too loose. Tighten it.

This is very important when sewing satin stitch. A slightly looser top tension will give a nice plump effect to the bar of close stitches. Use an embroidery foot. This has a wider groove underneath to allow the bar of satin stitch to pass freely underneath. The ordinary zig-zag presser foot will squash the stitches.

All zig-zag type stitches need to be fastened off. Draw the top stitch through to the back of the fabric and tie off or finish by sewing a few straight stitches in reverse. One machine has an automatic control that performs this function, whatever the width or pattern setting.

Stitches

The majority of semi-automatic machines have the basic utility stitches built in. These are selected by a lever or a dial and include a blind hem stitch and a choice of simple stretch and oversew stitches. These stitches can also be used decoratively for embroidery.

Semi-automatic machines with drop-in pattern cams also have a choice of simple geometric-type embroidery stitches sewn on a satin stitch setting. These stitches are all sewn forwards. The machine does not go back on itself automatically.

Automatic machines are provided with all the usual stitches, plus those that require the use of the automatic reverse feed – the trimotion stitches. The stitch patterns available in electronic machines are exactly the same, but the selection is by electronic circuitry.

The types of stitch patterns available are basically the same, whichever make of machine you use. Manufacturers have their individual stitch preferences and some machines feature a wider range than others. Some stitches have a variety of different names and this can be confusing. The machine stitch chart gives the most commonly used names first.

Automatic embroidery stitches

The few built-in stitches on semi-automatic machines can be used in a decorative manner. Even zig-zag and satin stitch used on their own can look attractive, especially when worked in a thicker or a metallic thread. These thicker threads are wound on to the bobbin and the material is sewn from the wrong side, the right side being underneath while sewn.

Using metallic cords and threads

The screw on the bobbin tension spring may need altering slightly when using metallic or thicker threads. The aim is to get the metallic thread to lie evenly on the material without distortion.

Open up the stitch-length slightly on the satin stitch setting when sewing with metallic threads. The metallic cords are more difficult to control and in some cases look better as a straight-stitch line or a very narrow zig-zag. The fine metallic cord worked through the needle is sewn from the right side and looks well on a not-too-close satin stitch setting. Use it in conjunction with the cords and flat lurex for a rich pattern effect.

Use any of the utility stitches worked in contrasting colours for decoration. Three step zig-zag can be worked in rows, parallel to one another. The blind hem stitch can be sewn first one way, and then a parallel line facing the other way. Try to keep the points of the pattern opposite each other to create a more balanced and attractive effect.

Three-needle position

If your machine has a three-needle position, this will provide more scope for decorative patterns, even on a machine with few embroidery stitches.

Select a stitchwidth about halfway and a close satin stitch setting. Machine a narrow satin stitch bar, about 1 cm ($\frac{1}{2}$ in) long, with the needle on the left hand side. Then, alter the needle position to the centre and sew a similar bar. Do the same with the needle on the right. Three little blocks of satin stitch will have moved across in steps. Repeat, going back the other way.

Using the needle position in conjunction with the stitch-width lever will give you a series of patterns very much like the simple automatic ones.

Automatic patterns

Most pattern cams are held in position by a lug or a notch and are marked to indicate the beginning of a pattern motif. Thus, a diamond shape would begin at the point and not half way through.

Some machines with built-in patterns have a pattern indicator to set to the beginning of a motif. On electronic machines it is possible to sew one pattern motif only; for example, one diamond.

If the length control is set for a longer stitch, the pattern will open up and the diamond will become elongated. On some machines a pattern density control allows an elongated pattern to be sewn in a variety of lengths without opening up the stitches. The diamonds would still be sewn in close satin stitch, however elongated.

Automatic stitches

Whether a machine is automatic with drop-in cams or fully automatic with built-in patterns, it can also have a selection of trimotion stitches, using reverse feed sewing in conjunction with automatic stitch-width. These patterns are all sewn on an open setting, normally the longest stitch-length. A short stitch-length or satin stitch setting would completely distort these stitches. The stretch and overlock stitches come into this category.

The width can be varied to some extent and some of the stretch stitches closed up slightly for certain effects. Many machines have the colour coding system to help choose the correct stitch-width and length settings. Sometimes all the close-type stitches are coded one colour and the open trimotion stitches another.

If the machine has a cam system, the pattern cams are formed from double discs with two separate contour formations round the circumference. Some fully automatic and electronic machines have automatic settings for these patterns, the correct stitch-width and length being set for you. However, it is possible to alter the width and length controls should you wish to do so. One machine has a control to make a slight adjustment to the trimotion stitches.

Working automatic stitches
The cloth needs to be guided very lightly when the machine is set for trimotion stitches. Let the machine and the pattern mechanism do all the work. If you pull the cloth at all, the stitching will distort. You will soon become used to the backwards and forwards motion of the cloth beneath the foot. Keep your attention on the outer side of the foot to guide a straight line.

How all these stitch patterns are used depends on the operator. They can be worked in rows, using shaded embroidery threads for effect, or metallic cord and flat lurex alternated with self-coloured thread.

The patterns can be sewn down one way, then the material turned and the same pattern sewn the other way around. If your machine has an even feed foot, or sews very accurately, it will be easy to make the motifs come dead opposite one another. On some machines this pattern alignment will need some assistance from the operator. It is possible to retard or speed up the sewing of a motif by placing one hand behind and one hand in front of the stitching area and either holding the cloth back or helping it forward.

Single pattern motifs can be combined and sewn in different directions to form larger motifs. For instance, a scallop motif could form the petals of a flower or a star. This is not difficult if the machine has a pattern start indicator.

Should you have any difficulty in sewing satin stitch or any of the close automatic patterns on fine material, place a piece of thin typing copy paper behind. This will hold the material taut and prevent puckering. It can be torn away afterwards. Iron-on interfacing can be used, but this is suitable only for stiffer fabric.

Automatic patterns can be used freely as creative embroidery to form a textural background or part of a pictorial design feature. Experiment with different threads and different settings.

Buttonholes
Semi-automatic or manual buttonhole
The controls are set at each stage by the worker and the cloth is pivoted half way through the operation.

The buttonhole has two parallel bars of satin stitching called *beads* and a bar tack at either end. The buttonhole can only be as wide as the stitch-width lever will allow. It can be any length determined by the operator. Mark the length with dressmaker's pencil, not tacking thread. Set the stitch-width control slightly less than half way (just under 2). This allows space for the slit in the middle of the buttonhole.

9 Sequence for making operator-controlled buttonholes.

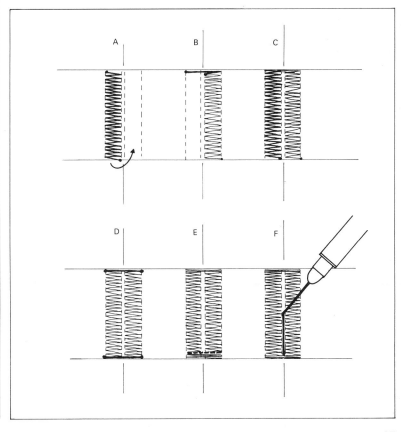

Set the machine for satin stitch and the needle position to the left. Stitch the required length and stop with the needle piercing the cloth on the right hand side of the satin stitch bead. Lift the presser foot and turn the cloth round so that the half-sewn buttonhole is facing the opposite way. Lower the foot. Raise the needle by turning the balance wheel towards you. Set the width to maximum and drop the feed. Sew a few stitches to form the bar tack, stopping with the needle on the left.

Set the feed to normal, raise the needle and set the zig-zag width to just under half way. Sew back to the other end of the buttonhole and stop with the needle in the cloth on the left of the row. Raise the needle and drop the feed. With the width control at maximum work a similar bar at this end. Secure ends by sewing a few straight stitches, either in one place using the drop feed, or along the inside of the bar tack.

Slit the centre space with a seam knife or ripper. If there is no drop feed control, try to keep the bar tack sewing in one place by retarding the feeding of the cloth.

Automatic buttonhole

This is dialled by the operator, but it is not necessary to turn the cloth. It can be called the four-step buttonhole. Sometimes a fifth step is used for the fastening off stitches, while electronic machines may have a two-step buttonhole. Follow your instruction book.

It is still necessary to measure the length. Some machines have a *float* or a *shoe* that fits on to the buttonhole foot. These come in different sizes and determine the finished length of the buttonhole. Other machines have graduation marks to use as a guide, or a sliding scale.

Most machines have a 'fine' control or density setting to ensure that both beads of the buttonhole are sewn with an equal stitch density. On some machines it is not possible to alter the width of the bead.

A thin cord can be inserted to make a firmer buttonhole. Fold the cord in half and locate on a lug on the rear of the buttonhole foot or hold with a pin in the cloth. The cord is pulled into position when the buttonhole is completed and the ends are trimmed off or taken through to the wrong side.

Accessories and attachments

The accessories are among the most useful, but at the same time, the least used of all the sewing aids. When all machines were of the simple straight-stitch kind, it was these attachments and feet for special sewing techniques that gave added interest as well as performing a highly practical purpose. As the machines themselves became more versatile, some manufacturers tended to concentrate less on the additions, although a certain number of feet for special sewing purposes are included with most machines.

The firms which have been in existence for a long time tend to include more accessories as this is part of a continuing tradition. In more recent years a series of specialized attachments have been developed to make use of the opportunities offered by automatic patterning.

Some of these accessories take the place of the normal presser foot, while others are in the form of guides or special sewing aids. Some are fiddlesome to put on – especially those that screw on. This is where those machines with easily removable foot and shank have an obvious advantage.

The simpler types of foot – mostly those for dressmaking processes – are changed by the snap-on or clip-on method; but certain attachments depend on the use of the needle bar movement to work a ratchet and need to be very firmly screwed into position.

The special feet and attachments used to come loose in a box. The very sight of this jumble of metal was enough to put people off. Now, some manufacturers have an accessory box or compartment with moulded indentations to fit each part, numbered or lettered for identification. Machine manuals illustrate the various feet, describe their purpose and method of use. Even so, many lie unused.

These attachments are essential additions to the simpler type of machine – in fact, they are part of it. Allow time to practice with each one of them on scrap material before embarking on any sewing project.

Special feet for most machines

These feet were first developed for the straight-stitch machine. Many are also available for the zig-zag machine and some have a wider slot for swing needle sewing. The feet

10 (Below) Buttonhole float or shoe with guide, or scale, underneath.

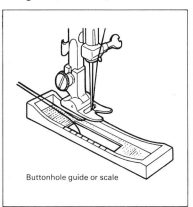

Buttonhole guide or scale

(Top row, left to right) Singer even feed foot; Riccar walking foot. (Centre row) New Home appliqué foot; Elna buttonhole foot and guide; Singer underbraider. (Bottom row) Elna tailor tacking foot, no snag foot and button sewer.

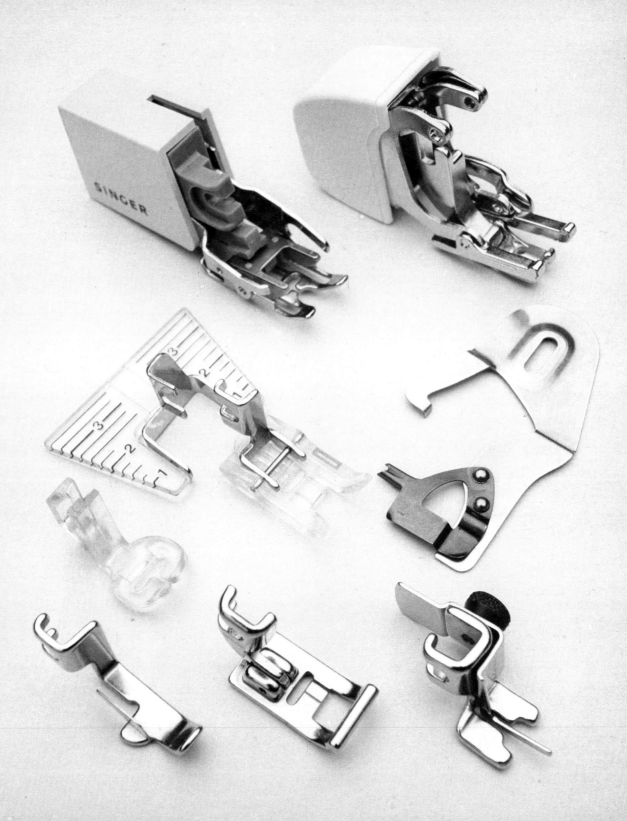

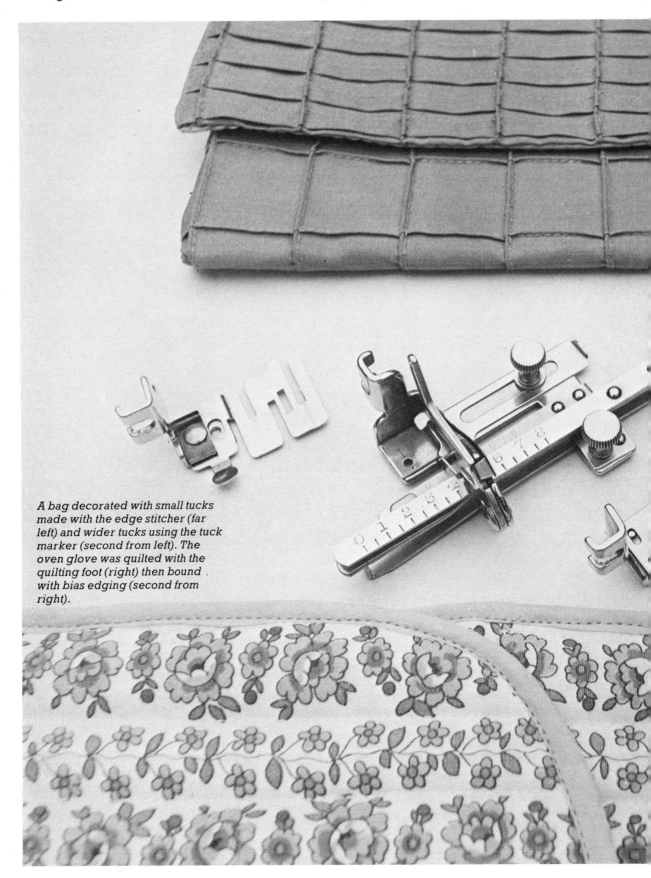

A bag decorated with small tucks made with the edge stitcher (far left) and wider tucks using the tuck marker (second from left). The oven glove was quilted with the quilting foot (right) then bound with bias edging (second from right).

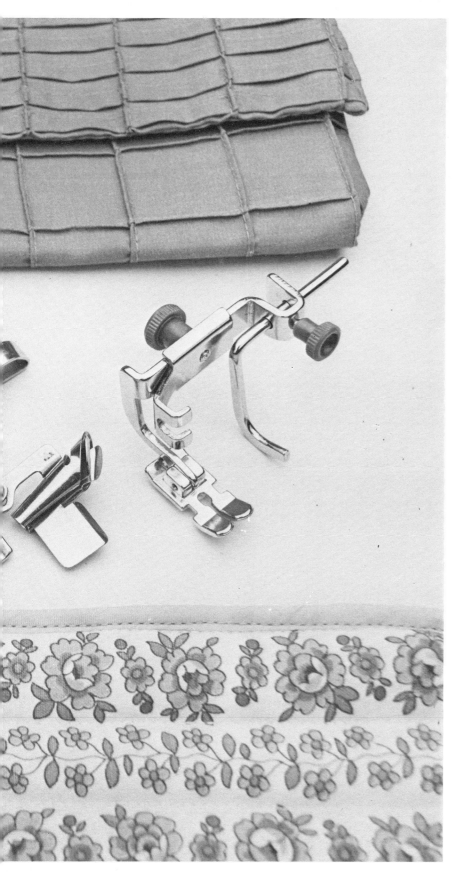

manufactured for some machines may be interchangeable with other makes but this partly depends on the height of the foot measured from base to top of shank. Some machines with removable feet have an additional screw-on system or an adaptor.

Adjustable hemmer
This is a straight-stitch foot for sewing the wider type of hems on household linen. A slide pointer is set to a figured scale, marked up to 2.5cm (1in). The material is inserted between the slide and the scale and drawn backwards and forwards until the hem is formed. With the needle in the cloth, lower the foot and sew carefully, keeping the cloth fed well into the hemmer.

For wider hems the slide is opened out and set towards the left. The hem is folded by hand before passing under the extension and into the folder.

Binder foot
Use cut strip or bought bias binding. Snip the binding to a point. Thread bought binding through the slit and flat binding into the scroll of the binder. Draw the binding out from behind and centre the edges beneath the needle. There is an adjuster. Sew a few stitches before inserting the cloth through the guide slit.

Turn round corners carefully, holding the binding up and towards you or against the guide if provided. Keep the binder full. If the binding slips to one side it will not be caught by the needle. Adjust the scroll to the left and avoid stretching the binding.

Braiding foot
This has a slot in front for threading braid or ribbon which is aligned under the needle.

Edge-stitcher
This versatile foot can be used for sewing a simple hem, for attaching lace or braid to an edge, for applying ribbon or lace on top of the material or for

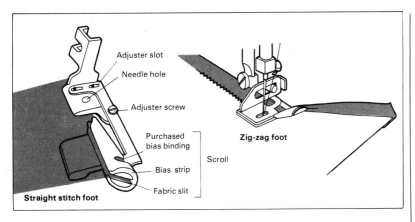

Adjuster slot

Needle hole

Adjuster screw

Purchased
bias binding

Bias strip

Fabric slit

Scroll

Straight stitch foot

Zig-zag foot

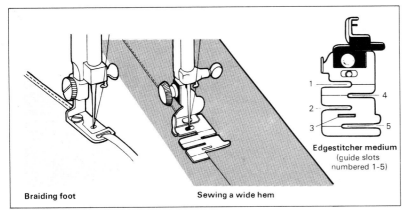

Braiding foot

Sewing a wide hem

Edgestitcher medium
(guide slots
numbered 1-5)

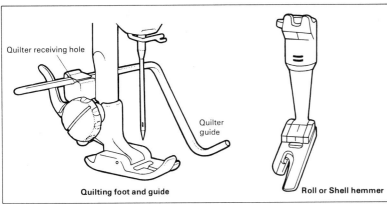

Quilter receiving hole

Quilter
guide

Quilting foot and guide

Roll or Shell hemmer

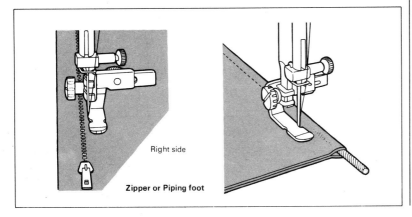

Right side

Zipper or Piping foot

edge-stitching two pieces of lace or ribbon together.

A series of slots or guide slits are arranged at various intervals on both sides. The lace is slotted on one side and the material on the other. A sliding adjuster centres the needle over the two edges to be joined.

Felling foot or lap hemmer

Similar to the narrow hemmer foot, it is used for sewing two pieces of material together with a felled hem. It is possible to use the narrow hemmer for felling, but the proper foot makes a better hem.

Gathering foot

This small, squat foot allows the material to gather up slightly beneath it before being sewn by the needle. It sews even, but very slight gathers. A shirred effect is obtained by sewing parallel lines at regular intervals. The gathering can be slightly increased by tightening the top tension and lengthening the stitch. This works well on fine fabrics of all kinds. Sew a measured test sample to determine the take up of the material. Some have a slot to allow ungathered fabric to be sewn on top.

Narrow hemmer foot

Turn the narrow hem under twice by hand and sew a few stitches. Leave the needle in the cloth and lift the hemmer foot. Bring the material across and feed into the scroll, holding it taut. Sew, making sure the hem is caught down. It is essential to feed the right amount of cloth into the scroll. Too much and the cloth will double over itself, too little and only a single hem will be sewn.

This does need practice, but once mastered, produces a very neat little hem. The roll

11–14 Special feet available on most machines. The design of these feet varies slightly from one manufacturer to another but the basic features remain the same and so does their method of use.

hemmer is used in a similar manner on zig-zag machines to make a shell edge.

Piping foot
This comes in two sizes with a groove to accommodate the piping cord.

Quilting foot and guide
Somewhat similar to the gathering foot, the quilter has a slightly raised front to lift it over the wadded material. The guide is used to keep the sewn rows of quilting even and parallel to one another. Sew the first line of stitching using the needleplate guidelines.

The quilting guide, an angled piece of metal on a moveable bar attached to the shank of the foot, is set to the required width. The next line is machined with the guide following the groove of the first sewn line.

Tuckmarker
Two adjustable metal slides can be set to a determined tuck width with a measured space between the tucks. The first tuck is folded by hand and sewn against the guide. The crease line of the next fold is marked by pressure to the selected measurement. Fold the fabric on the crease mark and sew the next tuck, when the following crease line will be automatically marked. The crease will not show on synthetics.

Underbraider or raised seam attachment
This attachment is easy to use and surprisingly effective. Use the quilting foot unless a special one is provided. A grooved piece of metal is fitted on to the machine bed in front of the needleplate. Braid, wool or soft cord is slotted into the groove and out behind the needle.

The design can be drawn on the material, wrong side uppermost. This is fed under the foot and on top of the braid, which, caught by the needle, sews in a continuous pattern. The right side is underneath. Turn sharp corners by pivoting on the lowered needle. Use only soft threads to prevent

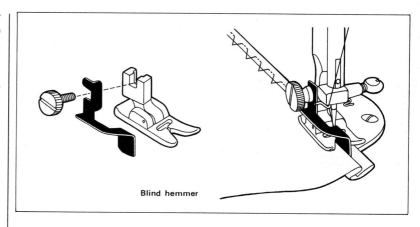

Blind hemmer

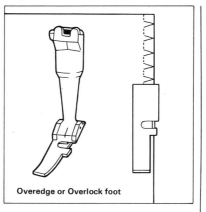

Overedge or Overlock foot

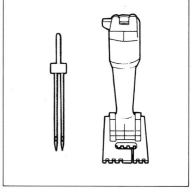

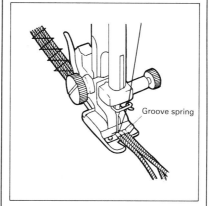

Groove spring

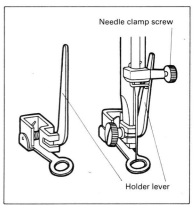

Needle clamp screw

Holder lever

15–19 Special feet for zig-zag machines. These feet can only be used on machines with a swing needle.

damage to the needle. On zig-zag machines this can be used in conjunction with twin needles.

Zipper or piping foot
This foot was first designed to meet the need for sewing close to the piping so popular on the dresses of the late 19th century. It comes either in the form of a very narrow presser foot or as a half foot, open on one side. Some are placed on a sliding bar held by a screw so

that sewing can be worked on either side.

Today, this foot does duty both as a piping and a zipper foot. To set for close sewing, place the needle down in the cloth and adjust the foot up to it. Tighten the screw. If the foot is fixed, alter the needle position.

Special feet for zig-zag machines

Appliqué foot

The appliqué foot is made of metal or available for some machines in see-through plastic to give a clearer view of the stitches. This foreshortened foot with a wider slot in the front helps when applying thick threads. Other machines use the embroidery or the cording foot.

Blind hemmer foot and guide

This is an indispensible attachment for use in conjunction with the blind hem stitch. The hem is turned up twice, then folded back on itself, fabric towards the left. The guide allows the needle to catch just the right amount of cloth when it swings out for the blind stitch.

The guide can be screwed on in addition to the normal zig-zag foot. Some machines have a special foot with the guide incorporated, while others have an adjustable guide altered by a screw for fine control setting.

Braiding foot

This has a large hole or groove in front of the foot to accommodate thick cord or braid. This passes under the needle and is sewn down with a zig-zag or suitable pattern stitch. Some feet have a sliding adjuster slot with a screw.

Buttonhole foot

A groove beneath the foot allows the raised stitches of the buttonhole to pass easily beneath. There are various systems of marking on the foot to aid the alignment of the buttonhole. A lug or spur on the back of some feet and on the front of others holds the folded filler thread in position for corded buttonholes. On some, the free ends can be held by a notch while working. This filler cord is sewn over during the buttonhole process and pulled into position afterwards.

Button sewing foot

The wide gap in front allows a clear view of the button. An ordinary zig-zag foot can be used instead.

Lower the feed and set the zig-zag to 0. Place a button in position on the fabric with the holes lying horizontally. Turn the balance wheel towards you by hand and lower the needle into the left hand hole. Still controlling the balance wheel by hand, open up the width control far enough to allow the needle to drop into the right hand hole. Set the width control to this limit. Sew five or six stitches, return the width to 0 and sew three or four straight stitches to fasten off.

For a short shank, place a needle on top of the button and sew over it. For a longer shank, lay a matchstick between the button and the cloth. Sew additional stitches. Some makes incorporate a spacer for the shank.

Snap fasteners and hooks and eyes can be sewn in a similar manner.

Cloth guide

This is an adjustable metal guide that can be screwed on to the machine bed to the right of the needle. The cloth is held against the guide and it is useful when sewing beyond the needleplate markings. Magnetic guides are available for machines made from aluminium alloy. These can be placed anywhere on the machine bed.

Cording foot

Cord is threaded through a hole or slotted under a grooved flange on the foot before passing behind and under the needle. The cord is held by a zig-zag stitch. Some feet have grooves or holes to accommodate up to five cords. These can be held down using suitable automatic patterns.

Cover plates

These are used to put the feed out of action when it is not possible to lower the teeth. They are used for darning, free embroidery and button sewing. Some fit or clip over the needleplate, others are interchangeable or a device is placed beneath to raise the needleplate.

Embroidery foot

This has a wider groove under the foot to allow the satin and embroidery stitches to pass freely beneath without the stitches becoming deformed. It can be made of metal or see-through plastic which may be reinforced with metal. This foot may do double duty for sewing buttonholes or when sewing pin tucks.

Nickel-plated sewing foot

A strong foot suitable for sewing heavy fabrics on a large scale – straight-stitch, zig-zag or overlock.

No-snag foot

The divided forks at the front of the presser foot are joined by a raised bar which helps when sewing shaggy fabrics, towelling, net curtains and curly knitteds.

Overedge or vari-overlock foot

Similar in appearance to a half foot except that it has a metal wire on the right hand edge. This helps to keep the fabric flat while the needle swings over when sewing overlock-type stitches.

Pin tuck foot

A series of grooves underneath the foot is used to space parallel rows of pin tucks. It is designed to be used with twin needles. These feet can be supplied with three, five, seven or nine grooves in different widths. These are for use with twin needles of 4 mm ($\frac{5}{32}$ in), 3 mm ($\frac{3}{8}$ in), 2 mm ($\frac{1}{8}$ in) and 1.5 mm ($\frac{1}{16}$ in) width.

The pin tuck foot can be used with or without the inclusion of a gimp thread in the tucks. Some machines have a cording plate fitted over the needleplate. The cord is slotted into the groove and fed beneath the needles which enclose it beneath the pin tuck. Others have a hole in the needleplate through which the gimp is threaded. Use a crochet cotton or coton à broder.

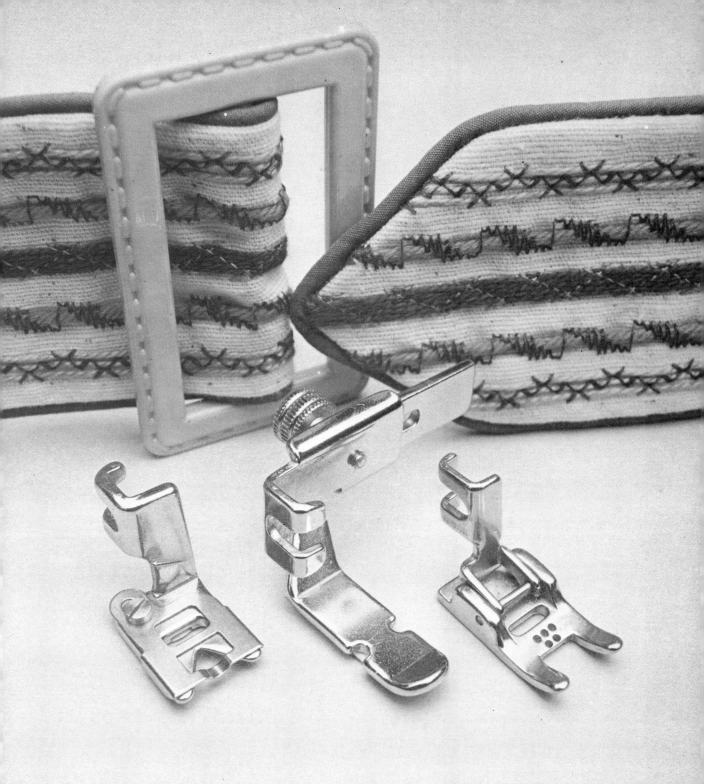

A belt decorated with braid and cording held with decorative zig-zag stitching using (left to right) the Elna braiding foot; New Home adjustable zipper or piping foot; Elna multi-cord foot.

Decorative stitching using (clockwise) the Elna monogram stitcher; New Home flower stitcher; New Home alphabet stitcher; New Home spiral stitcher.

Stretch stitch or tricot foot

This foot is used for sewing stretch stitches on jersey fabrics. A large indented space beneath the foot allows room for the action of the trimotion stitches. An ordinary foot would hold the material too firmly in the sewing area.

Teflon foot

This foot is Teflon-coated, like a non-stick saucepan, for smoother sewing on plastic, PVC and foam-backed materials. Some makers supply a Teflon plate to fit under the presser foot.

Zipper foot for invisible zips

This has channels which guide the zipper coils beneath. A different foot is needed for each make of invisible zip. The adjustable zipper foot can be used instead.

Attachments provided with some machines

Alphabet stitches

This attachment is used in place of the presser foot. A lever fits over the needlebar clamp to work a ratchet wheel which engages with a drop-in letter pattern cam. An under-plate is provided for fine fabrics.

Drop the feed. Use a fine needle and thread and stitch-width $1\frac{1}{2}$-2. Bring both thread ends to the surface of the fabric and sew a few stitches to lock the thread. Cut the ends close to the cloth. Continue sewing.

After the letter is completed a spacer lever can be pressed to move the cloth far enough for a full stop to be sewn. These letters are small, suitable for a handkerchief corner. It is not possible to vary the size.

Basting foot

One maker uses this foot in conjunction with a control on the machine for basting or tacking. The device allows one stitch to be sewn each time the foot control pedal is depressed with a sharp tap. Any length of stitch can be worked. It is also used for embroidery. A similar device is built into electronic machines.

Chain stitcher or looper

This device is inserted in place of the bobbin case. A single top thread is used to form a straight-stitch on top of the fabric and a chain stitch beneath. It is easy to unravel and is used for temporary seams and hems or for chain stitch embroidery. Avoid sewing round sharp corners as the chain stitch may break.

Tension is regulated by the upper thread tension control. The chain should be neither too loose nor too tight, but lie evenly on the fabric. The top thread may have to pass through a chain stitch guide.

Never sew in reverse. To finish, raise the foot and have the needle in the highest position. Draw a loop of thread out from the upper tension control, and hold before drawing the thread out and to the left of the foot. Remove the fabric from the machine by pulling towards the back. This forms a temporary lock. The seam will need to be fastened off by hand.

Circle stitcher

This is a device fitted to the bed of the machine for sewing decorative circles. A sliding scale with a spike at one end can be set for sewing circles with diameters ranging from 13 cm (5 in) to 27 cm (11 in) according to the machine. The guide may be attached to a separate needleplate or fit over it.

Work in an embroidery frame or back the fabric with iron-on interfacing or typing paper. Mark the centre of the circle on the fabric and centre on the spike. Sew with an even speed. A careful choice of automatic patterns combined with twin-needle sewing will give a rich, decorative effect. Circles can be overlapped or sewn inside each other. When joining, try to end with a matching pattern sequence. Take the ends through and tie off.

Darning foot

This enables the worker to move fabric freely beneath the foot for darning or embroidery.

The foot lifts when the needle is raised, but stays down when the needle is in the cloth. Speed of sewing gives this continuous motion. The makes vary, but all are worked on a spring-loaded principle, some using a lever that rests on the needlebar. Lower or cover the feed when working.

Even feed feet

These feet all help to feed the cloth at an even rate. They prevent one ply from creeping ahead of the other. They are useful for sewing difficult fabrics.

Use them for sewing knitted and stretch fabrics; shiny fabrics and plastic; stripes and checks; bonded fabrics; binding blanket edges; leather, suede and synthetic leather; pile fabrics; velvet; fake fur and brushed fabrics; layers of net; and waistbands, welts and slot seams.

Dual feed

Only one machine has a built-in dual feed device, located behind the presser foot bar. It takes the form of a foot with serrations underneath located on a hinged bracket controlled by a spring. It snaps into place and can be disengaged by pushing down lightly and pulling it out.

Even feed foot and walking foot

The presser foot is removed and the feed foot is screwed tightly into position with the forked arm resting over the needle clamp bar. This arm, activated by the up and down movement of the needlebar, operates a ratchet that raises and lowers an inner, serrated foot. This is surrounded by a static outer foot.

Use a slightly shorter stitch-length than usual for perfect fabric matching. To match striped fabrics, line up care-

Any combination of decorative patterns in all colours can be made with a Bernina circle stitcher attachment for dinner mats.

fully at the start of the seam. Hold temporarily with a pin set at right angles to the seam line about 2.5cm (1 in) in from the edge.

Hold the thread ends to the back of the foot when starting to sew. Release the ends and remove the pin when a few stitches have been sewn. Guide the fabric lightly and let the foot do the work for you.

Eyelet stitcher
The needleplate is changed or a cover plate fitted on top. To the right of the needle slot there is a semi-circular metal prong on which to place the eyelet. The needle dips into the metal prong on the right hand swing. Set the zig-zag width to $1\frac{1}{2}$ for small, and $2\frac{1}{2}$ for large eyelets. Drop the feed and use the special foot provided. The cover plate is for use on machines without a drop feed.

Stretch the cloth in an embroidery frame and punch holes with the awl provided. A square awl is used for holes in felt or leather. Place the hole over the prong. Lower the foot and sew with an even speed. Turn the frame in one continuous motion if possible. As the feed is out of action there is no automatic control of the stitch density. Sew round the eyelet once fairly quickly and then a second time a little more slowly. Do not continue to sew when the frame is at rest or the stitches will build up in one place.

Larger holes can be sewn round three times. To finish, set the stitch width to 0 and sew once round. Cut off.

Flower stitcher
This attachment will sew small circles, straight-stitch or zig-zag. When used in conjunction with automatic patterns, flower motifs can be sewn. A scale allows variation of circle size and one pattern to be sewn inside the other. It is so designed that a flower with five petals is sewn when used with the machine it is made for. The width of circle can be altered while the cloth is in position.

Set the needle to the left and drop the feed. Position the spring-loaded lever over the needlebar. This operates the ratchet on the circular stitching device. Back thin cloth with typing copy paper. Bring both threads to the top of the material and sew a few stitches on 0 width before re-setting for zig-zag or automatic patterns. To alter the position, loosen the screw and slide the cloth and disc holder together. Do not lift the presser bar. Finish off with a few stitches at 0.

Monogram stitcher
The foot is removed and a metal guide bar screwed behind the presser bar. The fabric is stretched in the circular metal frame provided. This has a slotted arm protruding to the left. One end of the metal guide slots into this arm. The other end is fitted into the groove of a chosen letter plate. This letter plate is located on to a pin on the other end of the circular frame. Lower the presser bar.

20 Ruffler foot and attachment.

The machine is set to a medium width zig-zag. As the sewing progresses, the guide works round the letter-shaped groove and moves the frame beneath the needle to produce an identical letter. There is a choice of four letter sizes to each plate. The largest one is suitable for embroidery on heavy linen such as table cloths and pillow cases.

Ruffler
This is a straight-stitching device for making pleats, gathers and ruffles. A forked arm fits over the needlebar to activate a ruffler blade. The size of the ruffle can be altered by a control determining the number of stitches to each pleat and by altering the stitch-length.

The material is passed through the steel blades one way only – from front to back. Never sew without cloth between the blades. The ruffles can be worked sewn on to a single layer of cloth or sandwiched between two layers. Lengths of pleating can be worked separately and attached afterwards.

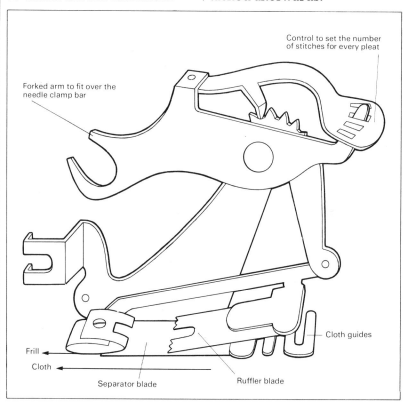

Control to set the number of stitches for every pleat

Forked arm to fit over the needle clamp bar

Cloth guides

Frill

Cloth

Separator blade

Ruffler blade

Roller foot

Two or more little rollers are fitted to the front and back of the foot. Criss-cross grooves help the foot to feed difficult materials evenly. It is used for sewing and quilting on leather, plastic, net, velvet and slippery fabrics.

Spiral stitcher

This is a more sophisticated version of the flower stitcher and works on a similar principle. The cloth is stretched on a circular frame which has grooved teeth on the inner circumference. These match up with the teeth on a smaller circle attached to the foot. A lever over the needlebar clamp works a ratchet to turn the circles.

The distance between the needle and the circumference of the small circle can be altered by an adjuster screw. The interaction of these circles produces a variety of spiral patterns which can be sewn as plain lines or with zig-zag width. Automatic patterns and twin-needle sewing adds to the number of possible effects.

A choice of two sizes of outer ring gives patterns with nine or nineteen spiral points. The thread must be brought to the surface of the cloth before starting and a few stitches sewn on stitch-width 0 before cutting off the ends.

These spiral motifs are very decorative. Use two colours in twin-needle sewing or one plain and one gold or silver cord.

Tailor tacking foot, fringe foot or looping foot

This foot has a raised flange over which the zig-zag stitch forms a loop. Loosen the top tension or reposition the top thread according to your machine instructions. Set the stitch width at $1\frac{1}{2}$-2. The needle must clear the flange on the foot on both sides.

Tailor tacks

Mark the pattern outlines on the fabric with tailor chalk. Use basting thread or two fine embroidery threads in the needle when sewing thicker fabrics. Use a single, finer thread for thin fabrics and the longest stitch length.

A contrast thread in the bobbin helps when the double layers of fabric are pulled apart and the loops between the cloth are snipped. This leaves a line of marking tufts.

Fringing or looped embroidery

A shorter stitch-length closes the loops up to form a fringed line. These loops will come undone and need fixing. Iron-on interfacing will hold, but also stiffens, the fabric.

Lay a worked fringe line to one side and sew a straight-stitch seam close to the first row of stitches. The fringe rows can be sewn close together to form a looped or tufted fabric. This could suggest feathers or animal fur for decorative work.

Loops sewn into a spiral are started from the outside, each succeeding spiral sewn to hold the preceding one. Stretch the cloth in a circular embroidery frame and turn with an even speed. This could be used for the centre of a decorative flower motif.

Wheel feed foot

This works on the same principle as the roller foot, but is made for sewing narrow edges on leather. A wheel with serrated edges is fitted to the left hand side of a very narrow foot.

Wool darning foot

This is similar to the ordinary darning foot, but is slightly larger and has a hole or groove in front for threading the wool. This is sewn over the area to be darned, carried backwards and forwards by the foot. Afterwards it is zig-zagged the other way, using the presser foot.

Special needles

Apart from the needles provided for normal sewing and those designed for sewing different types of fabric, there are certain needles to perform specific tasks. Some are expensive, but used on the correct materials, they are effective and fun to use.

Not every manufacturer produces special needles. It is worth seeing if those made to fit one machine will fit another. These needles can only be used on a zig-zag machine threading from front to back.

Basting needle

Many machines have a special foot or electronic control for basting stitches. The basting needle is an effective method of achieving these longer stitches if your machine is of the simpler zig-zag type.

This needle has two eyes positioned one above the other. The lower eye is used for normal sewing and the upper

21 Roller foot.

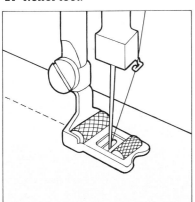

22 Wool-darning foot.

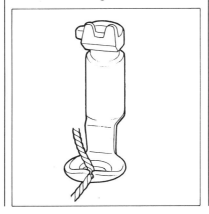

eye for basting or tacking. The needle does not need to be changed if your work entails a mixture of tacking and sewing. Although the machine is set for a zig-zag stitch, the upper thread will only loop with the bottom thread when the needle swings to the left. The position of the upper eye makes the needle shorter.

Thread the upper eye with a contrasting colour with the needle in the central position. Set the longest stitch-length and the widest zig-zag width. It will sew stitches of about 7 mm ($\frac{1}{4}$ in) long. Use them for marking out on single fabric. Draw the line with tailor chalk first then sew, using the zig-zag presser foot. The guide line should be sewn over at the extreme left of the needle swing.

When tacking two layers of fabric together, hold them with pins placed at right angles to the seam line, removing the pins before the foot approaches.

Twin and triple needles

Two or three needles are mounted side by side on a single shank which fits up into the needlebar in the normal way and screws firmly into position. The top threads interlock with a single bobbin thread which forms a kind of zig-zag stitch on the underside of the fabric. These needles produce parallel lines of stitching when the machine is set to straight-stitch. Zig-zag and automatic patterns can be used providing the stitch-width is less than half the maximum swing.

Use twin needles in conjunction with the pin tuck foot to produce parallel rows of tucking, with or without a gimp filler thread. Alternatively, a foot with a wide central space pushes up the pin tuck fabric.

Simple zig-zag, three-step zig-zag and curved patterns give variety to these pin tucks.

Before setting the width, test the swing of the needle to see that it does not catch on the sides of the foot. The extra needle decreases the available width. Some automatic patterns are not suitable for twin-needle work. The correct patterns will be marked on your machine or on the drop-in pattern cam, with a twin needle symbol where appropriate. Some electronic machines have a twin-needle sewing button.

Experiment to see which automatic patterns look best. The pattern motifs will repeat themselves, side by side. Sometimes they may overlap and look muddled. Two different colours in the needles will overcome this. One needle threaded in thin metallic cord will highlight and outline one half of the pattern.

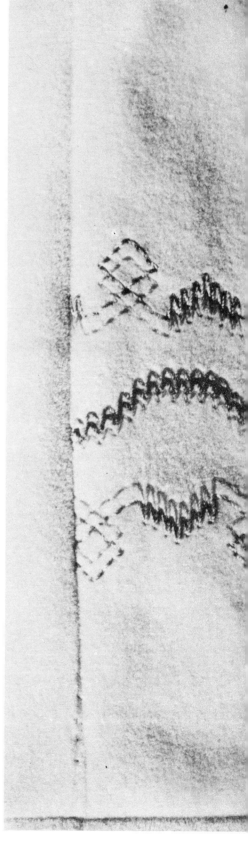

(Right) Example of decorative stitching worked on a Vigorelli using twin and triple needles and an oscillating needleplate.

23 Special machine needles.

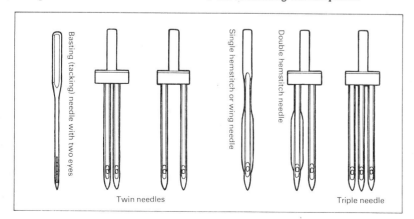

Basting (tacking) needle with two eyes

Single hemstitch or wing needle

Double hemstitch needle

Twin needles

Triple needle

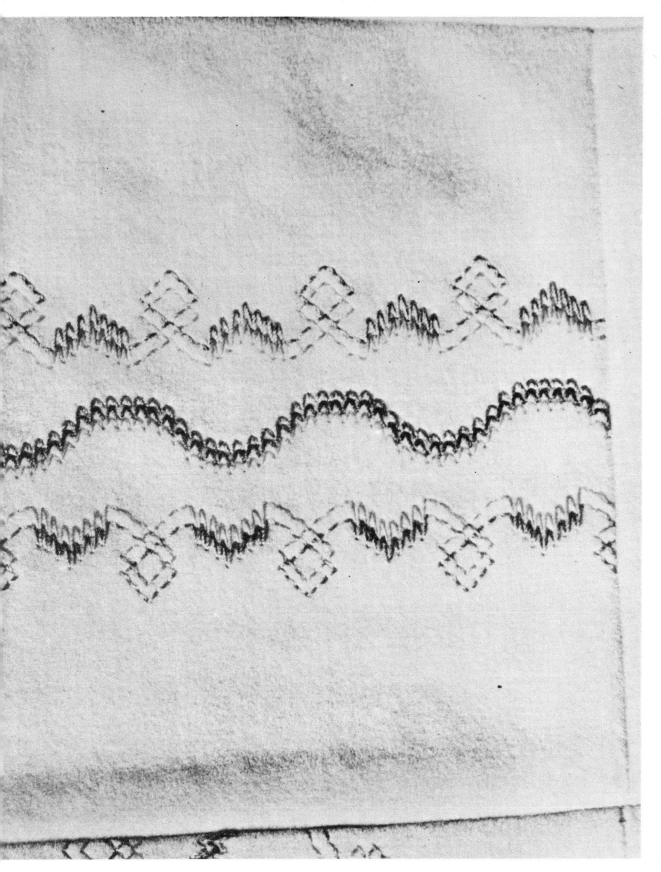

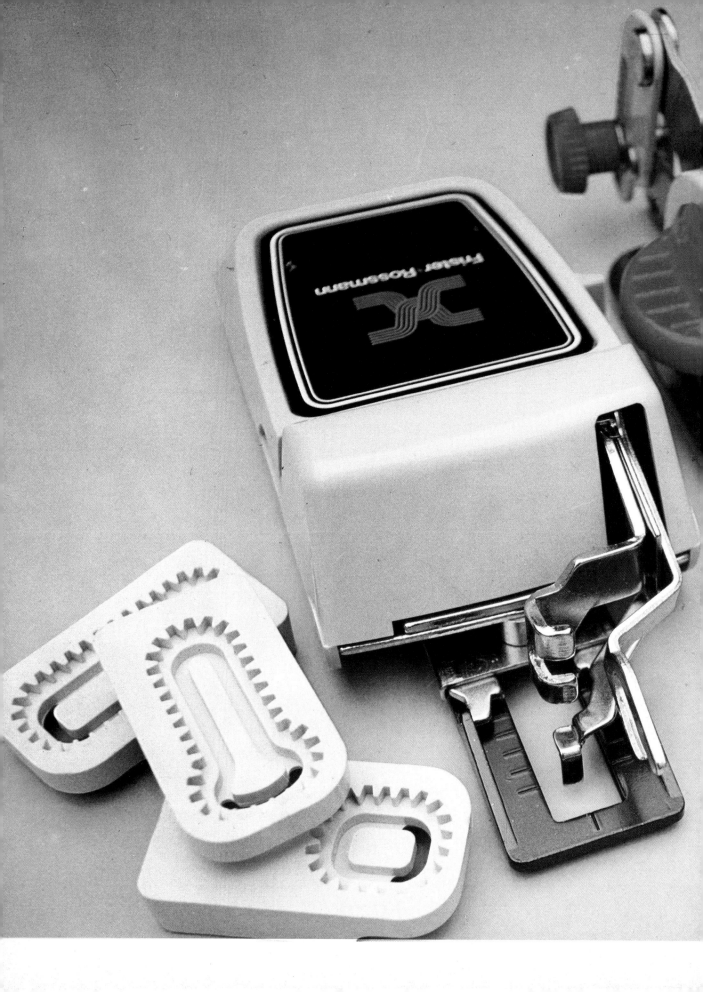

Top threading

Extra thread spindles are provided for multiple-needle sewing. On some machines there are extra thread guides and tension discs. Not all machines are equipped to take triple needles. The machine with the oscillating needleplate to give extra patterning width makes good use of triple needles. Three-colour sewing adds an extra dimension to the automatic patterns.

The threads may share guides until the double tension discs are reached where they should be separated. If there is only one set of tension discs, then try to keep the threads lying parallel. They may have to share the eyehole in the take-up lever. Some have two eyes. Most machines have two thread guides, one to each needle. Try not to get the threads twisted over each other.

When using triple needles, pass the inner thread through one tension disc and the outer needle threads through the other tension disc.

Turning corners

Because of the width of the needles, it is not possible to turn corners in the usual way. The cloth has to be turned in three stages, each time raising and lowering the foot. Gently pivot on the needles, turning the balance wheel towards you by hand. Try to keep the inner needle stitch in the same place.

Wing or hemstitching needle

This needle has a flange or wing on one or both sides of the needle tapering down to the needle eye. This is used in hemstitching to make a decorative hole in the cloth. It will not work on soft or synthetic fabrics as the holes tend to close up. Use firmly woven fabric, cotton or linen. Organdie is the most suitable. A twin-wing or double hemstitching needle is also available. This has one ordin-

Frister Rossmann (left) and Singer (right) buttonhole attachments.

ary needle and one winged needle sharing the same shank.

Stitch patterns are sewn first one way and then back the other, the broad blade sharing the same holes worked on the previous row. If your machine sews perfect, even stitches, this is not difficult. Guide the cloth lightly. On others the fabric may need a little help. A see-through embroidery foot is essential for this type of work.

A double row of straight stitching will have the large holes shared in the middle. Turn the fabric to the left at the end of the row. Raise the needles slightly so that they just touch the cloth. A slight adjustment may be necessary. The maximum possible zig-zag swing is less than when using normal twin-needles. Set the width control very carefully. Use a machine embroidery thread no. 50, or finer mercerized cotton no. 60.

Buttonholer attachments

These attachments produce a completely automatic one-step buttonhole. They can be set to produce buttonholes of different lengths.

Buttonholer attachment for straight-stitch machines

The presser foot is removed and a cover plate with a hole for the needle is firmly screwed to the machine bed. The buttonholer screws on to the presser bar and a forked arm fits over the needle clamp. The bobbin thread is brought to the surface through the needle hole.

There is a vertical sliding screw adjustment to set the buttonhole length and two horizontal screw adjusters. One sets the bight, or width, of the buttonhole bead. The other sets the width of the space between the beads.

A feeding foot with a marked scale is moved from side to side beneath the straight-stitch needle to produce the automatic sewing of the buttonhole

beads and end bar tacks. Sew round twice for firmer stitching and tighten the bobbin tension for a purl buttonhole. This gives the appearance of a hand sewn one. This is a useful attachment for straight-stitch machines.

Automatic buttonholer

This is for use on low presser bar machines with a central needle position. It will sew different sizes of buttonhole in standard, keyhole, eyelet, bound and purl edge shapes.

Remove the presser foot. The attachment is then screwed to the presser bar. A forked arm fits over the needle clamp. Drop in templates are positioned on to a pinion gear. A lever positions the buttonhole starting point. The marked fabric is aligned with marks on the guide support foot. The presser foot is lowered and the bobbin thread brought through to the top of the fabric.

The buttonhole is formed automatically. There is no need to hold the fabric. Light fabric can be supported underneath with tissue or typing copy paper which is torn away afterwards.

Purl edged buttonholes are made by sewing a narrow buttonhole over a wider one. First sew a standard buttonhole with a width of 3mm ($\frac{1}{8}$in). Change to a purl edged template of the same size without lifting the presser foot lever. Set the zig-zag width to 2mm ($\frac{1}{16}$in) and sew round once more.

Templates in different sizes are provided for sewing the straight-stitch rectangle used when making dressmaker bound buttonholes.

Automatic buttonhole sewer

This device is designed to work with one make of machine only. The presser foot is first removed. The buttonhole sewer has a feed shaft which is inserted into a shaft hole on the machine bed. It is swung into position beneath the needle and held on to the machine bed with a fastening bolt.

Plastic buttonhole plates are

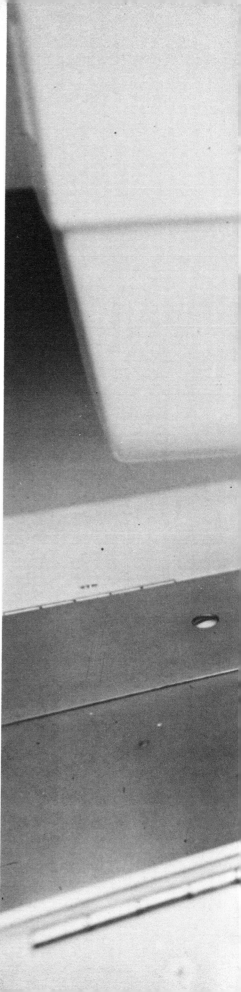

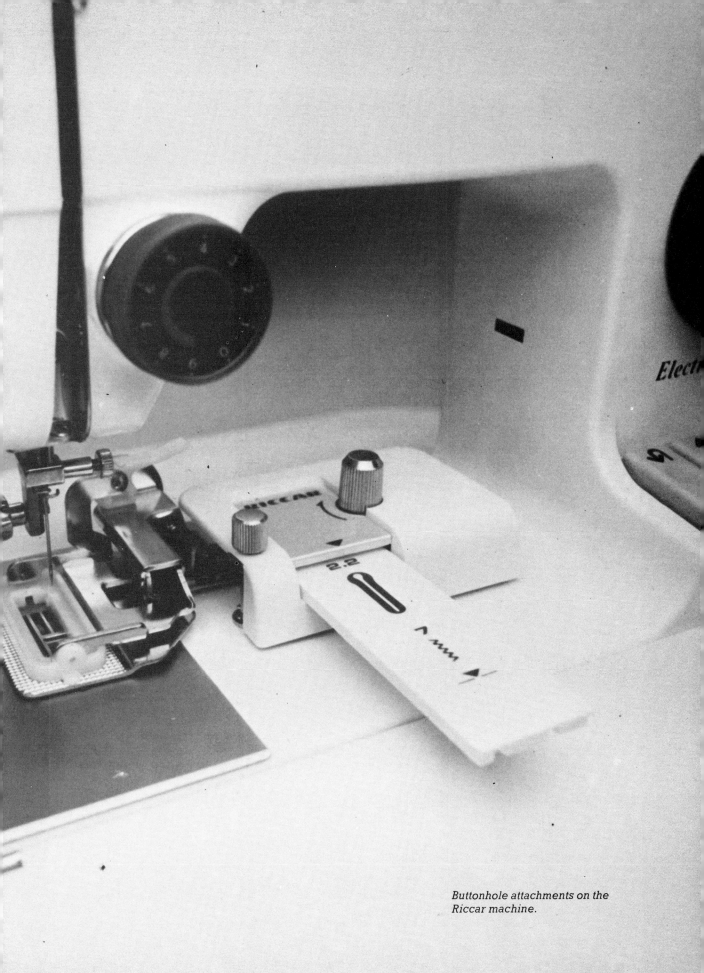

*Buttonhole attachments on the
Riccar machine.*

marked with settings for the machine selector dials. A drawing of a button is used for comparison with a real button when selecting the buttonhole size. The chosen plate is slotted into the buttonhole sewer. The fabric is fed under a presser frame which holds it in place while the automatic buttonhole is sewn.

The buttonhole can be sewn over by re-inserting the plate. A cord catch is located on the rear of the presser frame for use when sewing corded buttonholes.

One-step buttonhole foot

This foot, used on one electronic machine, makes buttonholes of up to 3.5 cm (1⅜ in) long. Two widths of buttonhole can be set. The zig-zag needleplate and one-step foot are attached and the machine switched to MIN. Select straight stitch. The lower thread is brought through to the top by turning the balance wheel towards you by hand.

A carrier clamp at the rear of the foot can be set for the correct length of buttonhole by placing a real button of the chosen size in the carrier. So long as the button is in position, the machine will sew a buttonhole to the correct length for that button. Buttons of unusual shape or thickness have to be set accordingly by hand. There is a density control on the machine to balance the stitching of both beads. Identical buttonholes are sewn by pushing the 'single pattern only' symbol after a satisfactory test buttonhole is sewn.

Zig-zag attachments for straight-stitch machines

Automatic zig-zagger or decorator

This works on the same principle as the straight-stitch buttonholer attachment and is de-signed to convert the machine for swing needle sewing. Pattern cams give some simple embroidery patterns. It sews best when used on a straight line or a shallow curve.

Blind stitcher

This converts the machine for blind hem stitch. Both these attachments and the zig-zagger are activated by a forked arm over the needle clamp.

Rug Fork

This accessory is a fork with two prongs, or tines, round which rug wool or some other type of thread is wound. The machine sews up the middle of the loops which can be sewn on their own or fixed to a background.

Thread the machine with synthetic thread for strength. Any type of thick thread can be used for the looping provided it can be pierced by the needle; thick or thin wool, braid, tape, ribbon or lace. Fine, hard threads are not suitable. If each loop is not sewn by the needle, it will unravel.

Wind the wool round the fork, starting from the open prong end. Secure the first end by binding over with the second turn of thread, keeping the layers of thread as even as possible. When it is full, place it under the machine foot.

Sew up the middle using straight stitch or a very narrow zig-zag. When the machine foot reaches the place where the fork is joined, stop and gradually withdraw the fork so that only a few loops are left on the prongs. Wind on more thread, this time slipping it down and over the fork. Continue sewing.

It is possible to sew continuous strips of loops or cut fringing. Use as trimmings on clothing, soft furnishings and lampshades.

(Right) Sample of work done using a rug fork.

24 (Below) Weaver's reed (left) and rug fork (right).

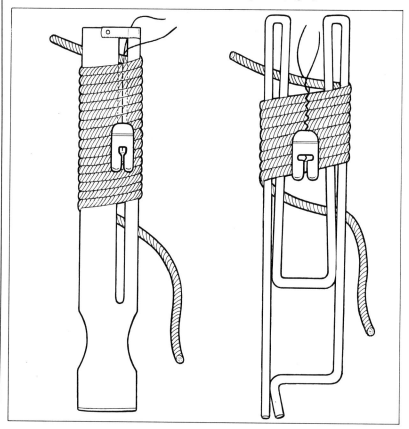

Use hessian as a backing. Mark the position of the fringe lines in felt pen 2.5-4 cm (1-1½ in) apart depending on the thickness of the wool. Place the full rug fork on top and machine the loops in position, following the guide lines. Start on the left hand side of the fabric. The rows of worked loops will be supported by the machine table. Push succeeding rows of loops to one side as you sew.

The loops can be left or cut into a pile. This adds texture to wall hangings. Decorative strips in a variety of threads can be sewn on for cushions, leaving parts of the background fabric showing.

Weaver's reed
This is a flat metal fork with one narrow and one wide prong. The machine foot sews in between the gap and it is used in a similar manner to the rug fork. The wider row of loops can be cut, leaving the smaller row fixed to the background.

The hemstitcher
This is another fork-shaped accessory used for making spaced hemstitches to join two completely separate pieces of material. It has two long, narrow prongs and a narrow space in the middle. The fork is sandwiched between two flat layers of material along the marked seam lines. Place both layers and the fork beneath the straight stitch presser foot and sew up the middle of the fork using a long straight stitch. Withdraw the fork.

Each piece of material is folded back on itself and the lengthened stitches stretch out to form a false hemstitch.

Common faults and how to correct them

Provided that the machine is well looked after, cleaned and oiled at regular intervals and the needle changed frequently, it should sew without any trouble. However, from time to time, minor sewing faults occur. If you do not know the cause, this can be very frustrating and time wasting. Sometimes people tend to think something has gone wrong with the mechanics of the machine when all it may need is a slight adjustment to the controls. It takes time to master all the control settings on a machine. Machine sewing requires patience and a calm attitude.

Once you are at ease with the machine, everything will come to you automatically, without thinking. This also applies to dealing with faults and their remedies. Try to prevent faults before they develop. Many are due to incorrect threading or setting of the machine. It is a good idea to check everything before you start to sew. It will save time in the long run.

25 Faults which can occur when winding the bobbin.

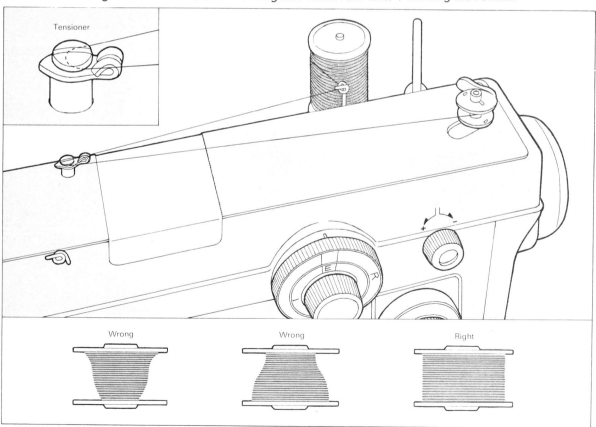

Tensioner

Wrong   Wrong   Right

If possible, store the machine in a warm, dry place. If the machine is kept in a cold room, the oil will harden and the machine will be sluggish to start. If it is impossible to store it in a warm place, then bring it out for a couple of hours before starting to sew. Keep the machine covered and out of the reach of children.

If the machine makes a nasty noise while you are sewing, stop at once. If something has gone wrong, this will help prevent further damage. It might be something simple like the bobbin falling out of the shuttle race because it was not located properly or the cover not being replaced in position.

Avoid sewing over pins. It is possible to sew a tacking seam with the pins at right angles to it, but only the very tips of the pins should protrude on to the sewing line. Do not force the machine to sew over fabric that is too thick or strong and take care when sewing several plies of material, especially where two welt seams meet.

If the machine is in constant use or when working free machine embroidery, the foot control pedal can get very warm and overheat. Most are provided with an automatic safety cut-off. This problem will not occur if the machine has an electronic foot control. An air-pressure foot control has no electrical parts; these are in the machine.

Do keep a check on the plug and the wiring to make sure all is in order. If the fuse in the plug should blow, insert a new one or consult an electrician.

Always check the basic fault first and work upwards. It is no use giving the machine a complete overhaul if the trouble is owing to a blunt needle. If however, the fault persists, even though you have made a check of all the faults listed, then consult your dealer or a trained mechanic. Do not be tempted to tamper with the machine workings yourself. These are carefully set and may only need a very slight adjustment which is best done by an expert.

Machine will not start and the light does not come on

Make sure the machine is connected to the power source and is switched on. Also check that the main power source is on. There may be a house fuse blown or a temporary power cut. In some machines the bobbin may have been wound too full and be jamming the mechanism.

Sewing light is on and the needle goes up and down, but the rest of the machine does not operate

On certain machines this means that the circuit breaker is closed. Re-set it.

Light comes on but the machine does not work

There is nothing wrong with the power source. The motor has failed. See your dealer or call a mechanic.

Bobbin winding mechanism does not work

The bobbin winding mechanism may not be properly engaged or the inner fly wheel inside the balance wheel may not be disconnected. Turn it towards you. On straight stitch machines with an outside winding mechanism, make sure the bobbin is placed correctly on the spindle and that the small winding wheel engages with the larger. If this small wheel is old and made of rubber, it may perish and shrink.

The thread may have come out of the hole or slot when starting to wind. You may have started the thread round the bobbin in the wrong direction or the bobbin is not placed correctly on the spindle. The automatic clutch-type bobbin may not be clicked home.

On machines where the bobbin is wound in the sewing position, the bobbin must be empty and the two halves tightened together. Make sure the bobbin push button is in position.

Bobbin does not wind evenly

You may have forgotten to guide the thread under or round the bobbin tension spring. The thread may have caught on some protrusion or in the slot on the thread reel.

The bobbin tension device may need adjusting. On some top-winding machines there is an adjuster screw to raise or lower the tensioner. Only a slight alteration is needed. Screw up tightly. Finally, the bobbin may not be empty and has thread left on.

Needle moves up and down but no stitch will form

The machine may not be threaded correctly. Check both top and bottom threading. Consult your threading instruction guide once more, you may have left something out.

The bobbin may be empty, the bobbin case not inserted correctly or the bobbin case and shuttle race may need cleaning. The needle may not be straight or it might be blunt or damaged or fitted the wrong way round. See if it is threaded from the correct side. It may be the wrong type or length of needle for the machine. The needle size and style could be incorrect for the type of thread used or it may not be pushed right up into the socket.

Needle will not stay threaded

The take-up lever needs to be in the highest position before the stitch is commenced. Allow a longer length of thread to pull out behind the needle eye. Modern machines appear to require longer thread for starting. This does not necessarily mean they use more thread. Anyone used to an old machine can find this very frustrating.

Needle will not move

The balance wheel has not been re-tightened after bobbin threading. The drive belt may have stretched. On some machines with an exposed belt there is a screw to tighten this. Buy a new belt or consult your dealer.

The bobbin case could be jammed. Thread may have caught in the bobbin case, around the race or under the needleplate. Remove the needleplate and unscrew or unclip the race ring. Take it apart and clean it out.

Machine is very noisy

The machine needs oiling and cleaning. Little wads of lint can form in the shuttle race. Clean it.

Inferior oil may have been used and the machine is gummed up. If so, consult your dealer.

The needle may be damaged or the stitch-width and length controls are incorrectly set for the type of work in hand.

Machine jams when starting to sew

The needle may be the wrong type or length or it may have been inserted the wrong way. If it is too loose in the needle clamp, tighten it. Make sure the width controls are properly set for twin-needle sewing. You may be pulling the threads without raising the needle and presser foot when finishing a seam.

Machine runs very slowly

The machine may need oiling and cleaning. Where a choice of speeds is available, the machine can be switched to a low speed. The machine may be cold. Bring it into a warm room one to two hours before you want to use it.

The tension belt may be too loose or too tight or something is wrong with the motor or the foot control. If so, consult your dealer.

Needle breaks

The foot may have been put on incorrectly and has been struck by the needle. Alternatively, the needle plate has not been changed from straight stitch when sewing zig-zag stitch. The needle could be bent or damaged.

The needle may be the wrong type or length or it may have been inserted the wrong way. If it is too loose in the needle clamp, tighten it. Make sure the width controls are properly set for twin-needle

sewing. You may be pulling the threads without raising the needle and presser foot when finishing a seam.

The fabric may be too thick or you may be sewing with the wrong thread. Check there is no knot in the thread and that you are not pulling the cloth. Let the machine do the work.

Upper thread breaks

The top tension is either incorrect or the thread has become knotted, caught on a protrusion or in the thread reel slit. Old or poor quality thread may break easily or it may be too thick for the needle. The thread may simply be wrong for the fabric or the top tension is too tight. If so, loosen it. Check that the hole in the needleplate is not damaged or rough.

Bottom thread breaks

The bottom tension is too tight or the bobbin thread has become caught in the mechanism. The bobbin may be too full or the needleplate hole damaged. Clean the bobbin case and shuttle race mechanism in case they are dirty and check that the bobbin is wound evenly. See that it has been inserted correctly and the case is properly threaded.

Fabric does not move

The feed teeth may have been lowered. Raise the feed and check that the stitch length is set correctly and the foot is lowered.

Bobbin thread will not draw up

The bobbin case may be inserted or threaded incorrectly. The thread end may be too short or the needle not properly inserted.

Fabric does not feed evenly

The foot is incorrectly attached or the pressure needs ad-

The Frister Rossmann Frister-Lock 4 domestic overlock machine, closely resembling the industrial version.

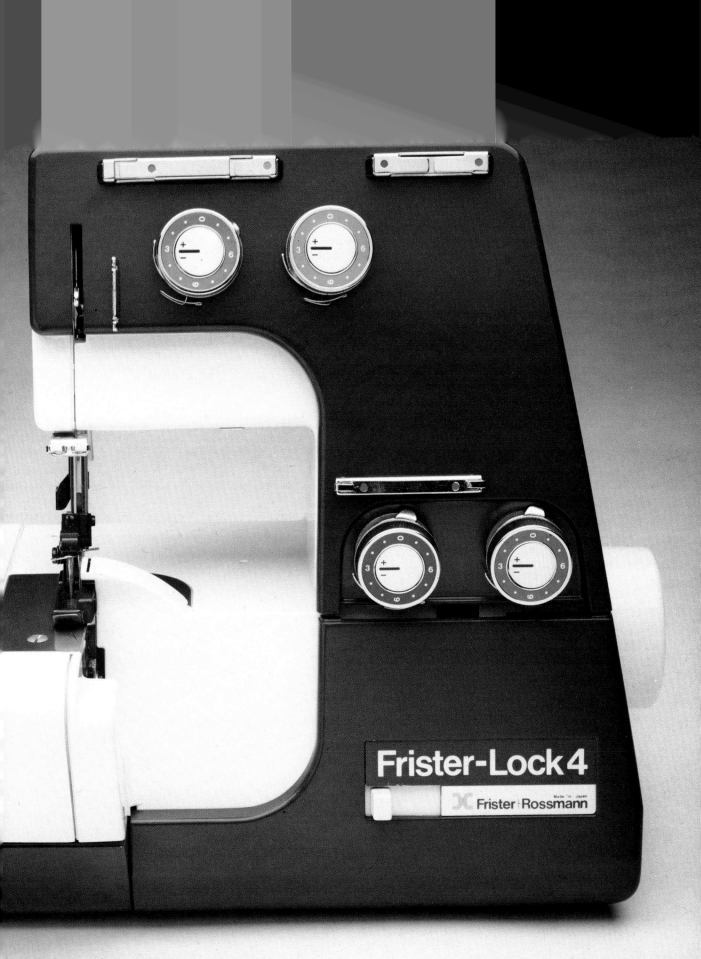

justing. If you are working on difficult materials, use an 'even feed' or roller foot.

Wrinkles in the fabric

The top tension is probably too tight or you are using the wrong type of thread. It may be too thick for the fabric or the needle may be too big or damaged.

The pressure may be too great. If so, adjust according to your machine instructions. If the fabric is too fine it may be damaged by the teeth. Place a piece of typing paper underneath it while sewing.

Uneven stitch length

The pressure could be incorrect, in which case increase or decrease it appropriately. The needle thread might be too thick or you may be pulling the fabric. Let the machine do the work.

Skipped stitches

You may be using the zig-zag needleplate when sewing straight stitch on fine fabrics. Change to the straight stitch needleplate if your machine has an alternative. Otherwise, the fabric is probably too close or has too much stiffening or sizing (as in chintz or glazed cotton). Wash the fabric or change the needle size.

Check to see whether the pressure needs to be increased and that the needle is the correct type for the fabric in question. Also check that the thread is not too thick and that it is not knotted.

Thread loops

The machine is either threaded incorrectly or the presser foot lever is not down when the foot is removed and the machine set for 'darning'.

Width control does not appear to work

This may be due to incorrect setting of controls on some machines. The drop-in cam for both straight stitch and zig-zag may not be in place. On certain machines the twin needle switch may not be in its extreme left position. The machine may be set to straight stitch or the stop controls on the width lever are in the wrong position.

It may help to have a note book handy to jot down any mistakes you have made or faults you have found and how they were remedied. This will save a lot of time in the future and may serve as a reminder when you are starting to sew.

Domestic overlock

In recent years machine manufacturers have introduced a variety of utility stitches both for sewing stretch materials and for neatening the edges of all types of fabric. These neatening stitches are called by a variety of names; overlock, double overlock, and over-

26 Holding two thread ends when beginning to sew with a domestic overlock (left); finishing off (right).

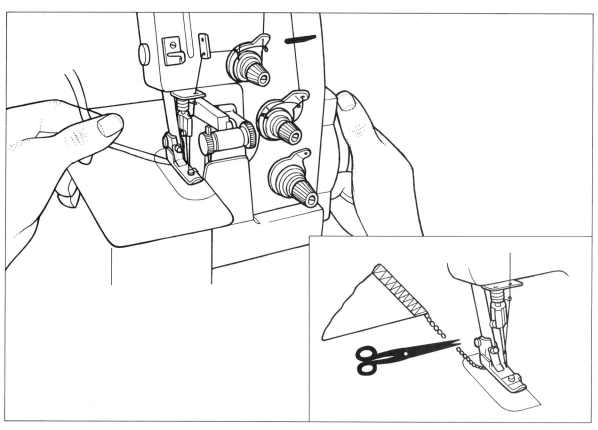

edge stitch to name a few. They are all trimotion stitches. They are efficient, but not quite the same as industrial overlock stitches.

Most mass-produced garments are finished with overlock stitches, binding together double seams. This is a feature of cut-and-sew knitwear in the lower price range. Fully-fashioned knitwear is expensive to produce. It is much easier to cut the knitted garment from continuously knitted fabric and seam it up by machine. These industrial machines can make a chain-stitch seam, overlock and cut off the surplus at the same time.

If you examine a garment bought from a department store, whether it is knitwear or woven fabric, you will see this double seam. Chain stitch shows on one side of the seam, straight stitch on the other,

while the overlock binds the edges. It is an extremely fast and efficient way of sewing and finishing a garment in one operation.

Choice of machine

There are several domestic overlock machines on the market. They all look very similar and most are made in Japan. One, however, is exceptionally well designed to a British specification.

The simpler models have only one needle and a top and bottom thread. The machine is an overlocker and does not make an additional chain seam. There is a cutting knife to cut off the seam surplus as the overlock stitches are formed. On every model there is a safety cover to guard the blade.

The three-thread model has one needle thread and two lower threads. The lowest thread forms a row of closing stitches with the needle at the base of the overlock stitch

which is formed by the middle thread. This is a true overlock. The stitch length can be adjusted from $1 - 5$ mm ($\frac{1}{25} - \frac{1}{5}$ in). The stitch-width can be altered by a mechanic.

The four-thread overlock machine has two needles. One shares a bottom thread to make a chain stitch seam line. The other shares a bottom thread to make the overlock stitch. They can be used separately or together. The overlocker can be used with or without the knife in position. When the knife is out of action, the overlocker will only sew on an outside edge. It cannot be used in the middle of the cloth as a decorative stitch.

At one time the only overlock machines available for home use were second-hand industrial machines. The professional dressmaker would find one of these machines a good buy. Certain machine dealers will provide these, serviced and with a guarantee. They come fixed to a stand and are heavy but sew excellent, very fast stitches.

Portable domestic overlock machines

Now, the home dressmaker is catered for as well. Lighter, portable domestic overlock machines are available. They perform the same task as the industrial overlock machine and although they are not as sturdy as their industrial counterparts, they are far more efficient at their specific task than the ordinary domestic sewing machine. Speeds of up to 1,500 stitches per minute can be obtained.

Anyone who does a great deal of dressmaking or is semi-professional, will find this machine extremely useful. Some dressmakers use this type of machine for all their sewing. Some models will do chain stitch alone, as well as perform the overlock functions.

The home machine-knitter who prefers the cut-and-sew method of making up, will find

27 Different ways of using the domestic overlock machine on its own and with a chain stitch.

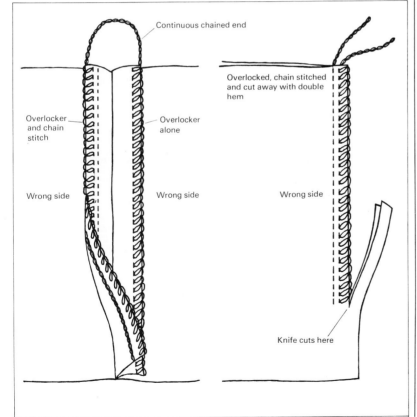

Continuous chained end

Overlocker and chain stitch

Overlocker alone

Wrong side

Wrong side

Overlocked, chain stitched and cut away with double hem

Wrong side

Knife cuts here

this machine indispensable. Often the time taken to make up a garment was as great as the knitting time before this machine came along. The only disadvantage is the amount of thread used but added to the cost of the garment it is not much. If time is your most precious commodity, then you can forget about the thread. Buy it in large spools or invest in some industrial thread which will be more convenient.

Threading

Overlock machines look more complicated than they are. Some models are fiddlesome to thread and do require a certain amount of patience. However, once threaded there is no need to unthread it until the colour is changed. In practice, you may need fewer colours than for normal sewing. When overlocking, basic colours will tone in with knitwear, tweeds and many dress fabrics. Remember that you will require two, three or four reels of the same thread each time you change colour.

Each machine comes with a threading chart located somewhere on it. The machine has two, three or four tension controls, according to the model. On some machines these are colour coded for easy threading. There is a spool stand to the rear or side and telescopic guide posts raise the thread above the machine. Nylon net sleeves may be provided to slip over smaller thread reels. These assist with the unwinding.

Two- and three-thread models

On the two-thread overlocker the upper thread tension control leads to the needle, the lower tension to the looper. On three-thread models, the upper tension control leads to the needle, the middle tensioner is threaded next and the outer tensioner controls the bottom thread.

Four-thread models

When the overlocker is used alone, the two threads use the central pair of tension controls. The upper mid-tensioner is for the needle thread and the lower mid-tensioner for the under looper thread. The needle is awkward to thread as it is placed to the right of the chain needle. Some manufacturers provide a pair of tweezers for this. Once threaded, pull a long end through and thread the under looper according to instructions.

Start by holding the two ends and lower the foot and sew a few centimetres without the cloth. This starts the overlock, which pulls to the back as a twisted chain. If you start with the cloth under, it may not take and you will waste time rethreading. When finishing, be careful to preserve this chain by sewing enough to form an end, about 5 cm (2 in) long. It is not a waste of thread.

Thread the chain stitcher separately, bottom thread first, through the chain looper. Leave an end about 10 cm (5 in) protruding underneath and let it hang there. Thread the needle and leave another long end through the eye. The chain stitcher will only start properly in the cloth. The needle thread is looped round by the thread from the bottom looper. Sew the first few stitches very slowly.

At first the machine is bound to come unthreaded. Do not lose patience. Remember the secret is to start with the chain stitching in the cloth and the overlocker out of the cloth. If you are making both seams at once, thread the overlocker first and get the chained end started. Then thread the chain stitcher, put the cloth under and sew. At the finish, sew long enough to form two sets of chain coming from behind both needles. Sew at least 12 cm (5 in) and cut off in the middle, leaving ends to be tied off on the work or it may unravel.

If you have the knife in position this will trim the cloth

as you go. At first this is so fascinating you may find all sense of direction is lost. Do not watch the knife but guide the seam line up to the blade and sew as normal. When the knife is out of use, a flat plate takes its place and guide lines aid sewing. This machine is much faster than the domestic sewing machine. It is not recommended for beginners or timid sewers.

Dressmaking

A completely different attitude towards the construction of sewing will help when using this machine for ordinary dressmaking. The machine is especially useful for making-up jersey-type fabrics. Since this is an industrial process, use industrial methods. If the fabric is fine, seam and neaten in one, in the commercial manner.

For narrow seams, allow the normal dressmaking seam allowance of 1.5 cm ($\frac{5}{8}$ in). Place the two layers of fabric right sides together, set the machine to overlock and trim and chain stitch, or overlock and trim in one operation. Hold the seam with one pin, placed at right angles to the seam, 10 cm (4 in) in from the top. When a few stitches have been sewn, remove the pin. Sew down the seam line, guiding the machine. Let the machine do all the work. Do not be tempted to pull or ease the fabric in any way. The machine will sew, overlock and cut the fabric away at the same time. Try it out on something simple first, an apron, a nightdress or a straight skirt. The results should be as good as anything bought commercially.

Seams can be sewn in the conventional manner, using the four-thread overlock to make a chain stitch seam. The edges are neatened first, using the overlock stitch alone. Allow a little extra seam when cutting out, then neaten all the seam edges using the knife to cut away the surplus. Do not be tempted to pull the work or it will become wavy.

Pin or tack your seams in the normal manner and sew using the chain stitch alone. Press the seams out flat. Hem edges can be neatened with the overlocker and a chain stitch line for extra strength. Seam edges can be neatened after they have been fitted and sewn. For some types of garment and fabric this may be preferable. The extra seam allowance can be cut off by the knife. It is far easier to overlock and cut off than it is to guide the overlocker over the edge of the fabric line.

Open the seam out flat and overlock and cut one edge. At the seam end, sew about 10 cm (4 in) of chain on its own. Do not cut it off but re-position the fabric and continue down the other side of the seam. This method does not waste thread, it saves having to stop and start each time. Use a fine thread when overlocking to prevent a stiff seam. It is possible to adjust the tension and stitch length. Try out a few test runs on the fabric in question until you have a satisfactory result. Remember to leave the chain 'tail' behind the needles each time you cut off.

Cut-and-sew

This method can be used on home-made machine knits or for making alterations to existing knitted garments. This can be to change their style or make them smaller for childrens' wear. It needs a bold approach. As in industrial manufacture, the knitwear is cut from a fabric length. The small amount of wool cut away is no more than the normal dressmaker wastes when cutting out her fabric. The waste can be saved to use as stuffing for pincushions or toys.

On a knitting machine, work your garment as a series of rectangles. These will have the usual ribbed welts at the base of the back and front. Knit straight up until the top of the shoulder measurement is reached. Start

sleeves at the cuff and increase until the underarm is reached. Continue straight up. Finish off all top edges with a few rows of waste yarn. Block out or press the knit rectangles according to the fibre content.

Either adapt a paper pattern or use your machine knit diagram for the shaping of the shoulders, neck and armhole edges. You only need the top part of the pattern. Make a similar one for the sleeve head. Place the pattern pieces on top of each single layer of knitting. Hold with berry pins and tack round the outline in a contrasting wool. If the fabric is ribbed, pull up the wool slightly so that it fits the pattern. Remove the pattern.

Set the machine for overlock and the knife to 'cut'. The procedure is to cut out and overlock each single layer in one operation. Do not stretch the work. Follow the tacked wool line, starting at the left back armhole edge. Machine and cut out the armhole, ending beyond the fabric at the shoul-

der edge. Leave a long chained loop of thread. Do not cut this off.

Now start again at the outer shoulder edge and machine straight up to the start of the neck. Go beyond and finish with a chain as before. Start again at the top and machine round the scoop of the neck. Work the other shoulder and, finally, the right armhole in the same way, then cut and sew the sleeve head as well.

The cut out, neatened shapes are now ready for sewing up. Use the chain stitcher or a suitable stretch stitch on the domestic machine or a very narrow zig-zag. The side seams are best sewn together as near the edge as possible. Machine the shoulders along the top. Press the overlocked seam allowances outward. These can be caught down by hand afterwards to make them lie per-

28 Cut-and-sew method for cutting out and joining knitwear in one operation using the overlock.

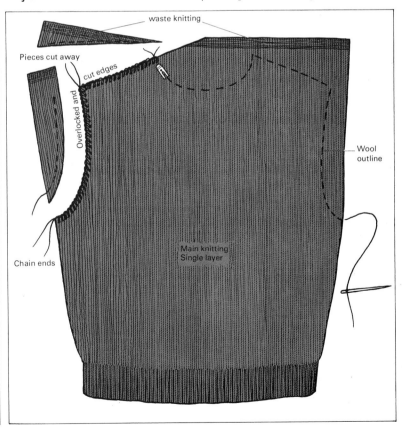

Cardigan made by the cut-and-sew method using a domestic overlock and chain stitch.

fectly flat. This method works particularly well on thicker knits.

On finer knits, the back and front shoulders can be placed right sides together and seamed with the overlocker again. On very stretchy knits add a stay-tape, machined on separately or caught in with the stitching. Always tack a sleeve head in position first with matching wool. These stitches need not be taken out. Machine round twice, using the overlock and knife. Finer knits are better chain stitched together very close to the separate overlock edges.

Use a 100% polyester thread for sewing knitwear. The under-looper on the over-locker can be threaded with a fine knitting thread. The industrial knitting thread sold on

29 Using the cut-and-sew method, sew pieces together using the overlocker without the knife. Side seams and front bands can be sewn together with the chain stitcher alone.

cones is excellent for this purpose. Use a tapestry needle with an eye large enough to take the thread, but fine enough to pass through the eye of the looper.

Double knit bands can be sewn on to edges, right sides together. Press the double seam away from the band. Opened-out double bands are sewn to the wrong side of one edge, then the band is folded over to the front and chain stitched in position, or finished by hand.

Alterations

Not all knitting comes out as you might expect. Wrong tension calculations can result in a garment being too wide, or with sleeves which are too long. To alter, cut the welts off just above the change to plain knitting. Replace them higher up, overlocking and trimming in one operation. Re-sew the side seams by tapering them from the welt to the armhole seam.

Cut pullovers down the middle to make a jacket and cut the sleeves off to make a waistcoat. Put a V-neck in for a change. Corners are not easy to turn on the machine, so cut a V-neck as a smaller U-neck first. Open it out and cut and sew a second time. Reinforce the V.

It is simple to make up a patchwork for a rug from tension square samples. Stripes are equally effective. Use alternating strips of knitwear and dress fabric. The machine will sew needlecord or suede just as easily. There are all sorts of mixture possibilities for creating fashion garments. Examine any commercially made-up knitwear you have and study the manufacturers' methods.

The chain stitch linking machine

This is a simplified version of the machines used in industry to link the various parts of knitwear together.

The domestic machine uses a continuous thread through the needle to make the chain stitch with a chain looper beneath. The knitwear or material to be linked together is fitted along the teeth of a metal comb which meshes in with a gear wheel on the machine. It moves forward one cog and one corresponding comb tooth for each stitch made. This comb slides in and out of a grooved plate running horizontally from front to back of the machine.

Machines with combs come in a choice of three lengths, with approximately thirty teeth to every 10cm (5in). Every twentieth tooth is marked for ease in counting and there is a centimetre scale alongside. The machine is turned by a handle and it will join any type of open fabric and can be used in conjunction with the over-locker.

Use a 100% polyester sewing thread or a smooth knitting

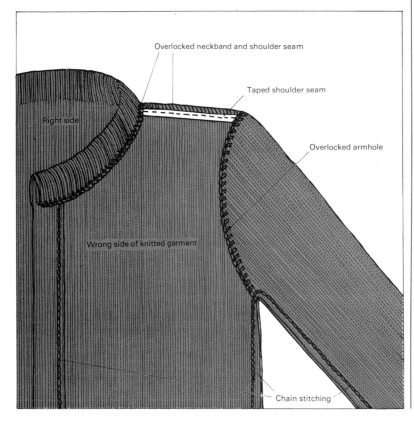

Overlocked neckband and shoulder seam

Taped shoulder seam

Right side

Overlocked armhole

Wrong side of knitted garment

Chain stitching

A Bellinky chain-stitch machine for linking knitwear.

thread, finer than the work to be linked. Thread up according to the instructions. Use a needle threader or cut the yarn to a slant and wax it before threading. The knitwear can be positioned on the comb stitch by stitch across the row. There is a guide in the booklet that explains how to set the different stitch tensions on the comb. Coarser knitting will have to be spread out. Finer knitting may have to share a tooth every so often according to the finished measurement. Lengthways knitting is stretched up to about 20%. To keep long or separate pieces even, mark the 'comb length' to be set with tailor's chalk.

Edges can be butt-joined, lapped or sandwiched between outer layers. Work can be 'bound off'. Leave several rows of contrasting waste yarn on all open edges and set the first main colour row on the

30 Starting off using the chain stitch linking machine.

comb teeth. The waste yarn is then unravelled after sewing. Slide the comb on to the guide until it reaches the gear. You will hear it engage and mesh in. Gently lower the presser lifter when the comb front edge is directly under it.

To remove it, lower the machine needle by turning the handle towards you. Hold the front of the comb in your left hand, lift it up and pull it towards you. Always start with one empty tooth against the needle free of knitting. Hold the thread spring while you make a few starting stitches, then release. Turn the handle clockwise. To finish off, turn the handle four times anticlockwise to disengage the chain looper. Cut the thread and draw through the last chain to secure.

To re-set stitches on the comb, finish in the middle of the work as if it were the end, securing the chain. Take it off, re-set and start again. Use the machine for matching stripes, sewing crochet squares, working with shirring elastic, attach-

ing neckbands, collars and cuffs, and for making pintucks and pleat crease lines.

The professional sewing machine high-speed zig-zag

This is a heavy-duty machine for the professional dress-maker or tailor. It will sew straight stitch and zig-zag at speeds much higher than those attainable on the ordinary domestic sewing machine. It will sew up to 2,500 stitches per minute on widths up to 5mm ($\frac{3}{16}$ in) and 2,000 stitches per minute for a 9 mm ($\frac{11}{32}$ in) width zig-zag.

There is a knee-operated presser lifter which allows both hands to be free for working. Pressure and tension controls are built in. A large lever sets the stitch width up to 9 mm ($\frac{11}{32}$ in). It can be moved easily for working free embroidery. The bobbin can be wound in the middle of sewing without removing the fabric.

The emphasis is on speed and precision stitching. These machines do not have the built in automatic and flex stitches provided with the domestic machine. Zig-zag is used for

31 Sandwich seaming.

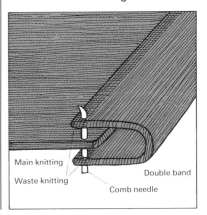

Main knitting
Waste knitting
Double band
Comb needle

Comb needle
Sewing machine needle
Knitting yarn
Knitting
Comb needle

neatening seam edges and a very small $\frac{1}{2}$mm ($\frac{1}{32}$in) zig-zag for sewing stretch fabrics. The industrial overlocker would be ideal for use in conjunction with this type of machine.

Industrial embroidery machines

Sometimes these machines are available for use by students in colleges of art and further education. They are heavy-duty embroidery machines, each one designed for only one or two special sewing procedures. They are used in a purely decorative context. The experimental worker will find they give scope for special textural effects that can make a valuable contribution to the machine embroidery repertoire.

A Singer Professional 20U heavyweight zig-zag machine. This machine will sew straight stitch and zig-zag at very high speed.

Irish machine (107 Class)

This machine is designed for free embroidery. It has no feed and the work has to be stretched in a wide, circular embroidery frame or backed with vanishing muslin. The machine has an extra-wide 'throw' to give a zig-zag width of 1.25cm ($\frac{1}{2}$in). The width control is worked by a knee lever which allows alteration to the stitch-width while working. There is one lever to set the width and one to set the needle position to the left, centre and to the right. Normally there is no foot on the machine, but sometimes it can be adapted for eyelet embroidery or Madeira work.

This is a very heavy machine powered by a large industrial motor. It will produce beautifully even, wide satin stitch embroidery. The embroiderer who has experience on the domestic machine will find this machine a delight to work. The knee-operated width control should not be used when the width lever is in a set position. It can be unscrewed and freed for this type of work. The tension can be altered to produce the same whipped and towelling stitch effects that are possible on the domestic machine. *Lurex* and metallic threads add to the decorative quality of the work.

Cornely machine

The first Cornely chain stitching machine was invented in 1865. Since then many variations have been introduced, some to perform specific tasks in the trade such as sewing cords and braid. They are used in industry among other things for embroidering net fabrics, sometimes with narrow ribbon for bridal and evening wear.

The simplest type of Cornely machine is the one most likely to be found in colleges. It has a universal feed and can be used to work chain stitch embroidery or moss stitch. This is a looped stitch formed by a not-

quite-completed chain stitch. It is used as a decorative technique in embroidery. A back-stitch is formed on the wrong side of the work.

The needle is a sharp, pointed hook which works a chain stitch on to the top of the work from the thread which is on a horizontal reel placed below the machine. A wire hook is used to draw up this thread into a position to be caught by the needle when starting the work. The hooked needle is positioned the opposite way round for moss stitch.

The stitch is formed inside the rubber-padded presser foot ring which moves up and down in conjunction with the needle. The machine is powered by a heavy industrial motor and has a large-area footplate control. The stitching is guided by a rotary handle beneath the machine. At first this is very confusing to work. It takes time to master the rotary guiding system. Circles are easy, straight lines need concentration and sharp corners require practice.

It produces decorative chain-stitch embroidery of a flowing type not possible to achieve on any other machine. The moss stitch is used mainly on embroidered panels and wall hangings as it is not stable. It can pull undone and has to be backed with iron-on interfacing or a minimum of fabric adhesive. However, it is a positive advantage when taking out mistakes or adjusting the density of the finished moss stitch.

Tufting machine

This industrial machine is normally used for making candle-wick bedspreads. The tufting threads feed from a series of telescopic guides down to a special needle. A straight back stitch appears on the top, wrong side of the work and a knife beneath cuts the tufting thread as the machine sews. Different machines are set to give varying depths of pile. Either one thick or a mixture of thinner threads can be used, treated and threaded up as one.

Bedspread tufting is sewn in rows 2.5 – 3cm (1 – 1¼in) apart, using a single needle or multiple needles. For certain embroidery effects, the rows can be sewn close together. The rows of tufts on the right, underside form a thick, close pile. Shaded effects are produced by altering the proportions of one colour to another when threading up. The inclusion of a *lurex* thread adds highlights. The spacing of the lines can be altered to give different densities as well as the shaded effect.

The machine will sew gentle curves and sharp corners can be turned by lifting the presser foot (knee-type lifter) and pivoting on the needle. Start at the top left of the fabric and work rows downwards, cutting off and starting at the top again for each row. Small areas of tufting can be worked separately on calico and applied to embroidered panels and wall hangings to give a variety of effects. They are particularly effective when used in landscape or seascape pictures.

Traditional crafts

A modern approach to a great tradition

Keeping up a tradition

In recent years there has been a renewed interest in all the traditional crafts. People feel the need to express their individuality as a reaction against the similarity of mass-produced goods. Embroidery, patchwork, quilting and many other fabric crafts have been revived. Up until now, it has been the traditional aspects that have held interest. Old books have been consulted, familiar methods re-learned, and workmanship equal to the standard of our forebears has been achieved.

It is a good thing that these traditions should have become part of our living heritage. At the same time, there is a need for change and for taking a look at the new ways of doing things that express our day and age. The old and the new should continue hand in hand, complementing one another and forming new traditions for future generations. Every craftworker knows how relaxing handwork can be, but it does require time – a luxury not everyone can afford.

The sewing machine can provide the answer to many problems. It has been used in the home for several generations, mainly for sewing clothing and soft furnishings. It is only recently that the sewing machine has been regarded as a tool in its own right.

The only exception was machine embroidery, and even this was regarded as a poor relation of handwork. The confusion is no doubt due to the invention of so many machines in the 19th century that could reproduce work that was mechanically even and perfect. These machines caused the unemployment of countless handworkers. However, they provided even more work in the factories, and most handworkers had, by the end of the century, become slaves to sweated labour.

The domestic machine, unlike its factory counterpart, is not set to a particular sequence or restricted to performing a specific industrial function; it can be used as the worker wishes, to carry out more sewing tasks and decorative processes than most people would believe possible.

The sewing machine can be regarded as a powered needle, to be used as the

An old appliqué bedspread worked by the author's great grandmother.

handworker uses a hand needle. Unlike the hand needle, it cannot pass right through the cloth but it can do many other things. It is up to the operator to exploit the potentialities of the machine and to express something new and different. Machine sewing is not the same as hand sewing, and should not be regarded in the same way. True creativity with the machine means working something that can be done in no other way.

Many of our traditional crafts can be sewn by machine. Often the stitching will be firmer and will wear better. It is no use forcing the machine to copy a hand process; the process must be adapted to be worked by machine. Each craft has developed through the years, together with the chosen materials and methods of working.

Embroidery is the addition of thread, passing in and out of an already finished fabric, to embellish and form a decoration. It can be worked with threads withdrawn from the fabric, or a thread can be laid on top of the fabric and couched in position with a second thread.

The machine can fulfil all these functions. The stitch is formed from a double thread, but normally only one is seen on the surface. The two threads can be manipulated through tension changes to produce decorative effects. Apart from all the set automatic patterns – which themselves can be used in a variety of ways – 'free' embroidery worked without the foot on the machine is an art in its own right, requiring skill and sensitivity on the part of the worker.

Applied fabrics and threads stand up to laundering and wear, making machine appliqué specially suitable, while the embroiderer will find scope for a less rigid approach when working on panels and wall hangings. The machine is used for reverse appliqué in a practical way for washable articles and in a decorative manner on felts and other fabrics.

The machine is very suitable for all kinds of patchwork, whether of the geometrical type worked in strips, or in random pieces. The sewing is firm and stands up to repeated washing. The worker has a choice of sewing methods and can use the zig-zag stitch to advantage. Some modern fabrics are easier to sew by machine, giving increased scope for texture and design.

The lace crafts, so popular at present, have been neglected in domestic machine work. Industrial machines produced such excellent imitations in the 19th century that handworking almost disappeared. Only a few were left to carry on the tradition. Until the 1930s a certain amount of domestic machine embroidery was worked on organdie, and there is always some experimental work being carried out in art colleges.

Machine embroidery can be worked on various types of net, while cut work and lace work can be used on fine fabrics. Many techniques have not been fully exploited, so allowing opportunities for innovation. Drawn and pulled thread work can lead to exciting textures and patterns and are used for soft furnishing and on clothing, or more freely in conjunction with embroidery.

The art of quilting has been with us for centuries – to give warmth to garments, to make padding beneath armour, for bed-covers or for pure decoration. Machine quilting can be executed in various ways, either as straight stitching using the foot, or as free quilting. Free work gives a distinctive, fluid effect. Corded quilting, trapunto or padded quilting add a textural quality to the work.

Machine work need not stand on its own, but can be used in conjunction with handwork. However, this should be part of an overall design concept and not a mere addition. A sewing machine is an investment, to be used to its utmost capacity. Its role as a creative tool has not yet been fully realized. The opportunities are there for those who are willing to take them.

Appliqué

This is the decorative application of one fabric to another and is probably as old as the art of weaving itself. Cut pieces of precious fabric would be saved and applied as decoration, with either plain sewing or additional embroidery stitches.

Appliqué forms part of the heritage of most ethnic and peasant societies. It was worked on saddle cloths by the ancient Scythian tribes from the Black Sea area, and in later centuries Hungarian shepherds applied similar felt motifs to their sheepskin coats.

Heraldic devices applied to the knight's surcoat and pennant aided identification in battle. Appliqué has been used throughout the ages for banners and flags of all kinds, religious vestments and ceremonial regalia.

After the dissolution of the monasteries, church vestments were cut up and the precious fabrics re-used for other purposes. Often, any materials in short supply were used as decoration for bed curtains and coverlets. The American settlers, with limited fabric supplies, made appliqué and quilting into an art.

William Morris and the late 19th century embroiderers explored many design possibilities. This led to the present day interest in applied fabrics and threads as a form of individual expression, whether from an artistic or practical point of view.

Applying thick threads

Threads can be applied using the straight-stitch machine. One method is to use the underbraider, a grooved metal plate attached to the bed of the

machine. Slot the thread through the groove and draw it to the back under the needle. The fabric is placed on top and the design sewn from the wrong side. This works well for any set pattern that is marked on to the cloth, but has the disadvantage that the work in progress cannot be seen. The worker is not influenced by contrasts in colour or by the way a thread behaves – which all helps in creating design.

The method using the braiding foot is more useful. This has a slot to take ribbon or thick threads, which are caught down by the needle. The thread should be soft, as well as thick, or the needle will not sew down the middle. There are many beautiful knitting threads available – slubbed, bouclé, looped or crinkle.

Turn corners by leaving the needle in the cloth, raising the presser foot and pivoting. Lower the foot and continue sewing. Designs can be made up as you work – turning corners and crossing over lines. The fabric may need backing to prevent distortion when working curves. It is also possible to sew thick threads using the presser foot. Anchor the thread with a few stitches before continuing to sew. Hold the thread taut, towards you and slightly up. Corners are turned as before.

Threads can be held down using a zig-zag stitch. When sewing cord or string the stitch goes right over the cord to enclose it. Do not let the needle pierce the hard cord.

Set an open zig-zag stitch and use a matching thread. A contrasting sewing thread can be used for additional decorative quality by opening and closing up the stitch-length control.

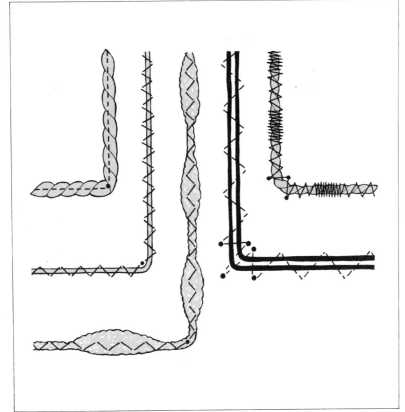

1 Applied thick threads. ● s indicate where foot is raised and fabric is pivoted round needle.

The front of a dress decorated with applied fabrics cut from the pattern given in figure 2 (below).

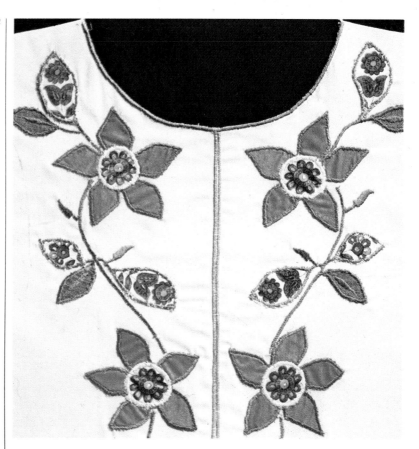

Some of the cord will show through to contrast. Turn corners by leaving the needle in the cloth on the inner swing. Raise the foot, hold the cord round the needle, pivot, lower the foot and carry on. The thread should be held towards you and up.

Some machines have a cording foot. One or more threads are held under a guide and can be sewn down with zig-zag stitches or suitable automatic patterns on open or close setting.

A narrow, but long zig-zag stitch can be sewn down the middle of thick threads (close zig-zag will crush the thread and it will lose its textured look). Slubbed thread, with contrasting thick and thin areas is best held in this manner.

Different-coloured threads can be laid side by side and held down, or the sewing thread itself can be shaded. Experiment with as many types as you can. Take the thread ends through to the back of the work with a large-eyed tapestry needle. Pull the zig-zag threads through to the back and tie them off. One of these threads can be used to neaten the thick thread – by hand if necessary.

Applying fabric

If you are applying fabrics that are to be laundered, they must be colour-fast, pre-shrunk and should have similar properties to the background fabric. Woven fabrics are the most suitable.

Stretch fabrics do not work well, unless they are backed with iron-on interfacing. This, however, has the disadvantage of stiffening the fabric, but is

2 Appliqué pattern dress front illustrated above. Design is drawn to actual size.

suitable for small areas like pockets, yokes, collars and cuffs. Any fabric that tends to fray will need backing and should be avoided if possible.

For making clothing or for household linen the safest way is to buy material of the same kind in two colours. Cotton-polyester poplin is an excellent fabric for this work, and has the advantage of not creasing. Machine embroidery thread can be used on most appliqué work. The stitching is meant to be seen and this thread gives a lustrous appearance to the sewing.

Working step-by-step

The applied fabric pieces should match the grain of the background fabric as closely as possible. The two pieces of fabric will then become as one, behave in the same manner and lie nice and flat.

At times fabric may have to be cut on the cross when cutting out motifs or matching pattern pieces to create new designs. Try to keep these pieces small. They can be backed with thin, iron-on interfacing or held in position with bonded interfacing, which has two adhesive sides. All these interfacings are bonded by heat from the iron.

Apply interfacing to the back of the appliqué fabric and iron it on before drawing on and cutting out the pattern shapes. The bonded type is cut out and slipped between the two surfaces before ironing it into position. All other fabrics are tacked down first, using a contrasting, soft basting cotton. Edges are left raw, and no hems are turned under.

Keep designs very simple. Complex designs are not only difficult to carry out; they leave no room for any additional embroidery. Shapes can be cut from paper first – coloured pages from magazines are excellent. Pin them on to the cloth and rearrange until you are satisfied.

The flowers and leaf shapes on the dress front were planned in this way – leaving room for the connecting stalks, which can be drawn in lightly with a hard pencil. Mark the centres of the flower shapes and use the cut paper as patterns. Try to use any distinctive fabric patterning to advantage. These shapes are small and can be cut as you like. Tack all leaves and petals in position with diagonal stitches. Set the machine to zig-zag, stitch-width 2.5 and stitch-length 2.5 according to the thickness of the fabric. Use a toning machine-embroidery thread No. 50, or a No. 50 mercerized cotton.

The small pieces are held in position with the zig-zag stitch. The needle pierces the appliqué fabric on one side and goes into the cloth on the other. Turn corners by pivoting the fabric and remove the tacking thread. If the work is purely decorative, it can be left at this stage, and just held with zig-zag stitch. For firm wear, the outline is sewn round once more, this time using a close satin stitch.

Ease round curves and pivot at the corners with the needle on the outside swing, ready to work back into the applied patch. Pull all thread ends to the back and tie them off securely. The stalks are sewn in after-

'Crowded Beach' by Joan Appleton Fisher, worked in embroidered appliqué.

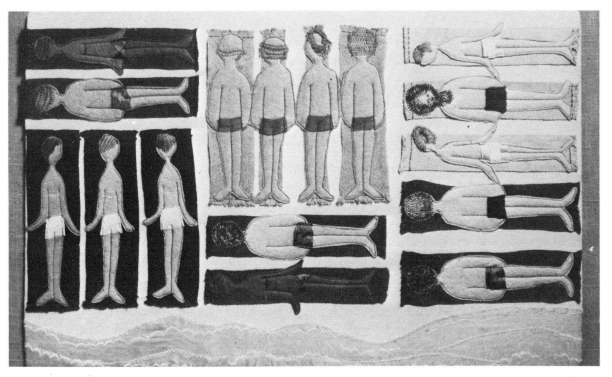

wards, covering the pencil line with close satin stitch. For a bolder effect, sew them over again. You may need to put typing copy paper behind the work to stop it from puckering, but this should be torn away afterwards.

This completes the basic method for machine appliqué. Any of the close automatic stitches can be used for sewing down the pieces. Larger areas need more careful handling and may be better worked as a double layer and cut away afterwards.

Methods for wall hangings, panels and banners

Work on banners can be treated more freely, but they need to be firmly sewn and must stand up to wear. Different types of fabric can be used together to give changes in texture. Remember that any banner is viewed from a distance and needs a bold approach. Banners should be interfaced and backed since they are to be viewed from both sides. Avoid too much iron-on interfacing as this destroys the original quality of the fabric in the finished work.

A wall hanging is one-sided, and seldom moved. Iron-on interfacing can be used if you wish. When the work is finished the background fabric can be mounted on to a panel, glued, or laced backwards and forwards, both top and bottom and from side to side, at about 2 – 3cm (1 in) intervals. This requires more effort, but gives a better finished effect and has the advantage that it can be removed if necessary.

A completely free approach can be used on this type of work. The fraying quality of some fabrics can be used to advantage and gives a softer quality to the work. Collect as many types of fabric as you can and sort them into colours or kinds. See-through plastic boxes or polythene bags with air holes in allow the contents to be seen. These containers may be labelled for quick identification.

Sort out your threads in the same manner. Sorting by colour can have the advantage of providing a ready-made colour scheme. Tip the contents of the bag on to a contrasting background fabric and you will see that ideas will come to you immediately. Net is available in a variety of colours and may be used to soften outlines or deepen other colours.

Choose a firm background fabric for any panel or hanging – iron-on interfacing can give support to a finer fabric – or place paper behind to be torn away afterwards. It is possible to paste calico behind a fabric using PVA glue or wallpaper paste. Be careful not to use too much adhesive and iron on the wrong side to bond.

This method of stiffening is sometimes used for hand-worked metal thread embroidery in ecclesiastical work. The machine will sew through the stiffened layers. Use a larger needle-size and a slightly longer stitch-length when applying fabric pieces. This stitching line can be covered with a metal cord, couched down by hand or zig-zagged over by machine. Hand and machine embroidery combine well with appliqué for this type of work.

You can mix fabrics and threads. Either keep to a simple design using larger fabric areas or use a variety of fabrics to create an interesting surface pattern. Sew them down with a straight stitch or zig-zag, or use a pattern stitch, adding the thick threads afterwards.

Simple designs can be taken from children's books or adapted from magazines. Trace their outlines and use them as pattern pieces.

Suede and unusual fabrics

Non-woven fabrics, felt, vinyl, interfacing, suede and light leather, fur fabrics, and plastic nets of various kinds, can all be applied to a background. Most of these will not wash, so they should be used for theatricals, 'fun clothes', belts, bags or panels.

Leather or suede should be sewn with 100% polyester thread, using a leather needle. A roller foot will help when sewing difficult fabrics. Use a longer stitch and a looser top tension.

Hold the pattern pieces in place with a little fabric adhesive before starting to sew – machine stitch holes will be permanent. Try not to undo work on suede, leather, plastic or felt. Bold zig-zag stitch may be worked over fur fabric.

Non-fray fabrics, leather and felt have the advantage that they can be worked on a straight-stitch machine. For these, use a longer stitch length and looser top tension and sew 1.5 – 2mm ($\frac{1}{16}$ in) from the edges.

Appliqué perse

This is the name given to appliqué designs made from a whole motif – such as a flower or a butterfly – cut out of patterned material, rearranged and applied to a background.

In Elizabethan times, plant designs, or slips, were copied from the herbals, embroidered on to linen or fine canvas and afterwards cut out and applied to other fabrics. It was quite common for Mediaeval embroidery to be worked on a fine linen stretched over velvet, and the surplus cut away afterwards. These are convenient methods of working on contrasting fabrics rather than true appliqué perse.

Appliqué perse flourished in the 18th and early 19th centuries. During the late 17th century exotic printed chintzes were first imported into England from India. After the original designs had been adapted to conform with English taste, they became all the rage. The government of the

3 Appliqué perse – small pattern motifs tacked in position then zig-zagged and satin stitched.

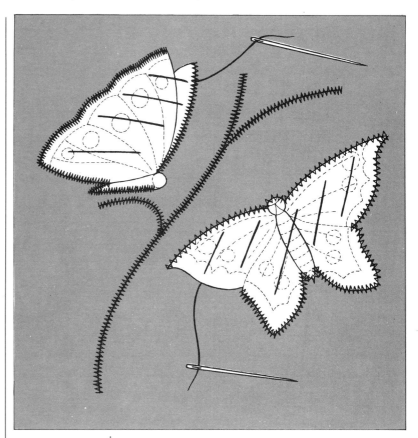

day, fearing that the home cotton industry would suffer, imposed heavy import tariffs, so that eventually only the rich could afford the imported fabrics. Consequently, any left-over piece of the patterned chintz, which was used for clothing as well as furnishings, was saved. The motifs were cut out and applied to cotton calico for bed curtains and coverlets. The most popular designs on the chintz featured exotic birds, plants, trees, butterflies and baskets of flowers. Many of these designs are still popular on furnishing fabrics today.

The cut pieces were sewn down by turning under and hemstitching, or by holding with feather stitch or buttonhole stitch. Long, trailing stems were glued to the background with a starch mixture and embroidered over.

Bedspreads of this type were very popular up to 1830. The next development was to cut shapes from patterned fabric to individual designs, at the same time using the fabric patterning to suggest the appropriate texture. This method was often used in conjunction with patch-work, which gradually took over. There was a renewed interest in appliqué perse in the 1880s and again in this century during the 1930s.

Appliqué perse is a very simple and satisfying way of creating new designs. Motifs can be cut from curtain fabric and applied to cushion covers, which may be re-embroidered or left plain. The pattern fabric can be used for the crossway strips to cover the piping cord, giving the finished cushion a uniform appearance.

Bold appliqué perse motifs look well on beach bags, screens, blinds or under glass

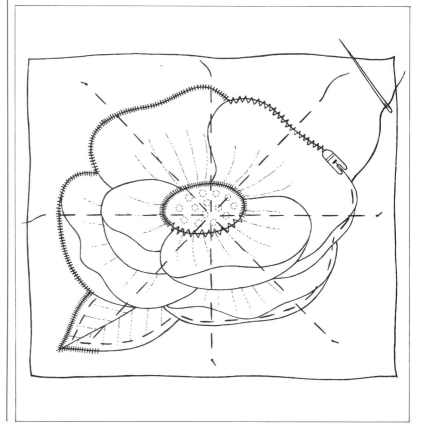

4 Large design applied to cushion cover held down with zig-zag and satin stitch.

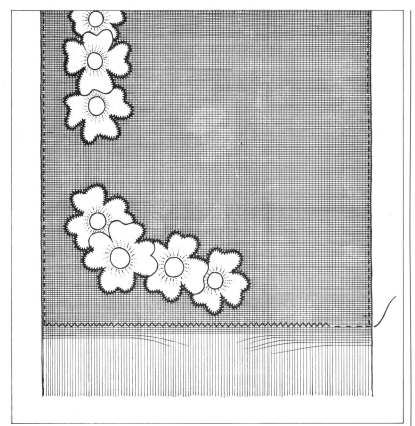

as a table top. Medium-sized motifs can be applied to table-cloths with matching table napkins, also to oven gloves, potholders or peg bags, pillow cases and sheets. The smaller and simpler motifs are useful as decoration for tea cosies and tray cloths and clothing.

It is better to keep to definite design areas when applying the motifs. Scattering them over the surface will not look nice unless it is expertly handled. The design areas can be planned to fit round the edges of rectangular articles, leaving the centre plain. A central design, on the other hand, may have an outer border, but parts of the background fabric should be left plain to show between the appliqué areas. For example, place a large cut-out motif in the centre of a round or square cushion, or on a beach bag, with smaller motifs sitting in one corner, or along two sides.

Appliqué perse on clothing or aprons can be confined to a hem border, pockets or dress yokes. Plan the border so that the designs are repeated or so that the motifs face opposite ways – if the pattern material allows. Borders for curtains in children's rooms could be decorated with cut-out motifs on a theme – a woodland scene or, perhaps, a townscape with people. Fabric pictures can be built up in this manner, but a large variety of pieces may be difficult to find.

It is possible to compromise by using the traditional method of cutting out your shape – whether a tree, a house or a boat – in suitable patterned fabric and combining with smaller appliqué perse motifs. But leave spaces for additional embroidery by machine. Tree

Tea cosy quilted freely using the darning foot and appliqué tray cloth worked under the foot.

branches, flower stalks and any other details can be worked in satin stitch or suitable automatic pattern stitches.

If you intend to use old fabric on anything but a picture, remember to wash the background fabric as well as the fabric you intend to cut up. This will prevent uneven shrinkage.

Working method

Back fine fabrics with iron-on interfacing before you cut round the pattern shape on the right side. There is no need to turn under any edges.

Pin the pattern pieces into position on the background fabric and move them around until you are satisfied with the result, discarding anything that does not fit in. Tack them into position using diagonal stitches. There is no need to tack round the edges on small pieces. In tacking the larger motifs work from the centre outwards, towards the edges.

Machine the pieces in position, using No. 50 machine embroidery thread. A straight stitch machine can be used for work on decorative panels and hangings, or when using non-fray materials. Anything that requires washing will have to be zig-zagged and then held with satin stitch. Alternatively, automatic pattern stitches may be used. Try to choose simple shapes for machine work, or there will be too many corners to turn.

Making a tray cloth

The tray cloth will be bordered with the same cotton print that was used to make the quilted tea cosy. When cutting a design from an all-over print, you have to make a decision on the areas you are going to cut. These patterns are designed to a definite repeat.

Choose a coarse cotton or linen type fabric for the cloth and then plan the overall measurement to fit your tea tray. Mark out the area with

pins and cut out along the grain of the fabric. Measure 2 cm ($\frac{3}{4}$ in) in from the outer edges and withdraw a thread on all four sides. Now zig-zag over the inner side of the drawn thread line with a small stitch in matching thread, withdrawing the remaining threads to form a fringe (you will find it easier if you start from the middle of each row).

Position your cut pattern pieces and machine them in place with toning thread.

Reverse appliqué

This is the term generally given to the practice of cutting through several layers of fabric, each of a different colour, to expose the colours beneath. The layers are first tacked together. The design pattern to be worked can be cut before hemstitching in hand-sewn work, and after stitching in machine work.

Simple reverse appliqué is worked on two layers of cloth only. It is possible to work up to seven layers of cloth, but this becomes very complicated. For any machine work, four layers will suffice.

Découpé is the name given to reverse appliqué worked on two layers of cloth, but with different coloured or patterned pieces of fabric slipped between the layers. The top layer is cut away to reveal these coloured pieces and the background cloth.

In some traditional work, reverse appliqué, découpé and small areas of appliqué can be combined in the same project. For example, the Kuna Indians of the San Blas Islands, Panama, work their *molas*, or blouses, in this manner.

Reverse appliqué differs from the normal method of attaching smaller cut pieces of fabric to a background, in that it begins with similar-sized pieces of fabric. It is much easier to work in two layers

than to apply an intricate design that first has to be cut out. The method is also a traditional form of patterning and is commonly found among different societies and racial groups throughout the world.

Designs made from folded cut paper were used by the American quilt makers in the 19th century. These were adapted from traditional Hawaiian patterns. The designs all have symbolic significance and they may be combined in different ways. A fan or a pineapple pattern might cover the entire quilt, but an alternative method entailed making up 43 cm (17 in) squares, often with the appliqué counter-changed. These blocks were quilted and sewn together afterwards. This method has found favour in the present American Block Quilt revival.

Place mats in Hawaiian block pattern

Simplification is the keynote when translating this type of work for the sewing machine. The large, traditional block patterns are too complicated and too large for easy handling. If they are to be quilted afterwards it is essential to keep the fabric flat beneath the machine needle.

Six mats can be cut from two separate pieces of polyester cotton each 60 cm (24 in) long and 90 cm (34 in) wide, in contrasting colours. Three mats can be cut across the width, each measuring 30 cm (12 in) wide and 27 cm (11 in) from top to bottom. This gives a better proportion.

You will need scissors for paper and card, dressmaking scissors, a dressmaker's marking pencil, a hard pencil, tracing paper and some thin card and machine embroidery thread No. 50 in two colours to match the chosen fabric. Now trace off the design in the diagram (fig. 7); it is a quarter of the pattern. Transfer the

6 Pattern for reverse appliqué mat. One eighth of pattern is drawn first to the actual finished size.

design to thin card and cut it out.

If you prefer, you can make your own pattern by folding a 23cm (9in) newspaper square in half twice and then folding this small square on the diagonal. You then draw and cut out your design. You may need to cut several before you are satisfied.

Using the dressmaker's pencil, mark out the mats on the fabric to the given measurements and cut out six dark mats and six light, keeping to the straight grain of the material. Fold one light-coloured mat in half from side to side and then from top to bottom to make creasemarks as guidelines. Then draw these in on the wrong side with your dressmaker's pencil. The card pattern template fits into each corner, with the dotted lines against the guidelines.

Next draw round the outer edges with a hard pencil (not biro), keeping the pencil point well into the corners. This line will be sewn over. Place one marked and one contrasting, unmarked piece of fabric together, matching the grain of the material. Tack these together, starting from the centre and working outwards, taking diagonal tacking stitches. Now tack round the outer edges.

You should thread the machine with the lighter colour on top and the darker in the bobbin. Set a medium straight stitch and sew round on the pencil lines. Now sew the shapes in the middle of the leaves and sew 1cm ($\frac{3}{8}$in) in round the outer edges of the mat. Pivot the cloth round the needle at all corners.

You have been working on the wrong side. Turn the fabric over and cut away the dark

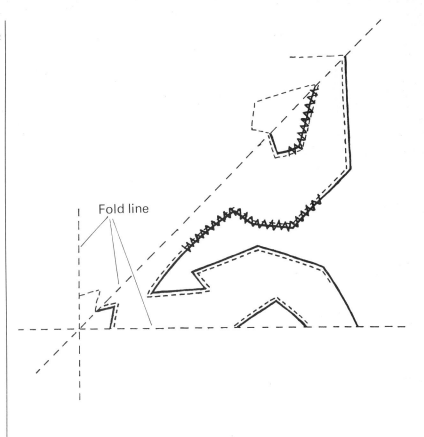

7 One quarter of the mat pattern drawn to actual size by making a mirror-image of figure 6 (above).

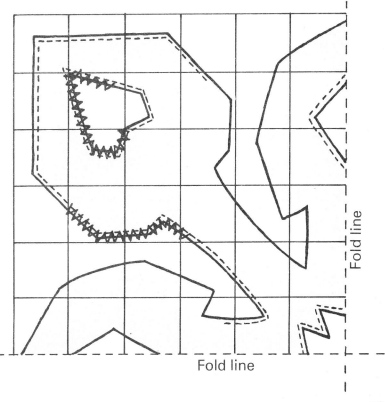

Reverse appliqué Hawaiian pattern mats worked under the machine foot.

fabric as close to the stitched line as you can, exposing the light fabric as a background. Now cut round the outer edges to leave a dark border and cut out the small central shapes. It is easier if you hold a finger under the cloth and feel as the scissors move along.

Re-thread the machine with the opposite colours and set for satin stitch. Sew over and enclose both the straight-stitch line and the raw edge, the outer swing of the needle going into the background only.

Turn the sharp outer points by pivoting round the needle on its outer swing and turn the inside corners by pivoting round the needle on its inner swing. This method will leave no gaps unworked.

Machine the central star shape next, then the cut-outs and finally the inner border. Sew round the outside edge twice. The next mat can be worked in the opposite colours to give a counter-change pattern. As long as the material is not pulled during the sewing, the mat will remain perfectly flat.

Using felt

It is believed that the linear patterned reverse appliqué worked by the Kuna Indians evolved from body painting. The early designs were geometrical or featured the mythological beasts and spirits that inhabited the various layers of the underworld.

The humidity in the air causes old *molas* to disintegrate and granny *molas* are now collectors' pieces. The newer *molas* depict birds and animals, and objects from contemporary life. They are designed, worked and worn by the Kuna women as panels at the back and front of their yoked, short-sleeved blouses.

These designs were marked on to the layers of cloth with

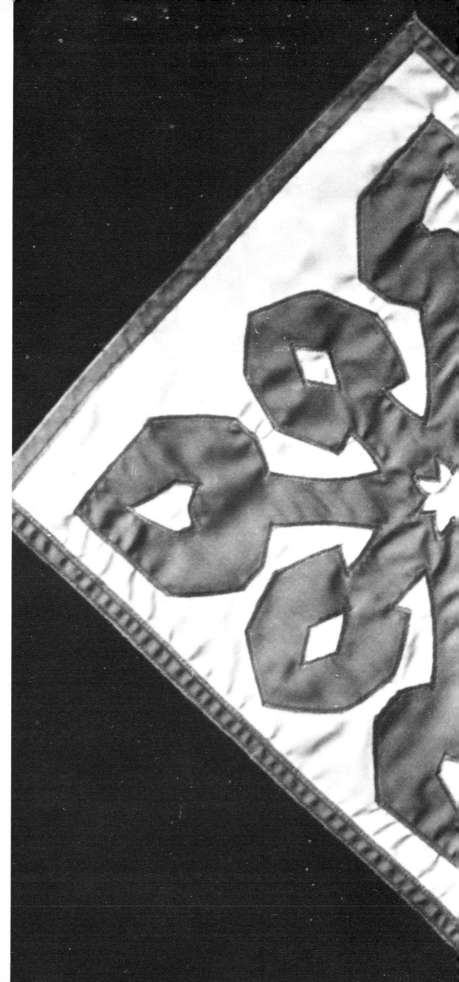

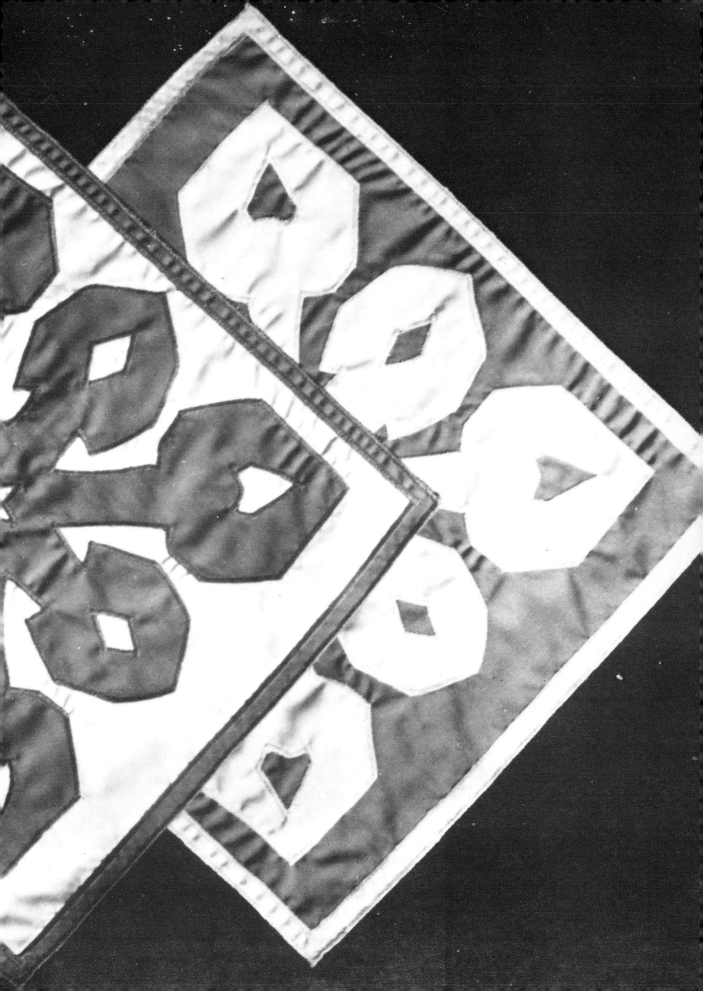

tacking stitches. An outline was cut and the seam allowance turned under and hemmed. A second or third layer could be treated in the same way. Some designs featured a zig-zag line, worked by turning under slit pieces of the cloth, but in later work this was replaced by ric-rac braid. This is a method that can be worked by straight-stitch machining through several layers of felt, cutting away parts of each layer. Pinking shears create the zig-zag lines.

Felt pieces can be purchased in sizes up to 30cm (12in) square – anything larger is difficult to handle. Choose one light square, one dark and one medium coloured, all of the same size. Next, using a ruler, divide the light felt square into smaller squares or rectangles and draw guidelines with a soft pencil or tailor's chalk. This is the underside of the work.

Sandwich the medium colour between the other two squares – dark looks best on top, but you can vary it. Now tack them together across the middle, using straight stitch. Larger squares will need additional tacking.

Thread the machine top and bottom with dark thread to match the top felt square. With the light layer uppermost, machine round each drawn rectangle, using a medium-length straight stitch. Now machine across the diagonals on alternate rectangles. Triangular spaces can be filled in with extra stitching lines but these should be kept at least 1 – 2cm ($\frac{1}{2}$in) apart. Turn over to the dark (top) side and cut away the dark layer of felt in some places to expose the second colour, using pinking shears on some areas.

Continue working from the top. The second layer can be machined in either matching or contrasting thread, to create

(Top right) A traditional South American Mola with a bird motif in reverse appliqué.
(Right) Reverse appliqué worked in layers of coloured felt.

more pattern lines. Make sure you leave enough space to cut some of the areas away to expose the lightest layer underneath.

Admittedly, all this takes a lot of thought, and you may like to plan a design on layers of coloured paper first. However, it is fun to create as you go along and no two squares need be the same. These large squares can be joined to make decorative panels, table tops under glass, 'fun clothes', bed-heads, or place mats.

Some of the more complicated *mola* patterns were worked by introducing different-coloured pieces of fabric between fewer layers of cloth. For these, you should use only two layers of felt. Sandwich the smaller, differently coloured squares between and plan the design to cut down and expose these extra colours.

Embroidery

In the Middle Ages, *Opus Anglicanum*, or 'English Work,' was famous throughout Europe. This superb embroidery was mainly for ecclesiastical use, and the Syon Cope in the Victoria and Albert Museum is a wonderful example. But fashion in embroidery changes, and by the Elizabethan period clothing was much more lavishly adorned. Precious stones, gold and silver thread proclaimed the wealth of the wearer.

This 'raised look' later found expression on the delightful Stump-work boxes – often made by young girls – during the reigns of the Stuart kings.

Embroidery in the 18th century featured naturalistic flowers and garlands on the costumes of both men and women. Superb whitework embroidery on caps, collars, baby gowns and bonnets was worked during the first half of the 19th century in Scotland and in Northern Ireland. But the invention of embroidery machines

soon brought about the decline of commercial handwork as the handworkers were unable to compete.

When the domestic sewing machine came into common use in the 1860s, home dress-makers were more interested in sewing frills and braid trimmings on to garments. Towards the end of the century, however, an interest in art embroidery was developing in America. This was free machine embroidery worked in a circular frame. The machine feed teeth were put out of action so that the movement and subsequent stitch pattern could be controlled by the worker.

It was not until the 1930s that this was taken up as a form of emboidery design in the Art Colleges. Machine embroidery gained acceptance very gradually, the turning-point coming in the 1960s when there was great interest in new techniques of all kinds.

Machines for embroidery

A machine that is perfect for dressmaking does not necessarily make an ideal embroidery machine. This is not a question of how many automatic patterns are included, but one of easily manipulated controls and knobs.

For free work it is essential to be able to drop the feed teeth. Some machines are provided with a plate to cover the teeth, or a plate to slip beneath and raise the needle plate above the teeth.

The other essential control is a free moving stitch-width lever or knob. The embroiderer needs to be able to alter the width while sewing. A knob that clicks into a variety of positions will not turn smoothly. Stop levers help to keep the width lever set at any chosen width, up to 7 mm ($\frac{3}{10}$ in) on some machines.

A flat-bed machine gives a firm work surface. If the machine is a free-arm model, see that the work surface extension is

firm and smoothly joined. It is possible to use a conversion table that will fit around the arm of a free-arm machine. The embroiderer will need this surface for resting the elbows on when working free embroidery in the frame.

Be sure to choose a machine that is easy to thread, with slotted guides and a bobbin case that can be easily changed. A front-loading bobbin will allow you to use twin needles. Some machines also have a see-through panel above the bobbin area.

Using the foot

The machine-stitched line is finer than handworked stitchery. Use this delicate quality of line to advantage. Lines will appear thicker when crossed or sewn close together.

On a zig-zag machine, the stitch-width control allows variation in the width of zig-zag line. The stitch-length control can be closed up to form a satin stitch, and opened out again to make areas of open and close texture.

Zig-zag rows in different colours can overlap or alternate with straight stitch lines. Try experimenting with white thread on a dark background, then adding colour to give a tonal effect.

If your machine has a selection of automatic patterns, make a sampler guide of all the stitches in contrasting thread on a plain white material and number them for easy reference. Use a machine embroidery thread and loosen the top tension slightly for zig-zag, satin stitch and all automatic pattern work.

Automatic patterns can be stitched in straight rows, to decorate borders and hems of garments. Combine them with zig-zag, plain satin stitch or rows of straight stitches. (They can also be sewn to ribbon or tape and added to braid.) Try sewing any of these stitches over felt, net, suede, or vinyl-coated material. A roller foot will help when sewing awkward fabrics. Automatic patterns can also be used to create additional patterns and textures. The Butterfly picture was worked using the various stitches to suggest wing-patterning and texture. Consult your stitch sample and try out stitches on a piece of the project material first to see which looks the best. Use a variety of threads.

Draw the outline of the butterfly (body, wings and large circles) on to thin typing-paper and pin to the wrong side of the bakground fabric. Set the machine to straight stitch and sew through the paper with the fabric beneath. Machine over the guidelines, using a contrasting thread. Now turn to the right side and work your design through the fabric and the paper. Paper will prevent the fabric from puckering and can be torn away afterwards.

Some of the automatic pattern stitches are sewn from the opposite way, to create extra patterns. You can use a single colour in the bobbin throughout. Loosen the top tension slightly and make sure you sew curves in stages, pivoting round the needle.

Free embroidery

Apart from the decorative effects possible using the foot on the machine, the embroiderer will find that free machine work will offer a greater scope for expression and design. Free machine embroidery is a direct, immediate form of decoration and can be combined with other types of embroidery. The design however, should be planned as a whole from the start.

Adjusting the machine

The feed teeth of the machine must be put out of action. In normal work they control the backwards and forwards movement of the cloth. In free work it is the operator who controls the movement of the fabric, which is stretched taut in a circular embroidery frame.

Consult your sewing machine manual for darning, to drop the feed. Some machines have a knob, or lever, to drop the feed; others have a cover plate to fit over the teeth. This latter

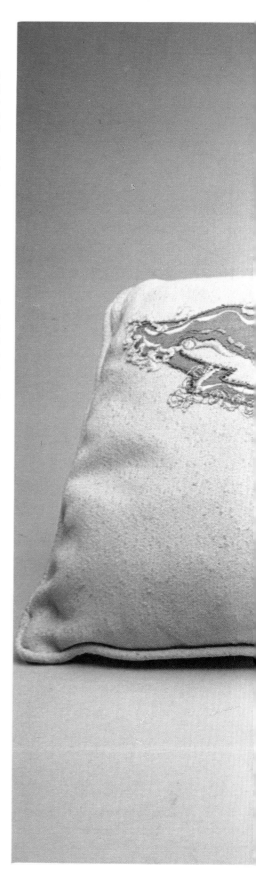

(Below) A picture of a butterfly embroidered on to a textured background using automatic stitches and the foot on the machine.

(Right) A cushion with an applied shell motif embroidered in cable stitch from the wrong side, both freely and under the machine foot as well.

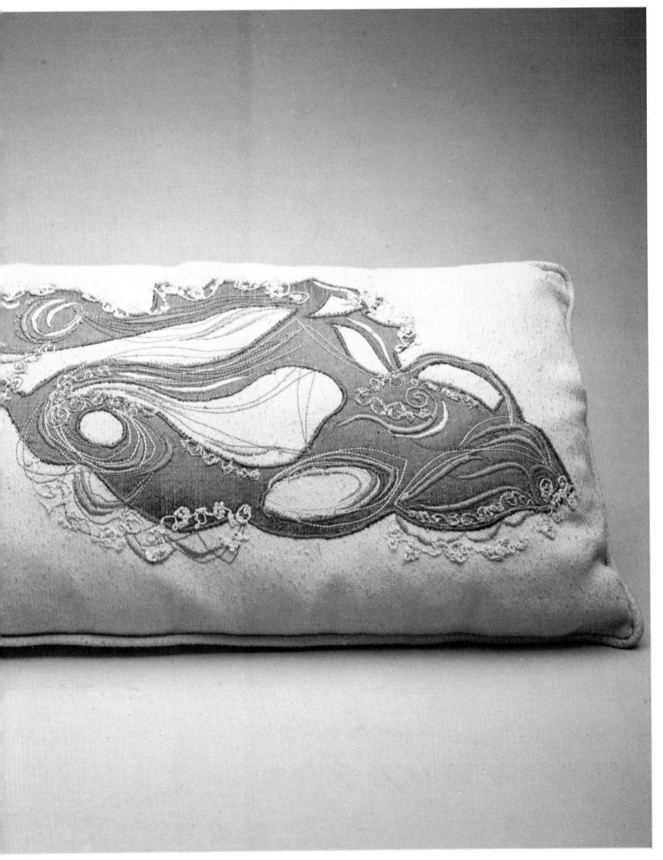

method is less satisfactory than the drop feed control: the framed material is liable to rock over the protruding cover plate. Because the presser foot has been removed, it is essential that the material is held as flat as possible on to the bed of the machine. If you have any trouble, use a darning foot, as well. This is controlled by a spring. Some makes have a lever that fits over the needle-bar, and this allows the cloth beneath to be moved at will. The darning foot has to be fitted after the frame is in position.

Framing the material

Choose a firm, but not too closely woven, plain material for your first experiments – cotton poplin, or even old sheeting, provided it is in good condition. Use a circular wooden embroidery frame, or a metal frame. Plastic ones are not suitable as they tend to warp. Normal sized frames for working are 18 – 20 cm (7 – 8 in), but they are available from 8 cm (3 in) up to 30 cm (12 in). Anything larger would be awkward to use. The space between the machine needle and the upright of the machine arm determines the area that can be worked, and a large frame would be hindered by the arm.

The frame should have a horizontal tightening screw so that it can lie flat on the machine bed. The inner ring of the frame should be bound with bias strip cloth, or bias binding, to prevent the fabric from slipping. The fabric should be secured with a few hand stitches on the inside of the ring.

Place the inner ring on the table and place the fabric over it. Now fit the outer ring over the top and tighten the screw. Turn over so that the flat material is on the table and pull each of the four sides of the material up and over in turn, to tighten the fabric. When it is drum tight tighten the screw again.

The presser foot should next

be removed – which will leave the needle unprotected. If you prefer, you may fit a finger guard or use the darning foot in conjunction with the frame while you practise.

Working free embroidery

Thread the machine with one colour on top and a different colour in the bobbin (both to contrast with the fabric). This helps when making adjustments to the tension.

Check that the feed teeth are dropped, or the cover plate is in position, and that the presser foot and screw have been removed. (Put these away in your accessory box.) Now set the machine to straight stitch.

Have your material framed and ready and push the inner frame so that it protrudes about

8 Embroidery with simple zig-zag stitch patterns using the embroidery foot on the machine.

1 mm ($\frac{1}{32}$ in) – this prevents the frame catching on any ridges on the machine bed. Raise the needle to its highest position and slip the frame underneath with the fabric flat on the machine bed. Some frames are thicker than others and you may have to tip yours to prevent it from catching on the needle.

Lower the needle into the cloth by turning the balance wheel towards you by hand. Remember to lower the presser-bar lever (even though the foot is removed); this engages the tension. Failure to lower the bar can cause looped thread and a jammed bobbin.

Draw the bottom thread up to the surface of the fabric. Hold on to the two ends and make a few stitches, turning the wheel by hand – this will lock the thread. Now cut off the ends and start to sew, moving the

9 Framing fabric for machine embroidery. The inner ring should be bound with bias strip.

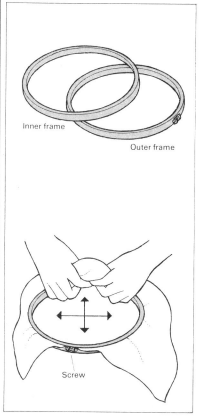

Inner frame

Outer frame

Screw

frame slowly beneath the needle with a circular motion.

It is as if the machine needle were a pencil, and the material beneath moved in order to draw a line. The faster you move the frame, the longer the stitches; the slower the shorter. Do not sew in one place or the stitches; the slower, the shorter. other and form a lump. Sew slowly and at an even speed. This will be easy if your machine has an electronic foot control, which will also enable you to stop and start immediately.

Next, set the machine to a medium zig-zag width. This will produce an entirely different effect. With the feed out of action, the speed at which you sew will determine whether the machine sews zig-zag or satin stitch. Do not, however, sew too slowly, or the satin stitch will build up and jam underneath.

If the frame is moved up and down within one plane to form a wave pattern, the thick line will decrease and increase in width, like writing with a flat-nibbed pen. Try writing your name. If you can do this, you have mastered the art of free embroidery. It takes time to gain real control and become proficient, but after 15–20 hours' practice you should be able to accomplish most things.

Next try altering the width control while you are sewing. You will have to guide the frame with your left hand only. This requires much more practice. The width control will open up from a straight-line to a wider, satin stitch and back again. All kinds of free patterns can be sewn like this, including leaves and flower petals.

Free embroidery is especially suitable worked on clothing and soft furnishing. The fine stitches become part of the fabric and do not look like an afterthought. For a more textured effect, you can combine free embroidery with beading or some hand stitches like French knots or detached chain.

Free embroidery will require careful planning. A machine-embroidered line is very difficult to undo, even with a seam ripper. It is far easier to machine over any mistakes or incorporate them as part of the design.

Embroidery can be worked on collars, cuffs, dress fronts, yokes, borders, pockets and hems. The design areas should be restricted. You will find fashion magazines a useful source of ideas for placing embroidery. Clothing should be embroidered before the pattern shapes are cut out to allow for working in a frame. Always buy extra material for design experiments since you may need to try out several ideas before selecting the one that is most suitable.

Mark the pattern shapes with tailor tacks through the sewing line, or cut out the pattern in paper and place it on the material. Tack around with running stitches, but do not tack on the outer cutting line. Alternatively, you can mount a cut-out collar or pocket shape on to thin backing material by tacking across and all round. This backing should be large enough to go into the frame and allow room for repositioning. The extra fabric will also act as interfacing on collars, cuffs or pockets. Toy pattern pieces can be cut out, mounted and embroidered in a similar manner before making-up.

Place the portion of fabric to be worked in the embroidery frame. It may be necessary to move the frame during the work if the design is a large one. This can be done without removing the work from the machine. First raise the needle out of the cloth, then push the inner frame out and move it across to the new area to be sewn. Finally, snap the frame back into the repositioned outer frame. This procedure is not difficult.

Fabrics such as velvet, needlecord or suede-cloth will mark when they are sewn in a ring frame. These should be sewn backed with paper or vanishing muslin, which is produced for the embroidery trade and can be ironed off on the back of the work afterwards. The muslin goes brown, and then shrivels – which can cause problems with synthetic fabrics. The paper will come away quite easily when torn off. You will need to use a darning foot when working on a backing alone, unless you are very experienced.

Embroidery can decorate sheets and the ends of pillow-cases, although it is not practical to decorate the middle. Tablecloths, place mats and napkins, can all be embroidered as sets, repeating the same pattern motif either on the edges, or in the middle. Tea cosies need a slightly bolder treatment, as do cushions and curtains. Machine appliqué can be combined with free embroidery, which has a softening effect on the harder appliqué outlines. Remember to ensure that all the fabrics you use are washable.

The design for the appliqué apron was taken from real leaves that had been pressed and dried. Free machine embroidery was added later.

Thick threads in the bobbin

Many kinds of thicker threads can be used for free machine embroidery. Over-sized needles can take a thicker thread, but it is much more practical to wind the thick threads round the bobbin and sew the work from the wrong side. Alteration in the tension will give a wider choice of design textures.

Some threads can be wound on to the bobbin in the normal way. If the thread is too thick to pass through the tension guide on the winding mechanism, control the tension by letting the thread pass between your fingers. Thick threads have to be wound on to the bobbin by hand. You can use any smooth thread that is not too hard. Rough or hairy threads, however, will catch on the bobbin tension spring or on the race hook, or in the feed teeth.

Sometimes very thick threads can be used if you bypass the bobbin tension spring. There is a special hole or by-pass on some bobbin cases. Beginners, however, are not advised to try this method as the thread is difficult to control and can get tangled up.

You will need to alter the tension on the bobbin case when using these thicker threads. Only a few machines have numbered bottom tension. But you will soon get used to gauging the correct tension by feel. The thread should just pull out tightly. When the bobbin case is held up by the thread and given a jerk, the thread should hold in position, and no more. If you prefer not to touch the little screw, buy a second bobbin case and save this for embroidery. It can be marked with enamel paint or nail varnish for identification. Keep the other, unaltered one for normal sewing.

Undo the screw, a quarter of a turn at a time only, in an anticlockwise direction, holding it over a box lid in case it should fall out. Choose a matching, or contrasting top thread – No. 50 machine embroidery or No. 60 mercerized cotton when using medium-thick bobbin threads, and No. 30 embroidery or No. 40 cotton for thicker ones.

Use a yellow or orange top thread when sewing gold threads in the bobbin and white or grey top thread for sewing silver. Be careful not to twist flat lurex thread. Hold the reel on a skewer or a knitting needle and do not put the thread through the tension guies. Let it wind on, keeping a slow, even speed on the machine.

You can use crochet cotton, cotton à broder, perle thread, goldfingering (in a choice of metallic colours), rayon floss thread, stranded embroidery cottons, knitting threads and many more. Gold and silver cords, incidentally, come in a variety of thicknesses.

Frame your material as usual, but choose a fabric that is not too closely woven. Lower the presser-bar lever, bringing the bottom thread through to the top of the cloth. Hold the top thread and lower the needle into the cloth by turning the balance wheel towards you by hand. Now gently pull the bottom thread up to the top – it may be difficult to get through. In which case, as soon as you see a loop, put a pin through to help it up.

Hold both ends of thread as you start to sew. This is the wrong side of the work so the ends may be cut off – but not too close. Sew slightly slower than normal, and move the frame more quickly. When you have sewn a test line, cut off the ends and turn to the right side to see the results.

Alter the top tension until you get the effect you want. A tight top tension will pull the bottom thread into the cloth; a looser top tension will allow the thick thread to lie flatter on the material.

The type of embroidery discussed can also be worked with the foot on the machine. This straight stitch-line embroidery is called cable stitch and can, by way of contrast, be used in conjunction with free work.

Straight line patterns can be sewn round rectangular or other geometric shapes. You should start from the outside and sew round in a spiral. Leave a space in the middle and work free cable stitch inside in a contrasting colour.

Free cable stitch or towelling stitch is worked by moving the frame backwards and forwards, sewing a series of small wavy lines. Set the machine to straight stitch and give a slight pull to the frame each time you change direction. If the bottom tension is loose enough, this should give a nice loopy texture. Be careful not to cross over lines or the thick threads might jam underneath.

This stitch will not work on all machines. The thicker threads could damage the mechanism on precision-built models. If in any doubt, consult your dealer.

Metallic cords work best sewn in straight-stitch lines with the foot on the machine. Flat lurex thread should be used for automatic patterns worked from the wrong side, with the stitch-length opened-up slightly.

Stranded embroidery cotton can be wound round the bobbin, either in the same colour or with the colours mixed to give a shaded effect. These work equally well with the foot on for free embroidery. Rayon floss thread is excellent and looks very rich on satin stitch or automatic patterns.

For embroidery on clothing, plan the design areas by cutting out paper shapes and placing them on the fabric. Since you are always working from the wrong side, these shapes can be drawn round with a dress-maker's pencil. If the fabric is finer use tacking stitches. But do not sew over tacking stitches; once caught they are a problem to remove. This type of embroidery is not so difficult to undo. Hold on to a free end of the thick thread, pull it up and snip the stitches between.

Decorate fabric-covered buttons to match your collar or cuff designs. Use a small 8 cm (3 in) embroidery frame. The circular button shape is cut out afterwards. This is an easy way of tying in embroidered decoration to give a complete look to a garment.

Thick threads can be combined with appliqué, and free embroidery sewn from the right side of the fabric. The cushion was worked in this manner. The shell design on the cushion was cut from paper which was pinned on to dark green material matching the grain of the background material. This pattern shape was cut out and tacked to the cushion material, then held down with a zig-zag stitch, using the foot on the machine. Next, the outline was held down with satin stitch using a matching machine embroidery thread.

Free satin stitch embroidery was worked on to both the appliqué and the background to soften the hard outline. Be sure to open out the satin stitch when crossing over already worked stitches; the needle may not be able to pierce hard lumps. The patterning was created by altering the stitch-width lever with the right hand while guiding the frame with the left.

Straight-stitch lines in a contrasting colour were sewn from the right side as a guide for the cable stitch embroidery, which was worked from the wrong side of the fabric. Three strands of stranded embroidery cotton were wound round the bobbin by hand. These lines were sewn under the foot, not in the frame. Free cable stitch was added afterwards, using perle thread in the bobbin to suggest encrustations on the shell.

Thick threads can be used to decorate all kinds of unusual fabrics. Rayon floss thread sewn on to fur fabric produces an almost quilted effect. Have the furry side facing downwards and sew a marked pattern outline from the smooth knit-back side. Let the rayon thread contrast strongly with the coloured fur fabric. Sew zig-zag rows, or very open satin stitch in patterns with crossing lines.

Metallic cords sewn from the wrong side to felt or suede sinks into, and becomes part of, the material. Try some experiments with similar thread on a variety of fabric types.

Whipped stitches

Other textural effects can be obtained by altering the tension, at top or bottom. In a normal, correct tension setting, the stitches should be evenly interlocked. Thread the machine with a contrasting colour, top and bottom, that will show up on the trial fabric. Have a fine No. 50 machine em-

Whipped stitch embroidery worked freely in the embroidery frame.

broidery thread in the bobbin and a coarser No. 30 machine embroidery, or No. 40 mercerized cotton, in the needle.

First set an even tension. Make a note of the number on the top tension setting. This will enable you to set up the machine correctly for normal sewing afterwards. Set the machine for free embroidery and frame the material.

If you tighten the top tension, more of the bottom colour will show through to the top. Move the frame slowly, in a straight line. The fine lower thread will wrap round the top thread to form what is called a 'whipped stitch'. The faster you move the frame, the more the stitches will be spread out, and the more of the top colour will show. Move the frame slowly and the bottom thread will cover the top thread. This technique can be used for creating tonal areas with different colours.

The straight lines can be sewn very close to one another to build up a solid area. Stitching with a circular motion will give a different type of patterning. If you tighten the top tension again spiky stitches will build up and radiate out from each tiny circle. This is called 'exaggerated whip stitch' or 'feather stitch'. But do not tighten the top tension too much or the top thread will break. To increase the spiky effect, loosen the bottom tension a quarter of a turn. Next, sew in spirals, letting the inner curve stitches build up as the circumference decreases. Give a definite pull to the frame as you go round.

Whipped stitches can be used to create areas of texture and they look well with added beads worked on clothing or on an evening bag. Sequins may be sewn on first and incorporated as part of the design as in the collar pattern.

The collar shape is marked out on to the fabric with tacking stitches. Sequins are then sewn on by hand at intervals, after the chosen place is marked with a pin. Whip stitch is filled in round the sequins, as a design

area rather than as a set pattern. Be careful not to machine over them. The even spacing of the sequins will give regularity to an otherwise random pattern.

Whipped stitches combine well with other types of machine embroidery. Cable stitch, for example, worked from the wrong side afterwards and using a metallic thread wound round the bobbin, can be sewn over the whipped stitches in circles.

Stretching and mounting

Embroidered fabric that is to be made up into an article, like the apron or cushion, will need stretching first. Some work will be impossible to iron; the fabric may not be suitable or bead work or metal threads may have been added.

Allow an extra 4 cm (1½ in) of cloth all the way round when working embroidery. The fabric is pinned out all the way

round with drawing pins on to a board and is covered with several layers of newspaper topped with blotting paper or clean, white material. Now sprinkle water over the blotting paper to dampen it. The newspaper needs to be damp, but not wet. Next pin out your embroidery, right sides uppermost, starting at the centre and working outwards, both top and bottom and from side to side. Stretch the fabric evenly, keeping the grain of the material straight. Leave it in a warm place and do not remove until the bottom layer of newspaper is bone dry. It will not always be necessary to stretch embroidery mounted as a wall panel.

String up wall panels in the same way as for appliqué panels. A wall hanging will need interlining and backing. Iron-on interfacing can be used, but try not to stiffen the work too much.

10 Stretching and mounting.

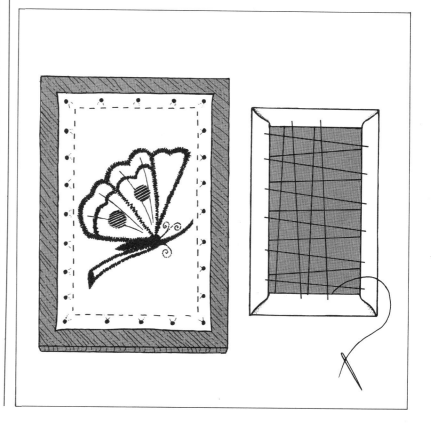

Lace

During the 19th century, various machines were invented to produce copies of all the main types of handworked lace. In some cases the results were so good that it takes an expert to tell the difference.

John Heathcote invented a machine for making plain net in 1809. Manufacturers employed lace 'runners', who darned the linear patterns in and out of the net meshes by hand. The patterns were simple at first but later became more complicated, and finally even these were worked by machine.

Chain stitch worked with a tambour hook was also used to embroider machine net, and was made at Coggeshall in Essex. The daughter of the factory-owner and her husband moved to Ireland and together they set up a workshop in Limerick to make similar lace.

Another type of Irish embroidered lace on machine net, made in Carrick-ma-Cross, was taught by convent nuns. This type of lace was popular until Edwardian times.

Cambric or muslin was placed over a machine net ground. The designs were couched or chain stitched and the surplus outer muslin layer cut away to reveal the net beneath.

These handworked designs were easily copied by commercial machines, but they are equally simple to sew on a domestic machine. Any competent machine embroiderer will find them well within her scope.

Carrick-ma-Cross lace

This method lends itself to domestic machine work. The best way to mark the design is to trace it on to typing paper.

Carrick-ma-cross free embroidery worked through organdie and net.

Lay the top layer of muslin or organdie on to a flat surface which has first been covered with a soft woollen cloth. Place the design paper on top of the organdie and hold this down with a weight at each corner. Using a blunt-pointed instrument, draw round the design lines, pressing hard, but not so hard as to tear the paper. In this way, an indented line will be transferred to the fabric. This will be quite sufficient to indicate the main design outlines for the embroidery.

Use nylon net with nylon organza, and cotton net with cotton organdie or muslin. Place the marked organdie on top of the net. Tack them together from top to bottom, across and round the edges. This double layer is then put into the embroidery frame ready for working, with the organdie on top.   With the machine set for straight stitch and free embroidery, embroider twice round all outlines and fill in any interior design lines such as leaf stalks.

The lace dress-front was worked in this way. Only the main lines of the stalks and leaves were marked, and the centres of all the roses. The design was drawn from a rambler rose and stylized to fit the shape of the dress front. Always keep your designs simple in outline and allow an equal amount of fabric to be covered.

Machine the entire design, moving the work in the frame so that each part can be embroidered with ease. Sew any border designs last. The fabric must be large enough to allow room for the border to be worked in the frame.

When all is finished, cut the top layer or organdie away, in between the design shapes – great care is needed not to cut the net. Approach the work in a calm and unhurried manner. Provided that you keep your fingers under the work, and help guide the scissors along, there should be no problem. If you do inadvertently cut the net, then machine over it as part of the design. Small pearl beads are sewn by hand afterwards to accentuate the centres of the roses.

Use the chain-stitching device to sew through a layer of organdie over net. As this can only be worked with the foot on, keep to linear designs. Right-angled corners can be turned by raising the foot and pivoting round the needle. Squares and rectangles should be overlapped and the overlapping parts cut away to disclose the net beneath. This work may be planned in more than one colour.

Machining on net

This is a simple form of machine embroidered lace, worked freely in the embroidery frame, with the machine set to straight-stitch and darning.

Use the firm, nylon net obtainable from multiple stores. This comes in a variety of colours and does not tear when stretched in the frame. Next, match the colour of your thread to the net. Any contrast can make the design look heavy. The only exception is a toning, shaded thread, matched to the darker colour.

For practice, cut a square of net and frame it in the manner described for free embroidery. You will not be able to mark the design on the net. Plan a continuous, circular design, such as a flower head or snowflake crystal, and start and finish, as always, at the centre.

Now bring the bottom thread to the top in the usual way. At first it may be disconcerting to see through the net, but once the sewing is started this can be ignored. Try not to go over lines more than twice, or they will become too thick. Make dots by sewing round in circles. Sew round a couple of times in one place to finish off the work. You will find that a smaller sized frame will help keep circular designs even. More than one layer of net can be embroidered, and parts cut away from behind afterwards. Try shadow work, with different colours of net behind.

The type of embroidery described is frequently used to decorate lace for cuffs, collars, dress fronts, and wedding veils. It can also be mounted over a contrasting fabric to cover box lids, evening bags, or to make a picture.

Detached work

Petals for flowers or butterflies' wings are embroidered on to the net and cut out afterwards. The outlines should be sewn round twice to give a firmer edge. A double layer of net will make the work stiffer, and a contrasting net can be used for shading.

Using thicker threads

This will give an entirely different character to the work. Wind coloured rayon floss round the bobbin by hand, and work on a dark-coloured net.

Try straight-line patterns, sewn in rows backwards and forwards, working in blocks and changing direction on alternate blocks. You will see how the work will catch the light differently.

Work with a fine metal cord in the bobbin and grey or white thread in the needle. Alternatively, use fine silver or gold in the needle and matching thread in the bobbin. Try experimenting, using metal threads sewn on to different types of net.

Darned netting

Another type of embroidered net work, called 'lacis', or 'darned netting', can be simulated on the machine by using wider-meshed curtain net.

Use a plain squared net, with holes preferably not more than 1–1.5cm ($\frac{1}{2}$in) apart. Darn backwards and forwards across the holes, using the free embroidery technique set to straight-stitch.   The machine stitches will interlock to form a chain across the space. Then sew across the other way to form the network. Fill in the net squares to a predetermined pattern, which can be planned out on squared paper first.

For bolder, more experimental work, use soft plastic netting or greenhouse net – see what you can find. Use thicker threads and work intuitively as you go along. This type of work is suitable for blinds, room dividers, lampshades and wall hangings.

Detached petals and leaves of guipure lace by Stella Bird.

Chain stitch on net

The development of the chain-stitch machine in the latter half of the 19th century brought about the end of the hand-tambour worked net lace. The Cornely chain stitch machine, which was guided from beneath by a rotary handle, is still in use today for specialized work on evening wear and bridal wear.

Some domestic machines have a chain-stitching device which is inserted in place of the bobbin case. The top thread forms a continuous chain stitch, which can only be worked with the foot on the machine. Al-though this stitch is best worked in straight lines or gentle curves, it can be added to free net embroidery to give a more textured look.

Some domestic overlock machines will sew a chain stitch that can be used without the overlocker. There is room for further experiment with both these types of chain stitching.

Chemical lace

Guipure lace, a heavy, raised needlepoint lace of the 17th century, was copied by machine in the late 19th century. The raised design was embroid-

ered in cotton on silk. Later, the silk background was dissolved away chemically to leave a lace pattern composed only of the cotton stitching.

This process is still used, working with modern materials to produce the guipure-type trimmings available in our department stores.

Machine embroidery can be worked on acetate fabric with cotton thread, and the background dissolved away with acetone. Normally this process is only used in commercial workshops and art colleges since chemicals need careful handling.

Embroidered lace with guipure motifs

Delicate embroidery was worked on fine muslin during the early 19th century. This white work embroidery, which suited the simple dresses fashionable at the time, was worked round the hems, on the high-waisted bodices and on the puffed sleeves. Later, it was used for collars, caps, and baby-clothes.

This type of embroidery can be sewn on the machine by combining free satin stitch embroidery with purchased modern guipure lace motifs. When used as trimming, the embroidery nearly always features flower designs. You should choose a pattern from which you can cut out the separate flower heads. Try to find flower patterns in a variety of sizes that are open in the centre, to give a 'lacy' effect.

The motifs are then tacked on to the organdie, or fine lawn background, and spaced out to a predetermined design. Plan this on paper by moving the flower heads into position and drawing connecting lines of stalks and leaf-pattern. Transfer the design to the background by the pressure line method.

(Left) Sample of free embroidery with purchased guipure lace.

Frame the fabric and set the machine for straight-stitch and free embroidery. The tacked flower heads are machined in position by stitching as close as possible inside their thick outlines. The fabric behind the flower head is cut away afterwards to reveal the lace pattern, or holes.

Embroider the stalks next, first in straight-stitch and then as a thicker satin stitch line. Leaf shapes are worked by altering the width-lever as you guide the frame with the left hand.

Other designs can be built up following this method, depending on the shape of the original guipure lace motif. Work border designs as repeats, round a collar or on the front and yoke of a christening robe.

Cutwork

The art of cutting away areas of cloth, neatening the edges and then filling in the holes with embroidery stitches was the forerunner of lace.

Cutwork took many forms, and was much used on hand-woven linen in peasant embroidery. Holes cut in the Ayrshire embroidery were enlarged, to be filled in with delicate lace stitches. This led to a type of embroidery composed only of holes that was at first called Madeira work, and later *broderie anglaise*.

Later still, more elaborate versions, with a greater area

Freely embroidered cutwork on a white organdie collar.

cut away, featured spaces linked by buttonhole bars. This style was called Renaissance embroidery, or Richelieu if there were picots on the bars. The 1930s saw a revival of this work, with naturalistic designs of flowers and leaves.

Broderie anglaise

This is also called 'eyelet embroidery' and can be worked on the machine using the eyelet attachment. This attachment, however, is only available for use with some machines.

A hole is punched into the cloth with a *stiletto*, and then fitted over a protruding metal spike on the special needleplate. The framed material is turned round while the machine sews satin stitches around the eyelet. Some buttonholer attachments will make larger, oval eyelet holes. The inner portion of fabric is cut away afterwards. The flower stitcher, an attachment available with some machines, will sew small circles in several sizes, and the central fabric will, again, have to be cut away.

Sewing across spaces

Victorian broderie anglaise work sometimes combines the finer eyelet embroidery with circular holes, filled in with needlepoint lace stitches or buttonholed to form spider-web or criss-cross patterns. These circles can also be worked freely by machine. You should set the machine for free embroidery and straight-stitch. But practise first on lightweight cotton material before working on finer fabrics.

Mark round a coin – either with a hard pencil or using the pressure method – and machine round two or three times. Finally, cut out the middle. For firmer wear on coarse fabrics, go over this line with satin stitch.

Make sure the tension is perfectly even and set the machine to straight-stitch. Start at the top of the circular hole and, pushing the frame away from you, sew evenly until the thread catches on at the bottom of the hole. The machine sews an interlocking chain of stitches across. You will find that the frame is easier to control pushed away from you. Carry on round the circumference and sew backwards and forwards across the circle, each time intersecting in the middle.

The spider's web can be finished by sewing round several times in the centre before catching on to the cloth edge, or by sewing round in an increasing spiral. If the thread breaks or tangles, cut it off and start again.

Cutwork collar

The collar in the picture was worked on two layers of organdie. The circle design was planned by drawing overlapping circles of different sizes on typing paper. Some of the overlapped areas were marked in black, to be cut away entirely, and some shaded to indicate that only the under layer of organdie was to be cut away. The design was then transferred to tracing paper.

The machine was set for straight stitch and free embroidery. The tracing paper design was laid on top of the double organdie, and everything placed in the embroidery frame. Design lines were machined through the paper, which was torn away afterwards.

The outlines were sewn over twice more before cutting away the layers to the design pattern. The material was reframed and the holes sewn across with straight-stitch lines. An automatic pattern stitch was used to make a scallop edge for the collar, which was cut out last of all.

11 Cutwork collar. Machining through the design lines drawn on top layer of tracing paper, then sewing across the holes.

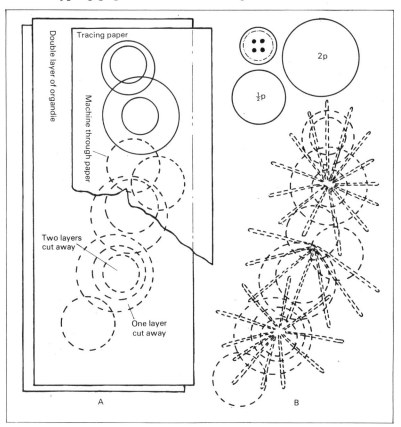

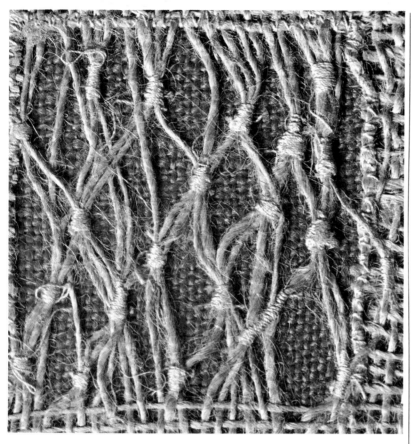

Pulled and drawn thread work worked under the machine foot.

Pulled and drawn thread work

This form of embroidery dates back to the early days of weaving. Threads withdrawn from the fabric weft were used to draw together the loose warp threads in new combinations and patterns. This was often time-consuming work, and was regarded as a sign of wealth in a hard-pressed agricultural society. A similar type of patterning was used on loosely woven fabric, where the threads were pulled together by embroidery, but not withdrawn.

All these methods are ideal for machine work. Choose a loosely woven material – even-weave linen, hessian, scrim, linen-type dress or furnishing fabric, tweed or woollen cloth. Some of the crossway or weft threads can be withdrawn to leave spaces and can be pulled out right across the width of the fabric – or over the planned design area. Snip the threads in the middle and withdraw them from either side. Neaten the side edges with zig-zag or satin stitch before cutting off any loose threads. These can be taken back at the sides and held in place if you prefer.

Set the machine to a medium satin stitch with the foot on. Sew down a group of threads, catching them together. Now move sideways and catch a different group. This can be done very neatly and methodically, but more exciting textures will result from a free approach. To turn, catch on to the top, or the bottom, of the withdrawn area and work back again.

The fabric can be stretched in the frame, and the machine set for free embroidery. Sew free satin stitch, catching in threads to create a design on loosely woven hessian or scrim. The small tree-shape was sewn first, and some areas cut away afterwards.

Pulled and drawn thread-work lends itself to experimental work. Satin stitch lines can be sewn backwards and forwards to form a chequered grid pattern, catching all, or only some, of the threads. Embroider wall panels and hangings, and back the drawn areas with a contrasting colour.

The threads need not be entirely covered. Some can be left free, without embroidery. Another method is to sew the threads together with small satin stitch bars. Lift the foot and pull the threads out behind before you start in another

12 Drawn thread work on loose-woven fabric. Threads are snipped in the middle and withdrawn from either side then neatened with zig-zag or satin stitch, cutting off any loose ends.

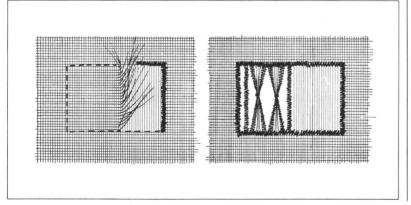

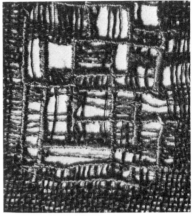

(Above and right) Three examples of using pulled and drawn thread work.

place. The bars are sewn with a continuous thread. This saves having to tie-off ends at the back of the work.

Similar patterns are worked over open-weave curtain fabrics. This obviates the necessity to withdraw threads. Work freely, or sew down on to a backing to make a firmer fabric.

This type of work also looks well on a cushion or a border for a curtain. Small, patterned areas can decorate a bag or a purse. Finer work should be used on clothing.

Embroidery on lampshades should be planned to fit into the spaces between the struts. Neaten the edges with zig-zag or satin stitch rather than turn them back, the threads would be revealed as heavy lines when backlit.

Patchwork

Patchwork, in one form or another, has been practised as a thrift craft since man began to weave. In later years, the decorative quality of precious scraps of material was used to form designs and patterns.

Patchwork is the creation of a new fabric by sewing together smaller pieces of cloth. Shapes are geometrical, random, or worked in strips, and can be sewn together in a variety of ways. Piece patchwork may be applied to a backing, but this backing is constructional and does not form part of the design.

In England, patchwork was worked during the 18th century, mainly for bed curtains and covers. These might be quilted for extra warmth, sometimes along the patch outlines, but more often as a continuous all-over design. The art flourished between the years 1750

and 1870. Emigrants from the British Isles took this craft with them to the New World. They developed their own pattern traditions and methods of construction. Many are well suited to the sewing machine.

Strip patchwork

Fabrics should be of a similar weight and type. It is not easy to distinguish between scraps of pure cotton and cotton poly-ester mix. The polyester does not crease easily and has a rather soapy feel to it when rubbed between the fingers. To prevent shrinkage, wash and iron all fabrics before cutting out. This ensures that the finished patchwork will lie flat and even.

Alternatively, use all tweed, or all needlecord, or wool and cotton mix. Even a firm synthetic jersey, like courtelle, will make successful patchwork providing the pieces are small, but it is wise to avoid any stretchy fabrics.

The joining seams show through very fine fabrics. Either this aspect must be incorporated as part of the design, or the pieces backed with light iron-on interfacing. This will stiffen them, but it is suitable for use on small areas of clothing or for decorative panels. Dressmakers will find the fabric pieces left at the sides when cutting out garments excellent for strip patchwork.

Cutting and sewing strips together

For the simplest and easiest type of machine patchwork the strips are cut into various widths, measuring 4–6 cm ($1\frac{1}{2}$ – $2\frac{1}{2}$ in), on the straight grain of the material. This allows for a seam width of about 1 cm ($\frac{3}{8}$ in) or the width of the straight-stitch presser foot, which is used as a guide. You should cut the strips as long as the fabric will allow.

Plan the choice of colours and fabric patterning to form a pleasing mixture, including one or two plain fabrics to present a contrast. Now cut the long strips into 12 cm (5 in) lengths. These are to be sewn together, long sides matching, to form a length of strips. Later, these lengths of strips are themselves sewn together to form the patchwork fabric. Use a toning thread and set the machine to straight-stitch.

First, arrange the cut strips of fabric so that there is a variety of patterns and colours and then lay out the next set of strips. Colour and pattern must not coincide, although the seam lines will not necessarily join across as the strips are of random width (fig. 13).

When all the strips are laid out, pick the sets up in the correct order and machine the long seams together. You may pin them if you wish. Do not break off the machine threads,

13 Angled and simple strip machine patchwork.

but pull them out behind and start again – this will save time. Once all the sets of strips are sewn together, press the seams open flat. Next, pin the lengths of strip sets together in the correct order and machine them together. Finally, press these seams out flat.

A second method is to cut the strips of varying widths as long as possible and to machine them right across to form a fabric. You then press all seams. Now cut this fabric into angled strips, turn them round, and sew back together again. This particular kind of strip patchwork has many variations.

Sewing machines were introduced to the tribes of the Seminole Indians of Florida at the beginning of this century. They machined strips of bright fabric together, cut the strips up and re-assembled them to form intricate patterns.

Seminole method

Long strips are sewn together and are cut either into different widths or to the same width. Using a ruler as a template, mark the material by drawing along both sides with a pencil. Machine the strips to form a fabric and press.

Again, use a ruler to mark strips going the opposite way, across the joins, and cut these into strips. These are then moved down, with the seams staggered, either half way, or to form a new square.

Sew them together for use as a border pattern. Alternatively, cut the fabric of joined strips on the cross, drop down the seam lines to create new patterns and sew them all together again. Seams on the cross are pressed to one side to prevent stretching. Place this crossway fabric on its side to make a diamond pattern.

Dark and light fabrics will give counterchange patterns and can be built up to form completely different design shapes and lines. It is advisable to plan out your designs with strips of coloured paper first. The Seminole Indians used

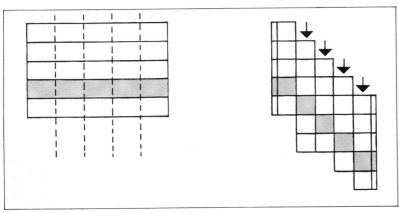

14 Method of cutting and arranging Seminole Indian patchwork.

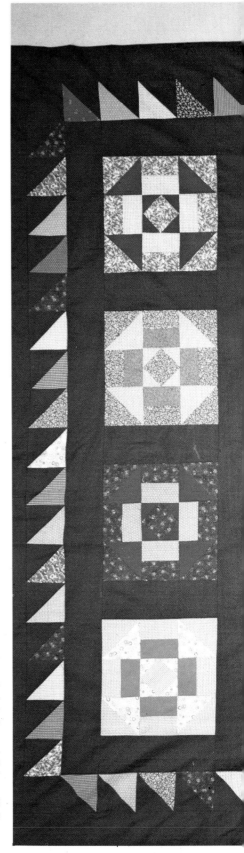

(Right) American-style patchwork bedspread worked by Jane Thompson.

dark and light patterning on their clothing. The strips were very narrow and gave a rich, mosaic effect, set within darker, plain bands of material.

Providing that the materials chosen are similar, any of these strip patchwork methods will form a fabric that can be cut out to make articles and will stand up to wear and washing. When used for cushions or on clothing, however, an interlining, held together at intervals with hand stitches, is tacked behind the finished, pressed work. Thicker fabrics will be firm enough on their own and can be made into squab cushions or a 'roly-poly' draught stop, with the strips going lengthwise.

Leather, suede, felt and vinyl-coated fabrics need no turnings and it is better to overlap the strips. Leather and suede can be held with a small amount of fabric adhesive before sewing. Use a roller foot, or place tissue paper over the seam, sew through and tear the paper away afterwards.

American-style patchwork

This can be worked as a form of strip patchwork, although it was developed from hand, oversewn patchwork. The geometric shapes of English patch-work are cut out, tacked over thin card templates and then oversewn together.

The American pioneers, travelling West in their cover-ed wagons, needed a simpler method and sewed simple geometric shapes together with running stitches along the seam line. These shapes were built up to form a block pattern, which could be quilted for warmth afterwards. The patchwork was sewn during the winter months and made up into a coverlet top. When the thaw came and roads were passable once more, the women got together for a quilting bee. The coverlet was stretched on a long frame and all shared the work and a welcome chance to gossip.

At first, all material was imported from England to the colonies. It only became freely available when the colonies started to manufacture their own cloth. Patchwork thus came into its own during the 19th century. Favourite designs were based on a block, divided into nine equal squares. These squares were subdivided into smaller squares and triangles, which were assembled in a variety of patterns. Some names echoed the settlers' new life – bear's paw, flock of geese, saw tooth, turkey tracks. This type of patchwork is easy to sew on the machine, but needs care in matching of seams.

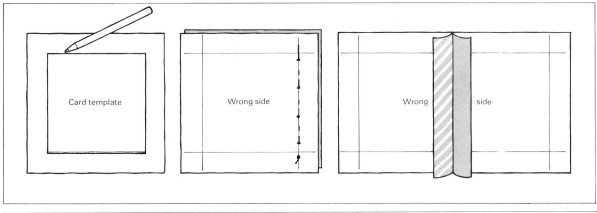

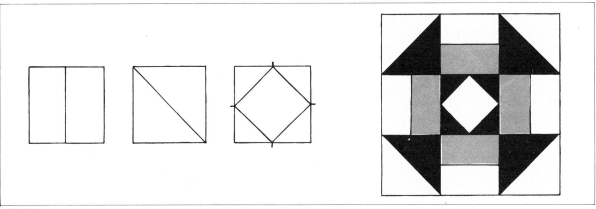

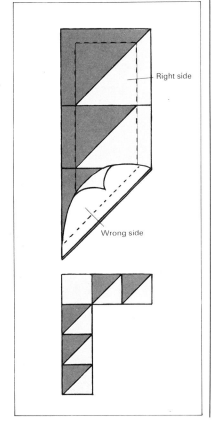

15 (Top) Marking out patches from a template and joining patches for American-style patchwork. The marked patches can be pinned together then machine stitched.
16 (Above) The nine-patch block pattern patchwork.
17 (Left) Saw tooth border.

Simpler designs were worked and quilted by the Amish of Pennsylvania, whose religious beliefs found expression in darker, more sober colours. These designs have a luminous quality, imparted by one small, bright piece of contrast fabric.

Patchwork need not be worked on a small scale. Carefully chosen purchased material or sale remnant lengths can be made up quickly on the machine. The Amish favoured wide, bold stripes and bars or large oblongs of cloth in closely related tones, but with a smaller square of the bright colour. Borders can be composed of smaller stripes, or strips of squares sewn together.

Random square patterns

This is a good way to start as it is less complicated. First, cut out a square template in medium-thick card – use the back of a letter pad, or a card with a ready-made right-angled corner. It is important that the template should be accurate.

Measure 5 cm (2 in) up one side and along the bottom of the card, to make a 5 cm (2 in) square. This measurement does not include seam allowances. Use fabrics of the same kind, and avoid any stretchy fabrics. For random patterns, choose from a selection of toning or contrasting fabrics. Careful planning will be necessary to achieve a balanced result.

Place the card template on the wrong side of the material – one edge to the straight grain of the fabric – and draw round it with a pencil on all four sides. Add a seam allowance of 1 cm ($\frac{3}{8}$ in) all round and cut out. Pin all the cut squares on to a piece of polystyrene or upholstery foam and move them about until the design looks right. Leave everything in position until you are ready to pick up and machine.

Making-up

Place two patches right sides together and pin them along the seam line so that they match. Machine along the pencil seam line, taking the pin out before you reach it, open out the seam allowances and press. Add more patches in the same way, picking them up in order.

Now machine the other sets of squares. Finally, sew the strips of squares together, matching the seam joins by pinning down each seam line at right-angles to the edges (Remove the pins as you sew.) Press out all the seams on the wrong side.

This patchwork fabric may be used for cushions, bedcovers, or cut out for dressmaking, allowing extra for paper pattern planning.

The nine-patch block

These blocks are sewn together in a similar way. All patterns are first planned out on squared paper – there are many variations. The patchwork bedspread, in plain and brushed cotton fabric, is based on a 10cm (4in) square, cut into oblongs and triangles.

Cut three 10cm (4in) square card templates and divide one in half to form two oblongs, 5cm × 10cm (2 × 4in). Cut the second square in half diagonally to form two triangles. The final square is marked half way along each side, and the marks joined to form a 7cm (3in) square surrounded by four small triangles. Mark round with a pencil as before and leave a 1cm ($\frac{3}{8}$in) seam allowance on all edges when cutting out.

Sew two contrasting oblongs together to form a square, and press the seam allowances out. Next, sew two triangles, long edges together, being careful not to stretch the fabric. Press these crossway seams towards the darker fabric and sew the four small triangles on to the central smaller square.

Make up the nine patches – four oblong pattern, four triangular pattern and one central square – and sew them all together. Careful planning of your fabrics, using darker and lighter tones, will give scope for many pattern variations.

Dark fabric strips, 12cm (5in) wide (this allows a 1cm ($\frac{3}{8}$in) seam either side) and 33cm (13in) long, are cut to join each block of squares together. Long, 12cm (5in) wide strips are sewn from top to bottom to join all the strips of squares together and to make a dark border all round.

The saw-tooth edge is made from 10cm (4in) squares – each made from one dark plain and one patterned triangle – added on all round. A final dark band, 15cm (6in) wide, gives the finished border edge. 5cm (2in) of the band is turned under all round and hemmed on to the lining, which is cut to the same size as the finished top.

This makes a full-size single bed cover to the floor, or a double bed cover to go over a valance frill. For a smaller coverlet, leave off the outer dark band.

Use needlecord or thicker fabrics for cushions, smaller squares for waistcoats and bags in leather or in suede scraps, and fine cottons for tea-cosies or place mats. Cottons should be pressed well on both sides, but needlecord should be pressed under a cloth on the wrong side only.

Oversewn patchwork by machine

(Author's original method)

Piece-patchwork, or mosaic patchwork as it is sometimes called, was popular in the 18th century, although it has a much longer history, going back to Ancient Egypt. Some fragments of silk patchwork of between the 6th and 9th centuries have survived in Central Asia. These examples, which were possibly from votive offerings to a shrine, are, however, very rare.

The earliest existing examples of English patchwork are the quilt and matching bedhangings at Levens Hall, Lancashire. These were made in 1708 from imported Indian calico. Since 1780 much more patchwork has survived. Sometimes old embroideries were cut up and used – or silk and velvet – as well as the Indian prints which were also cut out for applied work.

After 1840, piece patchwork gained increasing popularity. This was sewn even by warwounded soldiers as an early form of occupational therapy, while small girls completed so many patches every day – to be made into rosettes and added to the family quilt. Other types of patchwork were more favoured later in the century, and it was not until the 1930s that interest was revived. This renewed interest in piecepatchwork finally found expression during the 1939-45 war as thrift craft. Today piecepatchwork is as popular as ever and enjoys the advantage that small areas can be added as time and circumstances permit.

Construction is simple and based on interlocking geometric patterns. The equalsided hexagon divides into three equal diamonds; the long hexagon into two long diamonds and a square, and the octagon into long diamonds, a long hexagon and a square. This gives scope for both colour and pattern combinations.

Accurate shapes in thin card may be cut from metal templates. Seam allowances are added for the fabric patches, which are then tacked to the card shapes. In handwork, these patches are first oversewn together in pairs, with more patches added afterwards.

This method can also be

worked by machine. The papers for machine patchwork must be thin, for they will be pierced by the needle. The glossy paper from magazine covers or brochures works best. This is thin, but tough enough to hold its shape and, with care, can be used over again.

Most traditional patchwork materials are suitable, although closely woven cotton with a lot of dressing is difficult to sew since the needle must pass through many layers, including the papers. Thin wools and wool or cotton mixtures work excellently, while leather and PVC need no turnings.

Templates are measured along one edge only. Choose a patch length of 3 cm (1 in) and upwards. It is possible to work patches of a smaller measurement, but hardly worth stopping and and starting the machine. The modern tend-ency for larger patches can thus be fully exploited. Leave a seam allowance of 1 cm ($\frac{3}{8}$ in) all the way round.

Patches are prepared as for hand sewing. Tack the thin paper to the larger patch, folding under the corners all the same way for easier iron-ing.

Thread the machine top and bottom with a toning No. 50 mahine embroidery thread or No. 60 mercerized cotton and use a correspondingly fine needle No. 90. Be prepared to renew your needles frequently as paper blunts them. Set a stitch length of between 1.5 and 2 and a stitch width of 1.5. Slight variations are necessary for different materials and it is advisable to experiment.

Put your prepared patches right sides together, letting the working edge of the bottom patch protrude slightly (if this is just visible there is no danger of missing a stitch). Place under the foot with the needle piercing the top right-hand corner through both patches.

Place the presser-foot slit cen-trally over the edges of the patches so that the needle will sew beyond the patches when it swings to the right and will catch the patches together when it swings to the left. Always start with a left-hand swing.

Sew at an even speed. The last stitch should be over to the right, ready to start the next patch with the needle to the left. Leave enough thread to tie-off the ends and to start the next patch.

Simple square or oblong shapes can be sewn one pair after the other without stop-ping. When the work is opened out flat you will discover a criss-cross stitch at the back and straight stitches across the front – like very even hand sewing. Hexagons and similar shapes are sewn together in pairs to make a row. The rows are themselves then sewn together right across, without cutting off the thread.

Fit the shapes into one another by lowering the needle into the patches at the corner. Lift the foot, pivot the fabric and rearrange the seams to lie flat – ready for sewing again.

When a number of patches have been sewn together some of the papers can be removed. Take out the tacking threads,

18 Sewing together hexagonal patches by machine.

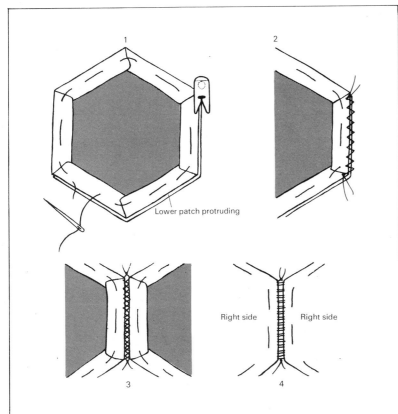

1

2

Lower patch protruding

3

4

Right side   Right side

Handbag worked in dark brown and cream P.V.C. patchwork.

19 (Below) Sewing separate patches into rows, then rows together in one.

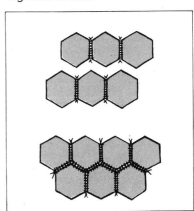

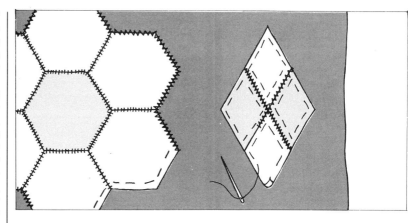

and the papers will come away quite easily, leaving a perforated edge where the needle has caught. If the papers are still in good condition, they may be used again.

For sewing diamond shapes use a softer fabric, folded over twice at the pointed corners. This makes a thick place for the needle. Help the needle by turning the balance wheel by hand for a few stitches if your machine does not have full penetration power. Either sew diamonds together in rows or sew two sets of three together to make a star, and machine straight across for the final seam.

Felt, suede, leather and PVC need no turnings and are easy to sew. Sharp points fit well into each other. The bag in brown, green and cream PVC-coated cloth is made from a pattern incorporating octagons, long diamonds and long hexagons on one side, and squares and triangles on the other. The method described may be also used for oversewing felt, or for sewing fur fabric for clothing or toys.

Applied patchwork

In some instances the definition of applied patchwork is quite clear; in others the distinction between applied patchwork and appliqué is so broad that either title is correct.

A made-up piece of patchwork fabric, sewn down to a background that is meant to be seen and not merely a backing, is called 'applied patchwork'. This could be in the form of a hand- or machine-sewn traditional hexagon double rose pattern, applied to the centre of a place mat, or in the form of four small hexagon roses, one

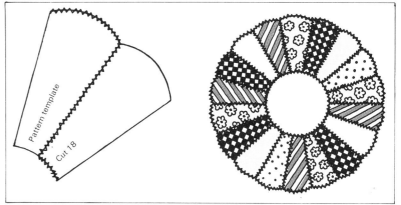

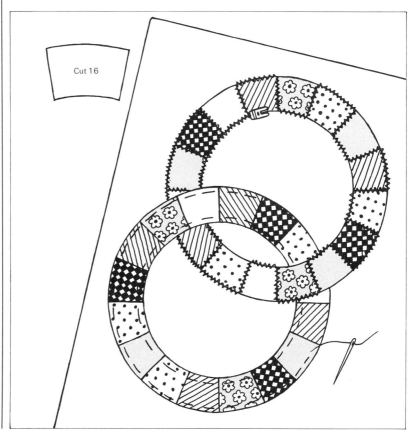

20 (Top right) Patchwork shapes applied to a background.
21 (Centre right) The Dresden Plate pattern.
22 (Right) Wedding Ring pattern.

applied to each corner of a cushion.

Use a medium zig-zag stitch on the machine, with a fine No. 50 machine embroidery thread or a No. 60 mercerized cotton in the needle to tone in with the patchwork. Let the bobbin thread match the background fabric. Press the pierced patchwork motifs on the wrong side before removing the papers from it, one by one, and securing the loose-edge turnings with hand tacking stitches. Tack the patchwork into position on to the background matching the grain of the fabric.

Sew down with a zig-zag stitch on the machine, with the needle piercing into the patchwork on the inner swing and into the background fabric on the outer swing. Now tie off all the ends. This method is a neat, firm, and at the same time decorative, way of applying this type of patchwork.

Single, applied patchwork shapes differ from ordinary appliqué only in that they are all cut from the same template, or are the same shape but different sizes. Free appliqué shapes are more diverse, whereas applied patchwork has more unity.

These can be used quite freely on panels and wall hangings. A square or oblong shape may be repeated, overlapped, elongated, turned sideways or emphasized by applied line decoration. The wall hanging was worked as a series of fabric pieces, some striped, some plain – all right-angled shapes – applied to a background with added braid and tape.

Large applied patchwork shapes – squares, circles and large hexagons – are zig-zagged or satin-stitched in position as for appliqué. For a stronger line, an additional braid or ric-rac may be sewn over the zig-zagged edge to cover the join.

Butt joining

Geometric patchwork pieces can be applied to a background by machine, using zig-zag stitch or, for heavier effect, a satin stitch or suitable automatic stitch. Patchwork shapes are cut out in fabric to template size, but without turnings.

These patchwork shapes may be placed in position on iron-on interfacing, edges just overlapping and bonded by ironing. Alternatively, tack them on to a fabric backing. Although a lot more trouble, this will give a softer appearance to the work.

The raw edges of the patches are covered and held together by the zig-zag or satin stitches. Diamonds are simple to sew. Start at the top and work down, crossing over at the points and making sure all is caught in.

Hexagons are not so easy to plan and cannot be sewn without some seams overlapping. This may, however, be avoided by setting the machine to straight stitch where the seams double up, and by opening to zig-zag again for the next patch (the coscote method).

Dresden plate pattern

This pattern can be sewn on to a background fabric, using the butt join method where the patches meet. A central circle of background fabric is surrounded by segments of patterned cloth that are curved at the top and require only one pattern template.

Mark a circle, 8 cm (3 in) in diameter, on to the background cloth as a guide for placing the segmented shapes. Trace a pattern from the diagram and cut this out in thin card. Use this as a template to cut out 18 pieces of fabric in a variety of colours and prints. Have the grain running lengthways.

Pin the fabric shapes around, with the bottom line to the drawn circle, and tack all in position. Use a toning thread in the top of the machine and zig-zag all round each segment, catching both in the next segment and on the long seam line. For a bolder effect satin stitch should be used.

Use a straight stitch line on felt, suede, leather or non-fray materials. For additional contrast, cut out a circle in plain material and apply it on top so that it just covers the base of the segments.

Clamshell

This traditional shape is also known as scallop or fish scale.

23 Clamshell applied with zig-zag (left); butt-joining method (right).

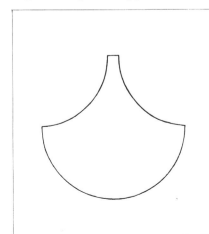
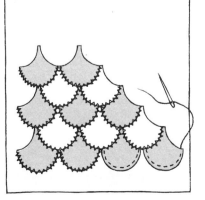
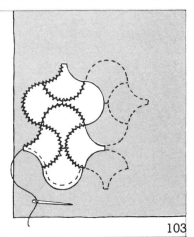

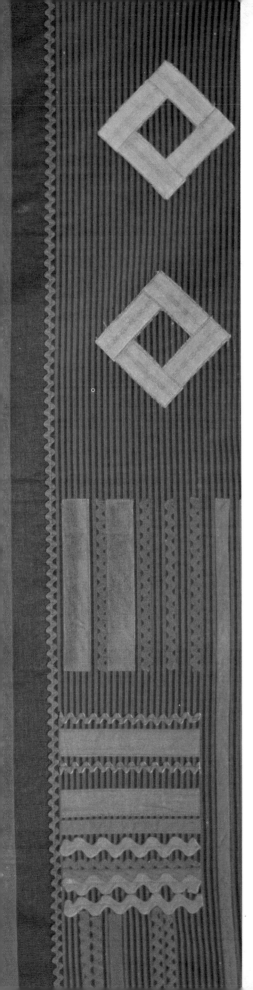

In handwork the patches are hemmed down, a row at a time, on to the preceding row to make a fabric. This style found favour in England and America during the 19th century.

It is easy to work by machine, using the applied method. Cut out the fabric exactly to the template shape. The bottom row of shapes is then tacked to a line marked on the background fabric and held down with zig-zag stitch on to the fabric or with straight stitch on felt or suede. The succeeding rows overlap, like fish scales or pantiles, and are then sewn in position.

Inlay

The clamshell patches can be fitted together as a pattern – like a jig-saw puzzle – in a form of inlay. (This refers to a method of 'letting in' a pattern shape that has been cut to exact size.) Felt is used for handwork, but suede or other non-fray materials would be very suitable for use with the machine with the butt-joining method.

Patches for rugs

Cut thick fabric patches, approximately 5 × 10 cm (2 × 4 in), or use rectangular shaped colour swatch samples. Fold them in half, machine up the two open sides, and turn them right side out. Pleat the top of the little bag so formed, or leave it plain. Select patches in various colours and sew these on to a hessian backing with zig-zag stitch along the raw edges. Let the second row overlap the first one, and so on (fig. 00).

Larger, cotton fabric bags can be padded for extra warmth before sewing down on to a calico backing. These would be suitable as chair backs or bed covers. Single fabric pieces can be stitched for wall hangings – use silks and fray the edges.

Applied patchwork by Ina Buckland.

Crazy patchwork

This is a patchwork made of random shapes in different materials applied to a background. Traditionally the shapes, which overlapped, were held down with a running stitch. Also, the edges were not usually turned under to form a hem. Raw edges were both strengthened and neatened with embroidery stitches.

Although this is one of the earliest types of patchwork made during the last two hundred years, no English examples exist before 1830 and it did not become popular until after the middle of the 19th century.

The earlier patchwork was made from heavier fabrics, such as wool or worsted, and used in a practical manner for blankets and bed covers. The later work was far more decorative, employing the velvets, silks and other fabrics.

Crazy patchwork is one of the few types where it is possible to combine different thicknesses and different types of material. Even so, this alone among the Victorian methods has sometimes not withstood the test of time. The fine silks frequently shred and pull away. Modern synthetic fabrics look like Victorian silks and satins, but are hard-wearing.

24 Applied patchwork for rugs sewing pleated tags to the backing with zig-zag or straight stitch.

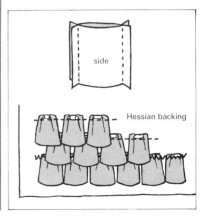

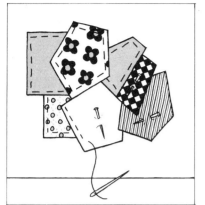

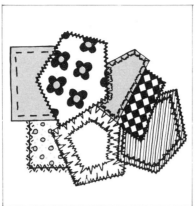

25 (Far left) Crazy patchwork. Hold the patches in position with a pin then tack round the edges.
26 (Left) Sewing down and decorating the patches.

work blocks are separated by plain bands in dark silk or velvet, giving the impression of a stained glass window.

Crazy work came into fashion again during the 1930s and 40s, making use of cotton fabrics instead of the mixture of silks and velvets.

Method

Crazy patchwork is always applied to a backing. Use white cotton, cotton polyester mix or any plain, finely woven, but strong, fabric. If you are using all cottons or similar fabrics, wash these and the backing first to prevent uneven shrinkage. It is inadvisable to wash the mixed type of patchwork – this is better dry cleaned.

Make a collection of fabric scraps. For the mixed kind you will need an assortment of both plain and printed velvets, fine needlecord, synthetic evening dress material – the kind with lurex threads interwoven as part of the design – and commercially embroidered materials: also, satins, heavy silks, corded or synthetic silk, lining materials, brocade and exotic scraps from sari cloth. Quite fine materials can be used on their own without a backing.

Choose a greater proportion of plain to patterned fabrics for your design, with colours that create a pleasing harmony – one or two bright patches among darker ones. The aim is to create rich, jewel-like patterning.

Shapes can be used as you find them, providing they are not too large. Bigger pieces of fabric should be cut in half, or smaller still. Ideally, the areas should be similar but the shapes different, to create interest. Avoid curves. Chop the pieces into a series of angled shapes; they are easier

27 Crazy patchwork squares joined by strips.

By the 1880s, the Victorian 'crazy quilts' (which were seldom ever quilted), had become all the rage. Not only were embroidery stitches used over the joins – such as double and treble feather, coral, herringbone and trellis – but additional embroidery was also worked, often in gold and silver thread. Hearts, kisses, stars and other shapes were embroidered in

the middle of the patches. As a final decoration beads, sequins, gold and silver braid or ribbon work were used, with frills in black or yellow added round the edge – all of which gave this work a bad name.

Some 'quilts', however, were far more restrained. One worked by Jenny Jones in 1884 featured velvet, brocade and embroidered silks made up into nine large blocks that were joined together, and with an embroidered border added. In another old design the crazy to sew and have more design impact.

Some special fabrics can be ironed, but heat will easily damage others. If your scraps are creased, especially velvet, hold them over steam from a kettle. Spike a row of patches on to a skewer – several can be steamed in safety this way without danger from scalding.

Shapes should overlap with no seams turned under. Any frayed edges should first be trimmed. Now lay the background fabric on a flat surface. Choose your favourite, or an eye-catching patch, and place it near, but not exactly in the middle. Pin down on all the edges. Working outwards from this patch, add others, some overlapping one way, some the other. Add or remove patches until you are satisfied with the overall effect. Then pin down the ones you are sure about. Tack them in position, round the edges, keeping it all as flat as possible.

Once this stage is over, everything is easy. Use toning thread for the patches which are zig-zagged over from the right side. These stitches will later be covered by automatic patterns in threads which match or contrast with the individual patches.

Catch down with zig-zag stitch half on one patch and half on the other. Many automatic patterns can suggest the feather stitches and herringbone used on the traditional work. Try them out beforehand to see which look the best on the various fabric types. Sew some patterns twice – first one way, then the other – to make new or broader patterns.

Flat gold or silver lurex is worked from the wrong side of the fabric – use as a guide the zig-zag lines which hold down the patches. Add goldfingering, rayon floss thread or thicker metallic cords, held down on the right side with a narrow zig-zag stitch. Alternatively, make use of your cording foot for this purpose.

A 60cm (24in) square will make up into a cushion cover, adding a border of velvet, 10cm (4in) wide all the way round. For a bedcover, join nine squares together, separated by dark bands, like the Victorian ones.

Using cottons

Crazy work in other fabrics, whether all cotton, all wool or all cotton and wool mix, has quite a different character, although the procedures involved are the same as before.

Mix plain with stripes, or spots or floral patterns. Sew the patches down with satin stitch or automatic patterns, as before. Use perle threads or thin coloured cords for outlining afterwards.

Log cabin – applied flat method

In England this was referred to as ribbonwork, and sometimes as log wood patchwork. It is probably one of the oldest forms of patchwork, and was worked in homespun wool and tweed cloth for making into bed covers. These were referred to in the north of England as 'strippy quilts'. The strips went across or down the coverlet top, or they could be arranged in a series of chevron stripes running from top to bottom. They were quilted afterwards along the strip lines.

During the 19th century quilts were sewn on the block principle, although the construction method is always the same. Alternating light and dark strips are worked into squares which are themselves arranged in a variety of ways to create numerous pattern permutations.

Fabric was always applied to a backing. This meant that fabrics could be mixed – sometimes silks and satins with velvet. Ribbons were often incorporated and also, in Ed-wardian times, the oblong swatches of silk from parasol and sunshade patterns. Modern fabric mixtures can include velvet and tweed, needlecord and suede, or tweed and snakeskin – as well as the more usual combinations.

Simple strip chevron pattern

This is worked on the strippy quilts. First, collect fabric scraps, preferably of the same weight and type, in a variety of patterns. Make a card template 3cm (1in) wide, or use a wide ruler to draw against on the wrong side of the fabric, keeping to the straight of the grain. Cut strips as long as the fabric will allow.

Cut the cotton background fabric 10cm (4in) wide and as long as the finished article. Fold the top over to make a diagonal crease, open out and use the crease as a guideline. Sew one strip against the guideline, right side uppermost. Take a second, contrasting strip and lay this on top of the first, right sides together. Machine across in a straight line, using the width of the presser foot as a guide. Cut off and press the strip over to the right side. Pin a third strip on top and machine in the same way. Each seam should enclose the raw edges of the previous strip.

When the background is covered, work a second, with the stripes meeting the other way in the same pattern sequence. Afterwards, sew the two finished pieces together to form a chevron pattern.

Cushion patterns

A simple design, composed of alternating light and dark stripes around a central square, does not require fabrics as diverse as those that rely on complicated light-and-dark shaded areas.

Choose a firm calico or cotton backing. 40cm (16in) square is a good size for a cushion front

Patchwork cushions worked by Jane Thompson and Stella Bird.

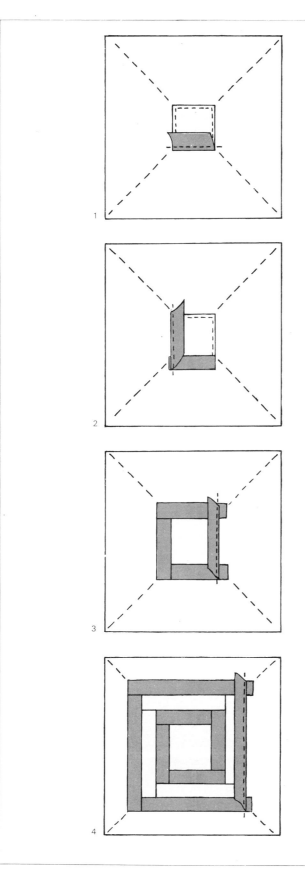

that is to be made in one piece. Four 20cm (8in) squares can be joined to make a cushion, or 36 for a bed cover. Borders may always be added, if required.

The cushions illustrated have strips sewn, in turn, round a central square. This may be in contrasting patterned fabric or may feature a flower or a piece of machine embroidery.

Fold the background fabric across on the diagonals, crease and mark in with a pencil or tailor's chalk. Plan contrasting light and dark strips to surround the square. There is no need to measure each one; the diagonal lines will act as a guide.

Cut the first strip as long as one side of the centre square. Place the right sides together and machine the seam across. Then press over to the right side. Working clokwise, lay a strip of the same colour measuring the width of the square plus the width of the strip. Cut this off and sew as before. Continue round until you have finished all four sides. Now change to a contrasting colour and work round in the same way. Make the final set of strips twice as wide to allow for joining to a cushion cover back.

A variation of this pattern is to start with the central square set on the diagonal. Draw a 6cm (2½in) square on to thin card, measure half-way down each side of the square and join across to form four triangle shapes. Cut out these five pieces for use as templates. Seam allowances can be added afterwards.

Sew a triangle on to each straight side of the fabric square to form a larger square. Continue round as before, adding on the straight strips. Another version can be formed of triangles and strips on each round.

28 (Left) Traditional method of assembling Log Cabin patchwork applied to a background.
29 (Far right) Variations on the traditional Log Cabin pattern.

American-style log cabin

Not all log cabin patches were sewn to a backing. They can be seamed together, in the same way as the American-style patchwork. Although this type of patterning is common to both America and England, it was adopted and developed by the American settlers to form part of their own patchwork and quilting tradition.

With the settlers pushing further West pioneer conditions persisted in America right up to the end of the 19th century. There were greater extremes of climate in the New World – Pennsylvanian winters necessitated the use of no less than five quilts on the bed. Since many of the patchwork coverlets were quilted for extra warmth the word quilt has come to be used for the finished patchwork cover, whether quilted or not.

The strip patterns, sewn into squares, were easy to handle and could be worked on the lap, often in cramped surroundings. In the early pioneer homes, which were utilitarian and drab, patchwork fulfilled many needs. It provided the very necessary warm coverlets and it made good use of any tiny scraps of precious material, whether left-overs from cutting out or the best parts of worn garments. But it also fulfilled another need – that for colour and self-expression. Although none of the early workers had any training in design, these eye-catching covers have an amazing affinity with modern art. The effect of the log cabin patterns is almost three-dimensional.

The name 'log cabin' was no doubt preferred because it reflected everyday life. The overlapping of the strips at the corners suggests the log construction, while the central patch, often in red, is said to have symbolized the hearth, and the light and dark patterning, the flickering shadows. Unlike their English counter-

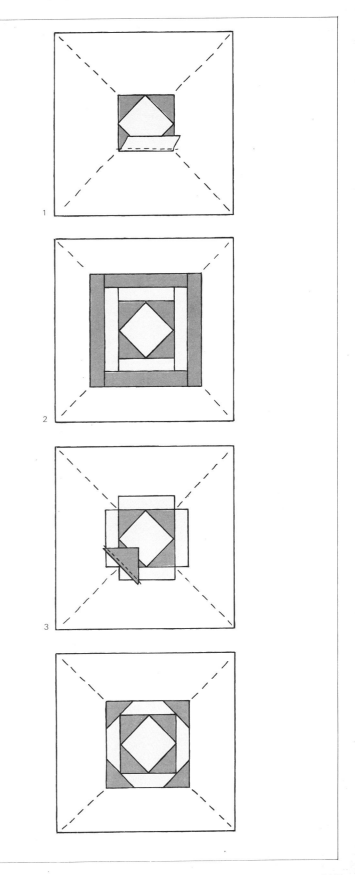

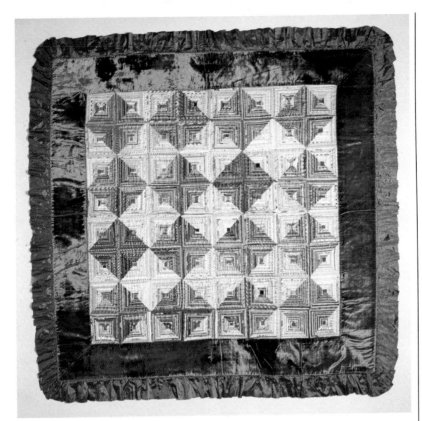

(Left) The author's great aunt Jane spent five years making this bedspread from silk cuttings.
(Far left) Log Cabin mats.

parts, the Americans gave names to their patterns like 'barn raising', 'long furrow' and 'pineapple'.

Choice of fabric

When working log cabin by this method try to find materials of a similar kind or weight. Fabrics are not applied to a backing and are more liable to strain. Mixed fabrics, however, are traditionally sewn to a backing – whether worked in Europe or America.

Use all needlecord, all tweeds, all suede or all cottons. Whatever type you choose you will need equal amounts of dark and light fabrics. You will also need a greater choice of colour

30 *(Below) Log Cabin assembly.*

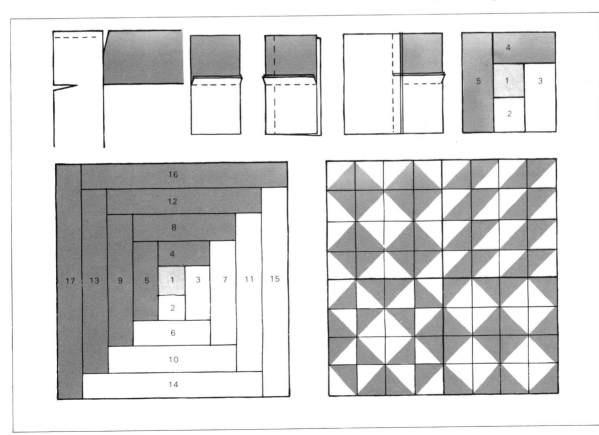

shades and patterns than for other kinds of patchwork. The light strips need to shade from pale to medium, and the darker strips from medium to dark.

Half close your eyes and try to gauge the tonal value of a group of colours. The order of the strips can be varied within the chosen colour range, but a really good contrast between groups is essential. This type of patterning will require considerable thought and planning.

Method

The width measurement of the strips is a matter of choice, but this must remain constant throughout the work. Either use a ruler as your guide, or cut out a template in strong card. Make a seam allowance of up to 1 cm (⅜in) on either side, or use the machine presser foot as a guide. Use a width minimum of 5 cm (2 in) to start with.

Mark out your strips as before – on the wrong side of the material and lining up the template to the straight grain. Cut the strips as long as the material will allow and chop the ends off square. Next, plan the order of the light and the dark strips. Pick up one light and one dark strip and lay their right sides together at right angles to each other. Next, machine the seam line with a medium straight stitch and cut off the surplus of both strips. You are left with two squares, one dark and one light, sewn together. Press the seam to the dark side.

Pick up a light strip and lay along one side and seam together. Chop off the surplus strip, keeping the end square, and press the seam towards the two squares. Now sew a dark strip on to the next side. Work in a clockwise direction, sewing alternate light and dark strips until the finished square is the right size.

Make four more similar squares, varying the order within the light and dark areas, and seam them all together. Press these seams out flat. The squares can be put together in different ways, to create new patterns and making good use of the light and dark areas. This patchwork is always mounted on a backing for strength.

Log cabin – folded applied variation

This variation of log cabin, or ribbonwork, is sewn to a backing. The strips are not applied flat, but folded over double and held at the seam edges only. This gives a raised look and provides far more warmth than the other types of log cabin since the soft folds trap the air. The method is less suitable for articles that have to stand up to wear, like cushion covers, but is excellent for bed covers, for fine silks on evening bags or

31 Folded applied method, yet another way of assembling Log Cabin.

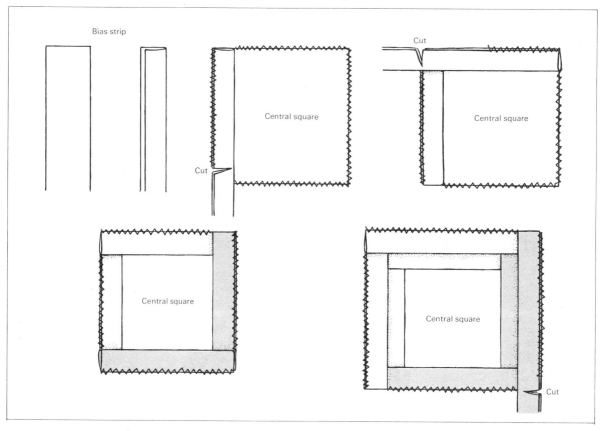

inset panels on clothing.

The normal method of working this kind of patchwork is to cut strips twice as wide as usual, on the straight, and to fold them over double. The first square is applied to the middle of the fabric backing. The folded strips surround all four sides, each row slightly overlapping the previous one. The colours should be shaded into light and dark as before.

The family heirloom quilt illustrated is worked differently. All the folded strips are cut on the cross, which gives the work a softer look. The central patches are in velvet, and the surrounding strips all from silk dress fabrics. The strips are held down by running stitches.

The quilt was worked between 1865 and 1870 by Jane Hughes. Before her marriage in 1860, at the age of 33, she worked for a Court dressmaker and later opened her own dressmaking establishment, calling herself Madam Rubery – it was considered improper for a single lady to go into business.

Fabrics take so long to collect that it is very probable that those used came from Jane's dressmaking activities. The coverlet shown here is not only a superb piece of craftsmanship, but also a treasure-house of mid-Victorian dress silks.

Method

Whether the strips are cut on the straight, or on the cross, the construction is the same. Fold the strips in half, lengthways, with the right sides outwards. Lay the first light strip against the central square so that the fold overlaps the edge.

Machine the raw edges flat on to the background, either with a straight stitch seam or enclosed with zig-zag stitch. Cut off the surplus and sew a dark, folded strip to cover both the first strip and the square, just overlapping. Carry on round in a clockwise direction and machine the four completed squares together to form a pattern.

The modern version of the log cabin pattern is worked in cottons on a cotton backing Four 12 cm (4¾ in) squares are joined to make a large one, and a slightly wider measurement allowed for the final surrounding strip. This gives seam allowance for joining up the big squares and permits the fabric to turn over and lie flat on single squares.

Patchwork balls and pincushions

Patchwork balls are made in sections. The five-sided template is used for cutting two sets of six patches to form the two halves of the ball. Pentagons cannot be sewn together to form a flat surface unless they are combined with a different shaped patch – sometimes a lozenge-shaped long hexagon.

Balls made from segments of a circle are simple to sew. Eight segments give a nice round shape, alternating light and dark patches. These balls are machined together on the wrong side, using a straight stitch.

Fabrics

Use printed needlecord, firm courtelle, tweed, felt, suede, thin leather, vinyl-coated fabric, fur fabric, strong cottons and firm woollens. Do not mix fabric types on one piece of work.

Segmented ball

Trace off the pattern shape in the diagram and cut this out in thin card. Lay it on the fabric, with the grain running from top to bottom, and mark around the template. Add seam allowances and cut four light and four dark segments.

The picture below shows a detail from an attractive table mat made in the log cabin method.

Match one dark and one light segment, right sides facing, and seam them together, starting and finishing on the seam-allowance marks, not at the ends. Add in alternate colours, keeping the points as accurate as possible. Leave 2.5cm (1 in) unsewn on the last seam and turn the ball inside out.

Stuff the ball until it is a hard, round shape, using kapok, terylene stuffing, cut-up woollies or tights – in fact, anything washable. Use foam chippings with leather, suede or vinyl cloth if you want a ball that bounces. To prevent hard edges of foam distorting the ball shape, first stuff with a little kapok and then continue with foam chips.

Pentagon ball

Either narrow seam together on the wrong side using a straight-stitch machine or use a zig-zag stitch to overcast the edges as in oversewn machine patchwork. This seam can be worked from the wrong side for fur fabric or as a decorative seam on the right side on felt or non-fray materials.

Method

Use felt, suede, thin leather, or vinyl-coated cloth. A ball in two colours will require six dark and six light-coloured pentagon patches, cut to template size, without seam allowances.

Sew five dark pentagon patches, in turn, against the five edges of the one light patch. Have the right sides facing outwards. Next, machine together the five dark seams towards the light patch.

Make another set of six patches, this time with light ones surrounding a dark centre. These two cup shapes are then fitted together, with the points intersecting. Sew this as a continuous seam, pivoting with the needle and piercing both patches at the corners. Align the seams as in the method for flat pieced patchwork, leaving one V-shaped section unsewn for stuffing. Finish off on the right side. Fur fabric seams are, however, sewn from the wrong side. Sew the opening up by hand after stuffing and the fur will hide the stitches.

Embroidery is worked on to the patch shapes before they are cut out. Mark out on the right side of the material as a guideline. Use a small 8cm (3 in) circular embroidery frame to limit the size of free-sewn motifs. To decorate, use the flower stitcher, eyelet stitcher, or spiral stitcher. Fabric covered with lines of automatic patterning can be cut up and alternated with plain shapes for good effect.

A collection of delightful articles all of which can be made with the aid of a modern sewing machine and scraps of fabric.

32 (Below) Segmented ball made up of pentagon shapes.
33 (Bottom) Joining patches and assembling a pentagon ball.

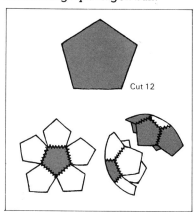

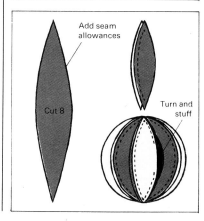

Pincushions

From a constructional point of view many of these can be treated in the same way as the patchwork balls. Pincushions were traditionally stuffed with bran or sheep's wool, which helped to prevent the early type of pins from rusting. Needles and pins were, at one time, all made by hand and were often in short supply. Many garments, or parts of garments were held together by pins. Sleeves were pinned to bodices, and collars and cuffs were held in position by pins. Pins were costly, and ladies were allowed 'pin money' to buy these small but necessary objects.

The pincushion was an essential item for holding not only sewing pins but also the longer dress pins. Pincushions

34 Heart pincushion. Cut one white, two large and one small red heart shapes in felt and trim each piece with pinking shears.

took many forms and were made in a variety of sewing and embroidery techniques. Some were square, like a little cushion, embroidered with a flower, a heart or other motifs, and finish with a cord to cover the join.

Simple, early Victorian shapes worked in canvas embroidery later gave way to more elaborate, sentimental pincushions, decorated with beads, sequins and mottos, held down with beaded pins and finished with fringing or bobble braid. Soldiers would give heart-shaped pincushions to their sweetheart or wives, and new arrivals were welcomed into the world with 'To Dear Baby' pincushions.

Working methods

Plain-shaped pincushions, based on a square, a circle or two patchwork templates, can be oversewn together by machine on the right side, or machined on the wrong side

and then turned inside out for stuffing.

The stuffing should be firm. Hampster bran is to be recommended and is obtainable from most pet-shops. But make sure that it is perfectly dry before stuffing. Stuff by trickling the bran through a funnel inserted in an opening left in the pincushion, or you can spoon it in. Sew up by hand, with additional machine stitches if necessary.

Make square blocks in felt or suede, with alphabet letters embroidered before cutting out. Sew flower petals in felt round a circle centre, using bright colours; or cut out a heart-shape and apply to a bigger heart.

The little fish are cut out of patterned furnishing fabric. The fins and tail are made from a strip of fabric folded in half, right sides outwards. The corners are folded over towards the middle before stitching in place along the seam line, sandwiched between the body pieces. Add a felt circle and a bead for the fish's eye. Enlarge the pattern by scaling up from a 1.25cm ($\frac{1}{2}$in) to a 2.5 cm (1in) grid, ad drawing out.

When making felt pincushions, cut some edges with pinking shears. For special occasions pincushions may be decorated with beads or sequins, held in position with a pin that is threaded with a small bead – like the Victorian ones.

Quilting

Quilting may have originated in Asia or the Far East, but nobody knows for sure. Somewhere, man discovered that two pieces of material with an inner layer of padding, held together at intervals, had surprising properties. It helped insulate from heat and cold; it was tough and could form a protection, whether as armour or floor covering; and at the same time it was highly decorative.

Quilted garments were worn during Tudor and Stuart times, but it was during the 17th and 18th centuries that the rich

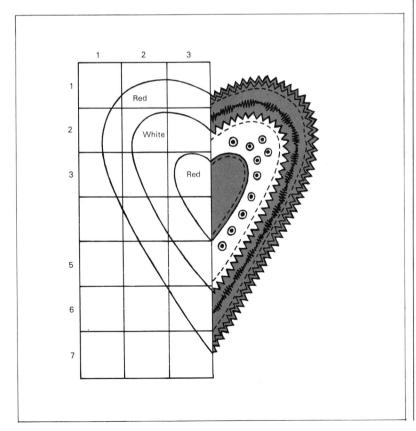

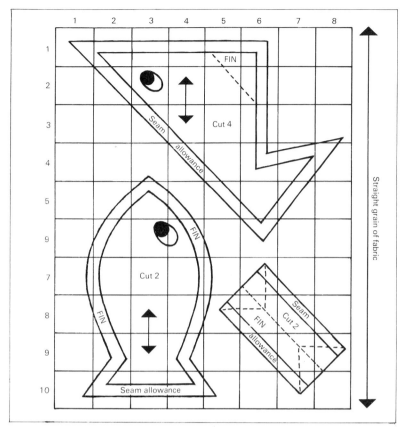

Choice of fabric

At one time, wadding, or batting, was made of cotton. The modern synthetic terylene wadding that is sold in large department stores will wash and is, in fact, better for machine quilting. It comes in several thicknesses and can be pulled apart to make thinner layers when required. Preshrunk, old blanket or soft woollen or cotton cloth will suffice as alternatives.

Most types of woven dress fabric can be quilted successfully. Thicker materials work better quilted in straight lines, using the quilting foot. Jersey, knits, velvet and suede can be quilted, but need more careful handling. For the free quilting, use cotton fabrics to start with. Choose a light cotton or muslin backing. Avoid slippery or shiny fabrics.

Preparing the fabric

The method is the same for all types of machine quilting. The three layers must be held together with tacking stitches at regular intervals in as even a manner as possible.

Lay the cotton backing on the table, place the wadding on top and place the chosen fabric on top of this, right side uppermost. Always start tacking stitches from the middle and work outwards – pushing and smoothing the layers away from you. Keep the layers flat on the table, use a long needle and keep one hand under the work to guide the needle. Tack as shown in fig. 37. Use straight tacking stitches; they will not catch on the machine foot so often. Even so, have a small pair of scissors handy, to snip the threads while you are machining.

Design

The design can be drawn on to the backing, and the quilting worked from the wrong side. Draw only the main outlines. It is far easier to work a design

silken court gowns with their quilted petticoats came into favour. Quilting is once again fashionable for use on clothing, after a period when the word 'quilt', which comes from the Latin *culcita* or 'sack', was synonymous with bed covering.

Wadded quilting

Wadded quilting and English or American quilting are the same. A layer of padding, wadding or sheep's wool was placed between the upper and lower layers of cloth, although this was sometimes omitted on bed curtains and coverlets during the 17th and early 18th centuries.

Sheep's wool was inserted between the flat quilts worked by the 'quilt wives' of Durham and industrial South Wales during the 19th century. The layered fabric was stretched on a quilting frame, and intricate

35 Little fish pincushions. Make a pattern for each piece, enlarging them on to a 2-cm grid.

patterns worked in running stitch – goose wings, feather and fan, as well as flowers, fruit and sheaves of corn.

Most people are familiar with machine quilting in the form of straight lines worked with the quilting foot and with the metal guide in position. Many attractive designs can be quilted, based on parallel or intersecting lines. Decorative stitches, automatic patterns and twin needle work, as well as the usual straight-stitch, can all be employed. Metallic cord and thick threads are wound round the bobbin and worked from the wrong side of the material.

A more exciting aspect of machine work is free quilting, or outline quilting. This can be worked in an embroidery frame with the foot removed and the machine set for darning, but it is far easier to quilt with the darning foot.

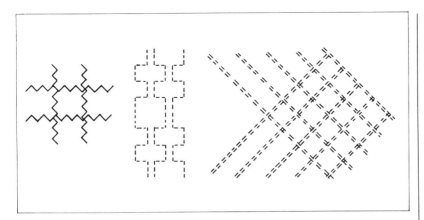

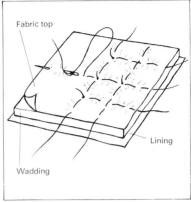

36 Line patterns for quilting.

37 Preparing fabric for quilting.

freely than it is to sew over guide lines. Another way is to start by working outline quilting. Choose a patterned material with medium-sized design elements – flowers, leaves, anything with curves – and sew these round.

Outline quilting

Set the machine for straight stitch and drop the feed, or use a cover plate. Use a darning foot which holds the cloth but also allows free movement. The thread should tone in with the background of the fabric print. Now loosen the top tension.

Starting from the middle, sew round the outlines, holding the wadded fabric firmly. There is no need to follow the lines exactly – a free approach makes for a livelier result – but try to sew a continuous line. When a group is finished, raise the foot and pull the threads – do not cut them off. Then start again at the next group. These threads are cut and taken through to the back afterwards. This method may be used for making cushions, bags, and quilted areas on clothing. Tie-dye, batik and screen-printed cloth can also be outlined. For special effects, use metallic threads in the bobbin and work from the wrong side of the wadded material.

Tea cosy

The tea cosy, illustrated on page 73, was cut out after the flower-printed fabric had been quilted. Some but not all of the flower heads, were outlined. Quilting that is too close, moreover, will flatten the work. Flowers that are small should be outlined in bunches.

Quilting tends to shrink the fabric, so allow for this. Cut a newspaper pattern to fit your tea-pot and have the material twice the height, plus 5 cm (2 in) for turnings. Also allow a good width and use thick wadding. The bag is cut from an oblong of quilting folded over.

Stuffed or padded quilting

This is also called trapunto quilting. Only certain parts of the design are raised, instead

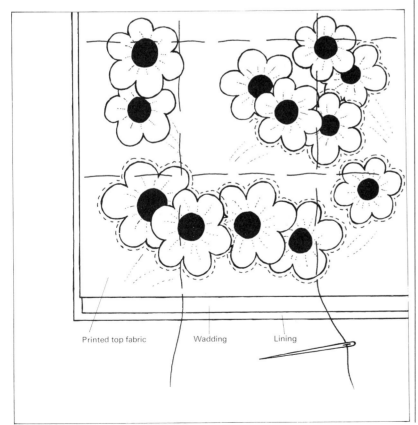

Printed top fabric   Wadding   Lining

38 Outline quilting.

of the whole area as in wadded quilting. The design outlines are first sewn through both top layer and backing. The stuffing is then introduced through slits in the backing which are sewn up afterwards.

The oldest examples of this work in existence are three Sicilian quilts, of which one is in London's Victoria and Albert Museum. These quilts show legendary scenes from the life of Tristram and include kings, knights, ships, horses and castles – each little scene bordered with leaf patterns. The outer borders are entwined with vines, flowering plants, ivy and oak leaves. The outlines are worked in backstitch on a double layer of heavy linen. Cotton padding raises the outlined shapes.

The running vine border pattern was popular during the 18th and 19th centuries and was worked on quilts. American, all

Quilted tea cosy and Victorian gown.

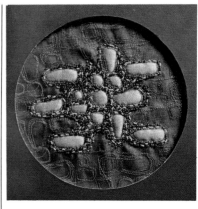

Sample of trapunto quilting.

white quilts contained raised designs – American eagle, the cornucopia, palm leaves and flowers. Sometimes piece patchwork was stuffed and quilted alternately.

Today, stuffed quilting is used on clothing as well as on soft furnishing, and can be used

to give additional depth to areas of wadded quilting. This three-dimensional quality makes it an ideal medium for expression in modern embroidery, wall hangings and soft sculpture. The highly padded areas of stump-work embroidery, worked on small pictures, mirror surrounds and boxes during the Stuart reigns, probably had their origin in simple stuffed quilting.

39 Straight-stitch line design for stuffed or padded quilting.

40 Outline stitching (left) and stuffing and sewing padded areas.

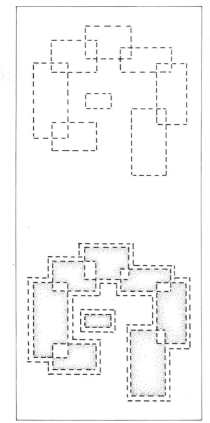

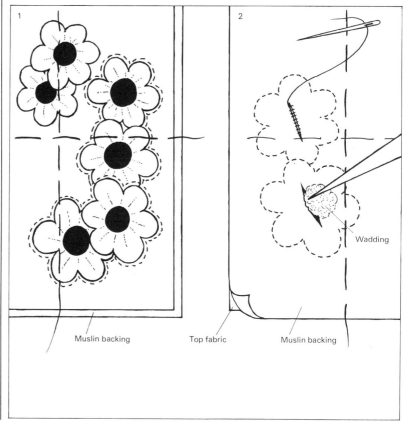

Muslin backing

Top fabric   Muslin backing

Wadding

Choice of fabric

In one context or another, most woven and knitted fabrics are suitable. The stretch quality of jersey fabrics is a positive advantage, but needs treating carefully when used on clothing. A more adventurous approach is possible when combining this method of quilting with textile construction. This work has the advantage that the design can be marked on the background and sewn from the wrong side.

Some thought needs to be given to the type of backing when this is combined with fabric for clothing. Traditionally, a very thin, open-weave muslin was used or, for heavier work, a loosely woven scrim. The threads could be parted and the stuffing introduced without cutting the threads.

A stretchy backing reduces the amount of padding protruding on the right side. A light cotton backing needs to be pre-shrunk before combining with synthetics. Avoid shiny fabrics or those that fray easily. They are difficult to sew up afterwards.

Design

Straight lines can be sewn with the foot on the machine. Make right-angled shapes, over-lapping squares and oblongs. It is not necessary to pad every one. Any embroidery is worked on the top layer of fabric before the design outlines are sewn through to the backing.

Printed, patterned fabric can be sewn round freely as in outline quilting. Stuff only certain areas, like flower petals.

Method

Choose a suitably patterned fabric print, and tack to the backing material from top to bottom and side to side, at about 5 cm (2 in) intervals. Stretch the double fabric in the circular embroidery frame or use the darning foot on thicker materials. Set the machine to straight-stitch and darning.

Sew round the outlines to be padded. If the padded areas are far apart, additional stitching can be worked round the outlines (this is called contour stitching). Next, remove the fabric from the frame. Take a quick-unpick tool or a sharp pair of scissors and slit just the backing material, behind the area to be padded. Keep the slits short on small areas. Stuff the space with small pieces of terylene wadding, cotton wool or kapok. When it is nice and firm, sew the raw edges of the slits together.

The beaded design illustrated was worked on a commercially embroidered organdie, mounted over a blue fabric which was backed with fine cotton. The design areas were worked over again from the right side in free machining. Some of the dark organdie was cut away to expose the blue material. Afterwards, these areas were slit behind and padded. Beads were sewn on by hand to give sparkle and emphasis to the repeat pattern of the original fabric.

Pillow quilting

This is a form of stuffed quilting. Cut out pieces of fabric, 12 × 7 cm (4¾ × 2¾ in), in different colours. Place two, right sides together, and machine round on three and a half sides, with 1 cm (⅜ in) seam allowance. Turn the right sides out. Now stuff well, fold in the raw edges and machine them together.

Arrange a number of these little pillows to form a pattern. This can be varied by making some into squares, cut from fabric measuring 7 × 7 cm (2¾ × 2¾ in).

The pillows may be machined together in any of the following ways:

1 *Oversewn machine patchwork method* Place two pillows together, ease the stuffing to one side and match the edges. Zig-zag over, with the needle piercing all the layers on the left hand swing, and sewing over the edges on the right hand swing. Open the pillows out flat and rearrange the stuffing.

2 *Butt joining* Either use a wide zig-zag stitch, or one of the automatic bridging stitches – feather stitch, three-step zig-zag, faggotting, smocking or lingerie stitch. Hold the pillows slightly apart, just enough for the needle to catch on either side. Alternatively, hold the two pillows apart on paper with sticky tape. Sew as before, tear the paper away and remove the sticky tape.

3 *Joining the corners only* Set the machine to a wide zig-zag and darning. Overlap the pillow corners, sew several stitches in one place and fasten off with a few straight stitches.

Pillow quilting is very similar to raised patchwork (sometimes called Swiss patchwork). This is made from geometric patchwork shapes, cut double and machined together on the wrong side. Leave a small opening for stuffing and sew up by hand or join by machining an edge-stitch all round. This gives a flatter edge and makes butt-joining easier. Join all to form the patchwork.

Make triangles by folding a square over on the diagonal, right sides together, and machine round as before. Always use larger size templates for machine work.

Corded quilting

Cords are inserted between narrow channels sewn on double fabric, both for decoration and to produce a firm fabric for garments. Another method is worked on a single layer of cloth with the cord held in place by double back-stitches. These cross on the back of the work, enclosing the cord. Tightly pulled stitches give the cord a very raised appearance. From the right side, it is almost impossible to tell which method has been used.

Some European work has

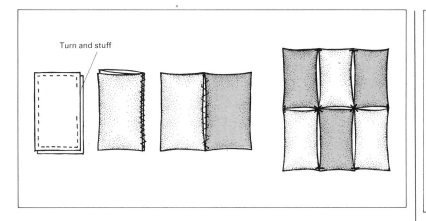

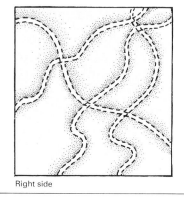

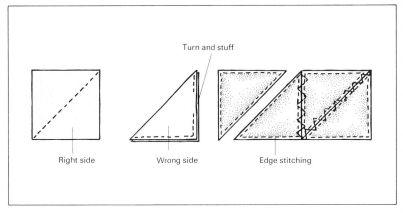

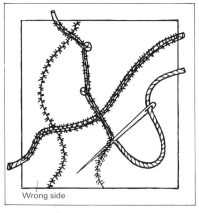

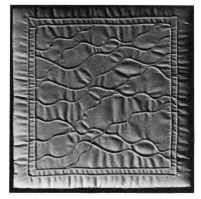

Corded quilting on a box lid.

41 (Top) Pillow quilting – joining.
42 (Above) Raised patchwork.

43 Corded quilting; right side (top); wrong side (above).

survived from the 16th century, but most existing corded quilting is from the 17th and 18th centuries, when bed curtains and coverlets were completely covered with linear patterns. Later, the cording designs were placed further apart and this was combined with stuffed quilting. Additional flat quilting, sewn through two layers only, made the raised cords appear even more pronounced.

Some of the work was delicately sewn on fine linen with thin padding cord. This was used for baby clothes and adults' caps, and on the elaborate petticoats that showed between the ladies' slit overskirts. Both men and women wore quilted jackets, and men's waistcoats often combined quilting with ornate pulled-stitch embroidery.

Method

Cording on the machine gives the same kind of results as the back-stitched method. A thin cord is held between the parallel lines of stitching made by twin needles on the surface of the material. The bobbin thread forms a criss-cross behind.

It is only possible to use twin needles with machines that thread from front to back. It is also necessary to have an underbraider, or raised seam attachment. This takes the form of a small-grooved metal plate fitted on to the front of the needleplate. In this way, the thread is held in the correct position to be sewn over and enclosed by the twin needle stitching. In some machines the cord is passed up through a small hole in the front of the needleplate.

If your machine has none of these devices, it is possible to make a substitute. Cut 2 cm ($\frac{3}{4}$ in) of plastic sleeving off a piece of electric flex. The diameter may vary in size. Choose one with a 2 mm ($\frac{1}{16}$ in) hole in the middle for perle thread No. 5. Now line up the flex in front of the needle and fix it on to the machine bed with transparent sticky tape. Poke the cord through the hole. Use a larger plastic sleeve for thicker cords, which should pass through easily and not catch.

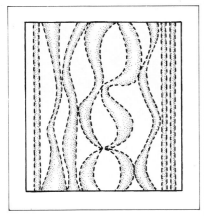

44 (Above) Two examples of Italian or padded thread quilting.

Thread the machine according to the instruction booklet. Part the threads at the tension discs and again at the needle-thread guides, one thread to each needle. Set the machine to straight stitch and loosen the top tension a little.

Place a piece of fabric under the wide-slot presser foot and on top of the cord. The twin needles will enclose this within two parallel stitch lines. Try to plan your patterns in straight lines or in gentle curves.

Corners can only be turned by raising the needles and the foot and turning the balance wheel by hand to make three stitches on each corner. Take care that the cord is still aligned under the needles before continuing to sew. Have it in your lap and let it unwind easily.

This may take a little practice before you get it right. It may be advisable to do a few test samples first.

Using the darning foot

Corded quilting can be sewn more freely by using the darning foot. Set the machine for twin-needle sewing and straight-stitch. Make sure the twin needles sew within the darning foot ring. Set for darning, or if your machine has it, half-dropped feed position. Sometimes this works better, depending on the fabric.

Sew undulating lines and curves. Avoid corners as the undercord may come adrift, but lines can cross over each other. This will give areas of raised contrast. Some fabrics work better double and treated as one.

An alternative method is to sew freely, using the darning foot without the undercord. More control is possible if the material is loosely framed. Fix the darning foot after the frame is in position, or tip the frame and slide it under.

Sew lines, circles and curves. Cross over, and work any flowing, free design. Thread a blunt-pointed tapestry needle with thin cord and insert this behind the twin-needle sewing. Go in and out at the same place for each new stitch. Loop round corners, coming out and back in again. Free embroidery can be worked inside the intersecting spaces before cording.

Some automatic pattern stitches are suitable for twin-needle work. Three-step zig-zag and simple curve shapes can be sewn with the normal foot in position. Thread extra cord behind in the way described for free work.

Italian or padded thread quilting

These are alternative names for the other form of corded quilting, worked on a double layer

45 Inserting the quilting wool in Italian or padded thread quilting.

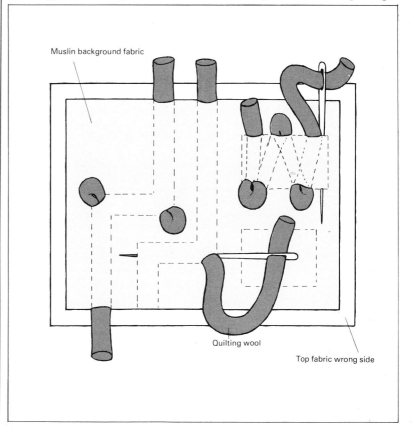

Muslin background fabric

Quilting wool

Top fabric wrong side

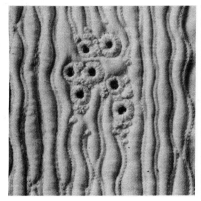

Padded cord quilting with eyelets.

of material. Parallel stitch channels are threaded from the wrong side with cord, quilting wool or other thick threads.

Traditionally, the backing is of soft, open-weave muslin or scrim. This allows the threads to be parted, but not cut, when the cord or quilting wool is introduced. A large, blunt needle is used to guide the filling thread between the channels. Alternatively, a thin cotton fabric that can be pierced easily by the needle may be used.

Although areas of soft padding had been included in with the harder, corded designs, it was not until the late 19th and early 20th centuries that soft corded patterns were preferred. Cushions and tea cosies in shiny satin were popular in the 1920s and 30s, featuring interlaced designs. Today, this quilting is worked on a variety of modern fabrics. Freedom of expression allows variation in the width of line and a more exciting approach to design. This type of quilting is very suitable for machine work.

Padding threads

These may be hard cords as in the early corded quilting. Piping cord, too, is excellent and comes in a variety of thicknesses. You can also use macramé threads or string. Always wash these threads beforehand in case they shrink – whatever the label may say.

Softer threads are easier to handle. Traditionally, these were always made of sheep's wool but nowadays quilting wool may be synthetic – this does not shrink.

Other kinds of thick threads, such as quick knit, or several strands of knitting thread will make a good substitute. Colour is a positive advantage in shadow work. It is worth experimenting with various types and thicknesses of thread as the results can be very different. Hard outlines can be combined with softer areas. The coloured stuffing thread can be brought out on to the surface of the fabric to create additional areas of interest on embroidered panels.

It is also possible to machine transparent PVC for use on wall hangings, bags or window blinds. Use a longer stitch-length when sewing any plastic fabric; if the holes are too close it will tear away. Sometimes this material is difficult to sew and sticks to the machine. Use a roller foot or a teflon-coated or glide foot. A little French chalk, talcum powder or a touch of oil smeared on to the material beforehand, may help.

Traditional padding threads are colour-fast, washable embroidery wools. Several strands may be needed to fill the spaces adequately. There are plenty of fluffy, coloured synthetic knitting threads available that will not shrink. The thick and thin slubs in some threads may be incorporated as part of the design.

Some shadow work is mounted on a background, or incorporated in dress embroidery. Other shadow work is mounted so that the light shines through and enhances the colours. The light will show through window panels and through lampshades.

A lampshade has to be designed so that it will look equally good whether the light is on or off. Thinner, coloured threads that can be inserted in rows down narrow channels, or worked backwards and forwards across larger areas, look all right on a backed fabric.

When held up to the light, these filling threads will give an entirely different pattern. In some instances this can be incorporated as part of the design, but it must be deliberate. The alternative is to stuff with coloured filling or wadding or the dyed synthetic fibres sold for hand spinning.

Twin-needle work

Narrow twin-needle lines give a decorative quality to this work. The stuffing is inserted between the rows of twin-needle sewing, not between the narrow lines. Use automatic patterns with twin needles, to give simple outline shapes. These may be sewn in rows and may overlap, cross each other and create new spaces. You should fill some of the spaces and leave others plain.

On organdie, combined with the hemstitching needle, a pattern of holes is formed. Work machine eyelet holes and back these with thread or coloured organdie.

Plan patterns on lampshades to sit within the areas of the struts. Alternatively, the struts can form part of the design. Emphasize with a line of shadow work to cover and coincide. Alternatively work a pattern right round, top and bottom, or on the bottom only.

Shadow quilting with guipure motifs in the shape of little flowers gives a delicate effect.

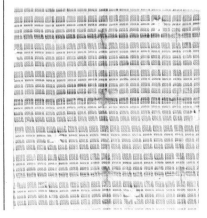

46 (Right) Inserting threads from wrong side in shadow quilting.
47 (Below right) Tacking felt in place in solid shadow quilting.

Try working this technique on other fabrics. Net is much more transparent. Tack several layers of coloured net to a plain backing. Machine double line designs. Thread with the same colour but darker. Some of the layers of net can be cut away in between the padded lines.

Solid shadow quilting

Cut out shapes of thicker fabric or felt are sandwiched between two layers of semi-transparent material and machined round.

Samples of machine shadow quilting were worked by Dorothy Benson in the 1930s, for the Singer workrooms. Later, she wrote the *Singer Machine Embroidery Book.* Shadow work in organdie, was used for tray cloths and as over-covers on tea cosies.

Felt will not wash, and a good modern alternative is the thicker type of plain courtelle fabric. This is less likely to fray.

Simple shapes work best. Use squares, rectangles and triangles. Cut out fabric or felt shapes, using geometric templates to make a form of shadow patchwork.

Lay the bottom layer of muslin or organdie on to a flat surface. Arrange the cut-out shapes on to the backing, either to a pre-determined pattern or move them around until you have a pleasing design. Leave plenty of space between to allow for machine lines and additional pattern outlines – 2-3cm (1 in), to start with.

Felt, on a firmer backing, can be held with a tiny spot of fabric adhesive. This may eventually show through, and tacking is therefore the better method. Tack each shape in position

48 Transparent shapes held in place with twin-needle stitching in transparent shadow quilting.

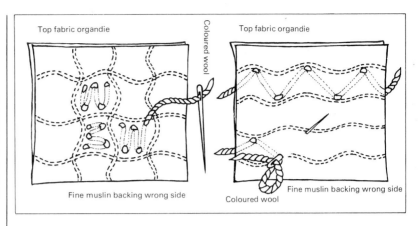

Top fabric organdie

Coloured wool

Top fabric organdie

Fine muslin backing wrong side

Coloured wool

Fine muslin backing wrong side

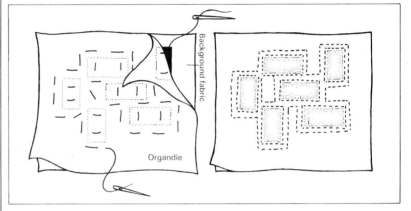

Background fabric

Organdie

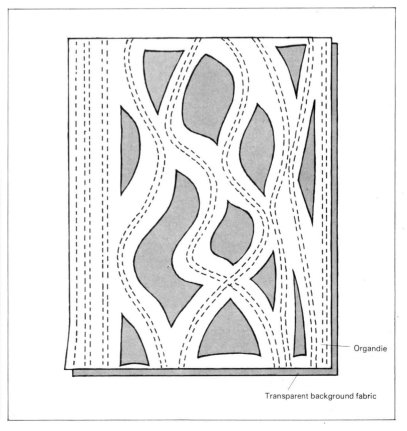

Organdie

Transparent background fabric

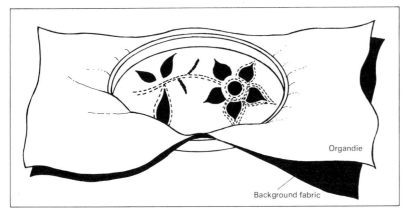

Organdie

Background fabric

49 Free shadow quilting in the embroidery frame.

before adding the top layer of organdie – machine work is more liable to slip than hand work. Additional tacking stitches will hold the two layers together between the shapes.

Design

The easiest way to design for machine work, of any kind, is to set the machine for the type of work in hand, prepare a piece of test fabric and see what you can do. A machined design where the stitching is forced to conform to the concepts of a different medium always lacks vitality. Let the machine dictate what it can do best, and then adapt and use your experiments to work something completely original.

Padded thread quilting lends itself to rows of undulating straight-stitch lines, varying in width and padding. More formally, machine round outlined shapes, squares, triangles and oblongs. Continue working inwards in a continuous spiral, and use the presser-foot width as a guide.

Designs can be suggested by ploughed fields, wave forms, fence posts, woodland trees, map contours, tree bark or ripples. Look through magazines and colour supplements, paying attention to the backgrounds of photographs as well as the subject.

Machining

Draw the main design outlines on to the backing fabric. Coloured tailor chalk works best on muslin; a hard pencil will drag the threads.

Tack the backing to the top fabric, right sides facing outwards. Straight lines of tacking at 5 cm (2 in) intervals, from top to bottom and side to side, are sufficient. For small areas, to be sewn freely or with the darning foot, an embroidery frame should be used. If you are careful two layers of fabric can be stretched in the frame as one, without the need for tacking. Whichever method you use, see that the straight grain of both fabrics is matching.

Either machine the design lines with the foot on the machine, lines no less than 5 mm ($\frac{3}{16}$ in) apart, or use the widest twin-needle size. Vary the width of the lines to make the work more interesting. Quilting looks best when the sewing thread matches or tones in with the background fabric. The patterning is partly created by the areas of light and shade formed by the ridged lines. Sometimes a design may need additional emphasis, in which case a single colour is used rather than a contrast.

Inserting thick thread

When all the channel lines have been sewn take any loose thread ends to the wrong side of the work. The thick threads are inserted into the channels, using a large-eyed, blunt needle. Take as long a stitch as possible through the backing and out again. Insert the needle in the same place for the next stitch. Try to plan these filling stitches to coincide with corners or line ends. Come out at a corner and back in again, leaving a small loop of thread on the corner point. Do not pull the padding thread tight while you are working.

Wider areas between lines will need an extra thickness of padding thread. This can be doubled, or trebled within the wide area, or worked backwards and forwards across, going in and out of the backing fabric at each step.

Corded quilting can be combined with small areas of padded quilting (trapunto), machine embroidery, eyelets, beading or hand stitches.

The small panel, 'Beach Sand at Ebb Tide', is worked on fine lawn with muslin backing. Italian quilting is combined with machine eyelet stitches. The padding is threaded between rows of twin-needle sewing worked on a curved automatic stitch to simulate ripple formation. Some hand-stitched French knots are added. (See previous page.)

Set the machine to straight-stitch and machine an outline round the shapes, using the presser foot as a guide. Machine additional outlines, again to presser-foot width, to unify the design.

Alternatively, machine straight across from top to bottom and side to side, enclosing all the shapes within a grid. Work from the middle outwards to keep the work flat. Threads can match the background, tone in with the padding shapes or be sewn from the reverse of the fabric using a metallic cord wound round the bobbin.

Transparent shadow quilting is worked in exactly the same way, but the padding shapes themselves are transparent. This will give a much softer effect. Cut several layers of coloured transparent fabric to give a deeper colour.

American block Hawaiian pattern. This design has been made particularly striking by the effective use of contrasting colours.

Cut shapes out from coloured sheet mica or from any other coloured transparent plastic and insert these between net or transparent plastic. Sew ribbons or tapes between layers, or combine line, tape and flat shadow quilting.

Free shadow quilting

The machine is set to straight-stitch and darning. Either use the darning foot or stretch the tacked layers of fabric in an embroidery frame. This is only possible if the design is small and fits inside the frame.

Plan curved or circular shapes. Cut out separate flower centres and petals and space them apart. Machine round these shapes freely. This method can be used on normal fabrics to give another type of padded embroidery.

American block quilting

The traditional quilting frame was big enough to allow a large portion of coverlet to be quilted at one time, with several quilters sharing the work. The frame was supported on trestles at either end, the intervening space giving room for the worker's chairs. The surplus fabric was rolled on to the side supports, and a new area exposed as the work proceeded.

The Dutch and English emigrants took this framing method with them to America. Established settlers had room to put up the frames, which could take a full-sized coverlet top, and were always worked on a neighbourly, community basis.

A young girl would start to make coverlet tops in pieced patchwork or appliqué from an early age. No less than 12 were considered necessary, the 13th being the wedding quilt. A quilting party was arranged when the betrothal was announced.

The 'freedom quilt' was made for a young man when he reached the age of 21. Sometimes the pieced cover top was worked by his mother, sometimes by the young ladies of his acquaintance. This was later quilted for the bride.

Pioneer settlers, still moving westwards, found this system impractical and developed the method of block quilting. Piece patchwork, often to the nine-block pattern and its variations, or appliqué and counterchange patterns, were worked to similar-sized squares. These were combined with a backing and an iternal layer of wadding and tacked together. They were small enough to be worked comfortably in the hand, could be picked up and quilted when the opportunity arose and were easily stored away. This method is also referred to as 'lap quilting'. When all the blocks were finished, they were sewn together to form the quilt, and backed with cotton cloth. All the pattern shapes could be cut out beforehand and assembled later – an early form of mass-production.

Appliqué patterns featured natural forms. Stylized flowers and plant patterns, cut from folded paper, were especially popular after the mid-19th cen-

Upper fabric with appliqué design

Background fabric

Quilting wadding

50 Tacking the appliqué ready for block quilting, adding a straight stitch quilted outline.

tury, when aniline dyes gave stronger colours and the American cloth industry was able to produce larger quantities of cheap material.

The American block system is extremely suitable for machine worked quilting. It is not easy to quilt a large area of fabric since the wadding builds up under the overhanging arm of the machine. The smaller-sized blocks are simpler to work and there is no danger of heavy work pulling out of position from under the foot. They are machined together afterwards and made up into cushion covers, garments, bed quilts, chair backs – anything that can be made up from a combination of squares.

Quilting the Hawaiian block pattern

The reverse appliqué design for the Hawaiian block pattern, can easily be used for the machine block quilting method. Any machine block quilted

design should be kept simple. Machine quilting tends to flatten the wadding if the lines are worked too close. Aim for a plump, evenly distributed quilting. It may be necessary to simplify a design outline, or to extend it.

Make up the Hawaiian block pattern according to the instructions, but do not machine a border line round the edge. Leave out this stage. The border width is used as seam allowance for seaming up. You can, if you wish, cut the squares a little larger to make for easier joining up. Take out any tacking threads.

Cut a fine cotton or muslin backing to the same size as the top squares. Next, cut a similar-sized piece of thick synthetic quilting wadding for each square to be worked. Lay the backing cloth on the table, wrong side uppermost. Place

the layer of wadding on top and the appliqué design on top of this, right side uppermost. Tack through all layers, using a long needle and basting cotton. To avoid tacking stitches catching on the machine foot, tack them in straight lines, working from the centre outwards along the centre portions of each extended arm of the design.

When all eight radiating lines have been tacked, add a tacking thread round the edge. For easy removal of threads, and 're-use' for the thrifty, make a large knot 2cm (¾in) from the thread end. Leave this end protruding from the tacking stitches. These are not fastened off, but left free. When the time comes to remove these threads, pull them out from the knotted end. This will save a lot of time.

The quilting is worked with either the quilting foot, the see-through plastic appliqué foot or a see-through embroidery foot. Set a medium straight-stitch and a looser top tension. The thread can match the background, but a contrast colour was used on the quilted blocks illustrated. Sew outside the embroidered appliqué area. Lining up the presser foot with the satin stitch line and using this as a guide.

Start at the middle and sew the inner star-shape first. Next, machine right round the outline of the entire pattern, sewing the shapes inside the pattern leaves last of all.

Work four counterchange squares to form one pattern unit and tack these together carefully along the edges. Quilting tends to distort the square shape, but take no notice of this. Keep to the straight grain of the fabric on both sides. Machine through all layers, take all thread ends to the back and remove all the tacking stitches.

Cut away the surplus quilting wadding from the seam edges and turn one seam allowance over to make a flat seam. Slip stitch in place by hand. This will keep all the inside seams flat. Four squares will make cushion cover, thirty-six a single-sized bed quilt.

A-Z of the sewing machine

A glossary of terms and techniques

Using the A-Z

The A-Z provides a quick and easy reference guide to machine methods for a variety of sewing processes used in dressmaking, millinery, soft furnishings, machine crafts and on household linen.

A dressmaking pattern gives instructions for making a particular garment; it does not offer alternative methods or explain ways of dealing with different types of material. Leather, suede and plastic-coated fabrics all require special sewing techniques. Fur fabric is easy to sew, once you know how. Many sewing enthusiasts are unsure of the correct way to deal with stretch fabrics. Often they do not know what kind of stitches to use or what is available for any particular type of machine.

It is possible to use the machine for more sewing processes than most people realize. Mending and darning by machine is not only much quicker, but a great deal firmer. Machine tacking and fabric marking give speed to the work in the initial stages. Decoration need not be limited to stitching and pattern sewing, but can take the form of tucks, smocking, quilting, braid sewing and decorative fringes.

More use can be made of the machine feet provided for special sewing purposes or for sewing various types of fabric. Not all these special feet are included with the machine, but they can be obtained as extras. Some will fit more than one make of machine, others can be used with a special adaptor. If your make of machine does not manufacture the particular attachment you require, consult a reliable dealer who will advise you as to which attachments will fit which machines.

They can help to make certain processes such as seam and hem sewing, binding and edge stitiching not only quicker, but also much easier. Other attachments, such as the eyelet stitcher, produce effects that are difficult to achieve by sewing in the normal manner.

Sewing construction

Some construction methods are included to help with the simple machine projects that do not require a pattern. These are attaching apron strings and tapes, interfacings and linings; applying tape, braid and lace; making casings for cord and elastic; making darts and sewing round curves.

There are instructions for matching checks and stripes and for making mitred corners. Three types of shoulder pad are also included. Instructions are given for making rouleau strips and loops, and for cutting and sewing bias strips. Methods for stay stitching, top stitching and stitch methods for millinery brims and crowns are also included.

Headings

A choice of methods for curtains is given.

Hems

These include plain, curved, blind stitched, scalloped and hem stitched. There are finishes for hems on all fabric types, also binding with tape or braid, piped and shell edges.

Seams

The types included are plain, lapped, machine fell, French, double welt, piped and corded. Special seam methods can be found under the appropriate fabric type headings. Seam neatening comes under 'Overcasting', with a choice of machine stitches.

Reducing fabric fullness

Various methods are dealt with under a series of separate headings: gathering, shirring, waffling and decorative smocking; similarly, in the case of the use of elastic thread, sewing on elastic, making tucks, pleats and ruffles. Alternative methods are given for straight stitch and zig-zag machines.

Fasteners

This section includes sewing on buttons and fasteners. One machine buttonhole method is illustrated, and there are two dressmaker-type buttonholes, fabric bound and fabric piped. Instructions for making belt carriers, loop closures and for using velcro are given. Alternative machine methods for zip fasteners will give additional choice. The experienced dressmaker will be able to insert these very quickly. The beginner is advised not to omit any extra tacking procedures.

Darning, mending and patching

This section covers a variety of methods and machine stitches for all simple repairs, including darning on wool, darning socks, using the darning foot and the circular darning frame. There are also mending and patching methods for different fabrics.

Decoration
Automatic patterns

Instructions are given for motif embroidery, the building up of new designs from single pattern elements, and for pattern sewing and pattern matching. It is surprising what can be achieved on the simple type of zig-zag machine. The instructions will be found under 'Operator controlled patterns'. Working methods are given for twin and triple needles, hemstitching or wing needles, and include turning corners and pattern matching.

Decorative effects

This section deals with the use of thick threads in the bobbin, using shaded thread and sewing patterns over braid or ribbon. Other decorative methods included are feather stitching, circle stitching, eyelets, fringing, smocking, faggoting and quilting. Instructions are given for applying and joining lace and for inserting lace into fabric.

Corners

This section shows how to turn using straight stitch, zig-zag, automatic patterns and twin and triple needles.

Improvization

Suggestions are given for sewing circles without an attachment and for making raised seams for pintucks.

Fabric types

There are guidelines on how to sew, using the correct needles and thread and the best stitches.

Thick fabrics

Woven, bonded and laminated fabrics come under this heading.

Fine fabrics

These include both natural and synthetic woven types

Jersey and stretch fabrics

Details are given of special sewing feet, stitches and edge finishes.

Knitted garments

Cut and sew methods using the domestic machine are included; also, sewing on bands and facings.

Leather and suede

Preparation, special needles, thread, and treatment of seams are all dealt with.

Plastic-coated fabrics

The correct types of seams and methods for sewing are considered, together with the use of special feet and other sewing aids.

Fur and fur fabric

This includes instructions on how to cut, how to sew and on dealing with long pile fur.

Net and pile fabrics each have their own section.

Stitches

These are listed both according to type, for easy identification, and under the uses to which they can be put. There is a choice of stitches to suit the kind of machine in use.

Finding your method

First look up the fabric type. This will indicate the best method for seams, finishes and stitches. After the correct stitch has been chosen, look up the method to be used; for instance,

gathering or sewing on elastic or lace. Find the appropriate finishes under 'hems' or 'decorative edges', and neatening under 'edge stitches' and 'overcasting'. Consult *applied braids*, *threads* or *automatic stitch patterns* and *decorative effects* to add interest to the finished sewing project.

A

Applying
Braid and tape

Apply narrow braids centred under the machine foot, either with a straight stitch or a wide zig-zag. A braiding foot with a guide slot is available for some machines.

Wider braids, tapes and ribbons can be held down by sewing down the middle or on either edge, using a straight stitch or zig-zag stitch. Either sew the zig-zag stitch on to the braid edge, or centre the braid edge under the foot and sew half on to the braid and half on to the background (fig. 1). Satin stitch (closed up zig-zag) will make a bolder line, and automatic patterns can add decoration to a plain braid or tape.

1 Different methods of sewing down braids, tapes and ribbons by machine using either zig-zag, straight stitch or satin stitch (closed zig-zag).

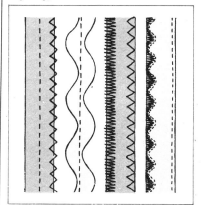

Edge of a skirt decorated with applied ric-rac braid and automatic embroidery stitches.

Turning corners

Straight-stitched narrow braid
Lower the needle into the braid and fabric on the corner point. Raise the machine foot. Hold the braid and pivot on the needle, lining it up with the new stitching line. Lower the foot and continue sewing.

Straight-stitched broad braid
Machine on the outer edge first. Stop at the corner with the needle in the cloth, raise the foot, turn the fabric and braid and then machine across to the inner edge at right-angles. Pivot round the needle again and sew up the inner edge to the width measurement of the braid (fig. 2). Fold the mitred corner under, as illustrated, and machine across the diagonal fold back to the corner. Continue sewing. Machine round the inner edge afterwards.

Swing-needle machine
Hold the outer edges of the braid with a zig-zag stitch. Change to straight stitch at the mitred corners and back to zig-zag for the edge stitching.

Matching patterns

Hold a pocket mirror diagonally across a patterned braid to plan a corner repeat. It may be necessary to cut the braid to make the pattern fit in. Machine the first piece into position. Cut and lay the second piece on top, allowing for turning under at the mitred corner.

Machine the mitred folds into position afterwards (fig. 2). In the case of thick fabrics cut the corners first, machine them together and press seams flat.

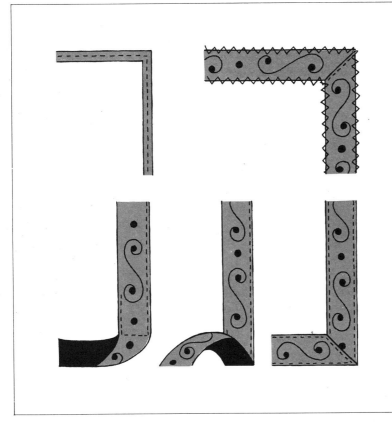

2 Different methods of turning corners neatly with narrow braid and straight stitch (top left); with broad braid and zig-zag stitch (top right); and with broad braid and straight stitch (bottom row).

Fabric and patchwork

An applied fabric shape should match the grain of the background fabric. Tack into position. Zig-zag round the outline of the shape, centring the fabric edge under the middle of the machine foot. Set zig-zag stitch and length at about half way. For a firmer line, machine over the zig-zag with satin stitch.

For a bolder effect, machine narrow tape or braid over the first line of zig-zag stitches.

If using a straight stitch machine sew round three times and apply a cord to cover (see *Cording*). Alternatively, machine a larger piece of fabric into position and trim away any excess afterwards.

Ric-rac braid

Machine straight down the middle, either using straight stitch or zig-zag. Alternatively, machine straight across one edge, ignoring the wave formation of the braid. It is possible to use an automatic pattern; some machines feature a waved or serpentine stitch. Adjust the stitch length to conform with the braid indentations.

Threads See *Cording*

Attaching
Apron strings and tapes

To prevent tapes from pulling away under strain, turn under at least 2.5cm (1in) and apply with the fold of the tape 3cm (1¼in) from the garment or edge of the article.

Using a medium-length stitch, machine round all four sides of a square, and then across the diagonals. Alternatively, sew a triangle shape. The tape can be applied to the wrong side with straight stitching, or to the right side using an automatic pattern stitch, satin stitch or zig-zag.

Automatic patterns

Use a wide-grooved embroidery foot for all automatic pattern work. This will not crush the stitches. A see-through plastic foot is ideal. Use machine embroidery thread no. 30 or for finer work no. 50. Loosen the top tension slightly for a plumper stitch. To prevent the stitches from puckering, put a piece of typing paper beneath the work and tear this away afterwards.

Automatic stitches

There are two main types, whether the machine works by selector dials or has drop-in pattern cams. The first kind is sewn on a short stitch-length setting to produce close, satin stitch, patterns. The other kind is sewn on a longer stitch-length setting and makes use of the automatic reverse feed to double back on itself. These are the trimotion stitches.

Stitch-length alterations

These will affect the look of the stitch and will increase pattern diversity. A longer stitch-length setting will open out the close type pattern and increase the length. Some machines have a control that keeps the satin stitch density on elongated patterns. Some stitches distort when elongated; others give the effect of cross stitches in hand sewing. Make a trial sample of all the stitches on both open and close settings.

3 Decorative automatic patterns worked with a swing needle.

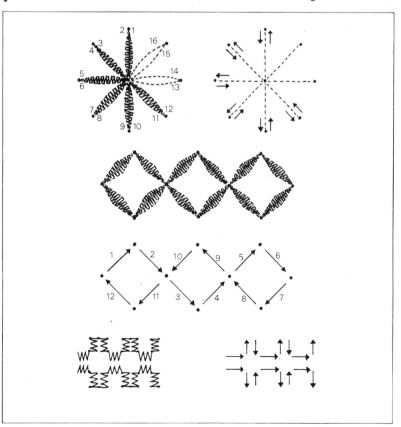

Applied felt motifs and decoration worked on a Bernina machine using a variety of automatic patterns.

Motif sewing

Some machines have a pattern indicator to show the start and finish of a pattern motif. Fully electronic machines sew one motif automatically. This helps when a single pattern element is used to create a new design or motif.

Continuous borders

Choose a one-sided, close-stitch pattern such as a scallop. Working in the order indicated in fig. 4, machine one pattern and stop with the needle in the cloth. Raise the foot and pivot to sew the next pattern at right angles. Stop and pivot to sew back to the middle.

Stars and flowers

Work as for border sewing, but continue round in a circle, always starting and coming back to the exact middle of the work (fig. 4). Some pattern shapes, such as a leaf or a petal, have to be sewn over again on the return journey.

Mixing the patterns

Change patterns or cams half way – a diamond and a leaf shape, for example. Alter the length or change the colour, either within the same pattern row, or on alternate rows. Do not cut off the threads when moving to a new position, but pull the fabric and threads out towards the back of the machine and start again. Cut all threads afterwards, take them through to the wrong side of the work and tie off.

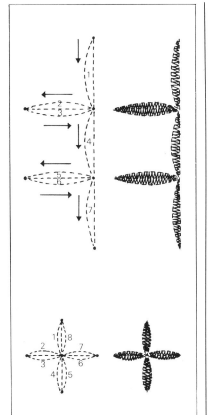

4 (Left) Automatic patterns used to make border and flower motifs.

Utility stitches

These are for stretch sewing, oversewing and triple seaming, but can be used as decorative stitches.

Patterns

Sew in rows facing each other, or back to back by machining in opposite directions. The second row may need some adjustment by the operator to keep the points of the motifs opposite one another. Either retard or push forward the cloth as necessary – it needs a little practice, but the results are well worth it (fig. 3). Alternatively, use an even feed foot. Use the pattern length selector, provided on some machines, to alternate long and short versions of the same pattern motif with constant density.

B

Basting

Basting, or tacking, is used to mark pattern or sewing lines on to single fabric, and also to hold two pieces of material together temporarily for fitting in dressmaking. It should be easy to remove, and yet firm enough to hold safely in place.

Using a long stitch

This is the simplest method. Use an unmercerized cotton thread in a contrasting colour. Set the machine for the longest straight stitch and loosen the top tension. Machine on the guidelines for pattern marking, and just outside the seam line, when joining two pieces of fabric. To remove the tacking, pull the under, tighter thread.

Basting needle

This needle has two eyes, placed one above the other: the bottom one is for normal sewing, the upper is threaded for tacking, or basting. Set the machine for a wide zig-zag stitch. The needle only forms a stitch when it enters on the left-hand side, and thus makes a stitch twice as long as normal, about 7 mm ($\frac{1}{3}$ in).

Pin along the seam line, points towards the foot. Machine with the guideline under the left-hand needle swing. Remove the pins before they reach the foot. For a longer stitch-length, up to 22 mm ($\frac{7}{8}$ in), use the blind hem stitch (fig. 41).

Chain stitch

Some machines have a chain stitching device which can be exchanged for the front-loading bobbin case. This enables a continuous thread through the needle to form a chain stitch underneath the cloth, and a normal stitch on top.

This unravels very easily and is useful for any temporary seams or marking. It is essential to fasten off well at the end of the stitching line, either by pulling the thread end through the final loop or by hand back-stitching.

Pin basting

Place pins at intervals of about 2.5 cm (1 in) at right angles to the seam line, and with the points just touching the line. Machine up against – but not over – the pins, either using the normal presser foot or the one-sided zipper foot, which allows closer sewing (fig. 5).

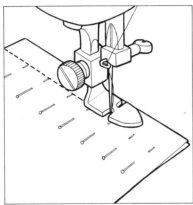

5 Machine basting with pins placed at right angles.

Basting foot or electronic control

This allows one stitch at a time to be sewn when the foot control is tapped sharply. The needle remains up and the fabric can be moved at will ready for the next stitch.

Belt loops or carriers

Fold no. 40 cotton over to form four threads. Allow 5 cm (2 in) extra length. Hold taut beneath the machine foot from front to back and work over with zig-zag stitch.

Chained loop

If the machine has a chain stitching device, sew a length of chain and secure the end by threading it through the last chain stitch.

The fabric is sandwiched between the fold and held with a straight stitch on the edge, or a zig-zag stitch to enclose the edge.

Also see *Rouleau strips*.

The binder foot

This attachment has a slotted scroll into which the binding is fed. A screw adjusts the position beneath the needle. Cut the binding to a tapered point and feed through the narrow outer slot on the scroll. Pass the fabric through the central slot and under the needle. Lower the foot and sew, holding the fabric well into the binder. Do not stretch the binding out of shape.

Turning corners

Machine to within three or four stitches of the corner and stop. Lift the foot, have the take-up lever right up and pull both bound fabric and threads to the back of the machine, just far enough to make a mitred fold on the binding. Reposition the fabric and binding, wind back the top thread and continue sewing.

Binding outside curves

Let the curved edge pass easily through the binder. Do not pull or distort it, but guide from the rear of the binder, and towards the left. Small curves should be fed in gradually, matching the sewing speed. Adjust the scroll to the left if the stitching comes off the binding edge.

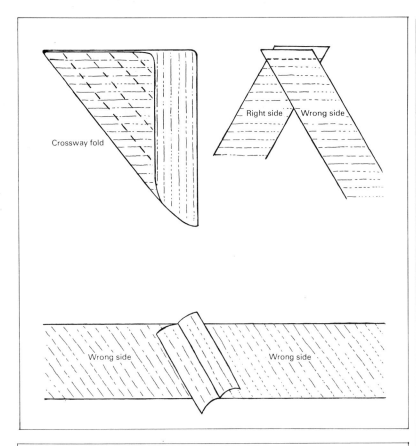

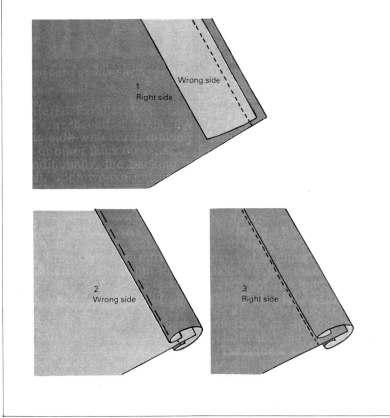

Binding inside curves

The edge needs to be held as straight as possible into the binder. Open out the curve, but not enough to distort it.

French folds

The binding is sewn on to the surface by passing the fabric beneath the binder foot, and the binding through the scroll.

Bias strips

A diagonal fold, at right angles to the grain of the fabric, is on the true cross (fig. 6). This will give maximum stretch for binding sharp curves and scallops. Jersey and stretch fabrics are better cut on the bias, which is just off the true cross.

Strips can be four times the finished binding width, depending on the fabric. Use a ruler or card template and mark with tailor's chalk.

Joining

Always join the strips on the straight grain of the fabric. The join will lie diagonally across the strip. Press out the seams and trim off the surplus.

Using the binding foot

Cut a strip 2.5cm (1in) wide to a point and feed this into the inner slit on the binder scroll. Pull the strip backwards and forwards, under the needle, until the folds are correctly positioned in the scroll. Place the fabric in the slot and machine as before.

Straight-stitch seam

Place the strip against the fabric edge, right sides together. Machine a narrow straight-

6 (Left) Joining bias strips.
7 (Bottom left) Attaching strips.

8 (Right) Braid-bound edges.
9 (Below right) Butt joining.

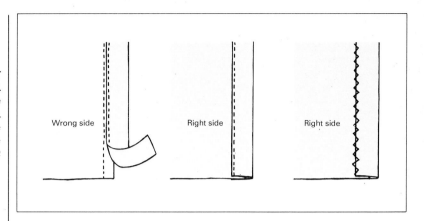

stitch seam. Turn the binding over to the wrong side, fold in the hem and slip stitch in place by hand. Alternatively, tack in place and machine from the right side, close up against the bound edge. Stitch the fabric with matching thread.

Blind Hems
See *Hems*

Braid-bound edges

Reinforce the edges to be bound by machining all round with a medium-length straight stitch, whether on single or double fabric. On the wrong side of the fabric, mark a line parallel with the edge, measuring just under half the braid width. Lay the braid up to this line and hold in position by machining on the edge with a straight stitch in matching thread. Turn the braid over to the right side and pin or tack into position. Machine the braid in place using straight stitch or a zig-zag. Ease the braid round the curves and corners (fig. 8).

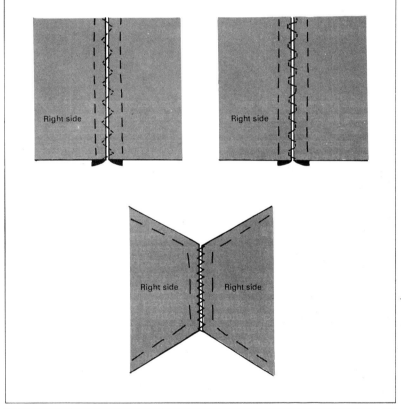

Butt joining
Seams

Prepare the seams by turning under the seam allowances. Hold by tacking stitches, machine basting or pressing well. The seam is joined on the right side, with the edge folds close up to each other, and held flat

Butt-joined patchwork waistcoat using a swing-needle machine.

beneath the machine foot. Non-fray fabrics, such as felt or interfaced fabrics, are joined without the seam allowances (fig. 9).

Stitches

Any open stitch that will bridge and hold the two pieces of fabric together is suitable. Use zig-zag, three step zig-zag, cross stitch, honeycomb, feather stitch, faggoting, bridging, closed overlock or double-action stitch.

Sewing

Any medium-weight to heavy-weight woven fabric can be sewn by holding in position with the fingers. Stretch fabrics are not suitable. For finer fabrics see *Faggoting.* If one side has a tendency to creep up on the other, use a roller foot, even-feed foot, or a black Teflon-coated foot which has a slightly matt finish and is less slippery than the ordinary metal foot.

Leather and plastic-coated fabrics

These need no turnings. Hold them together on the back with small pieces of adhesive tape at intervals. The tape is torn off afterwards. For sewing see sections on *Leather* (page 170) and *Plastic-coated fabrics* (page 177).

Patchwork

Choose simple shapes – squares, oblongs, diamonds or triangles. Prepare the fabric patches in the normal manner and tack through on to a strong paper shape. This can be left in position and torn away after machining, or the papers can be removed and the patches well pressed with the iron. Either retack round the edges; or on firmer fabrics leave them as they are. Join in the same manner as for seaming.

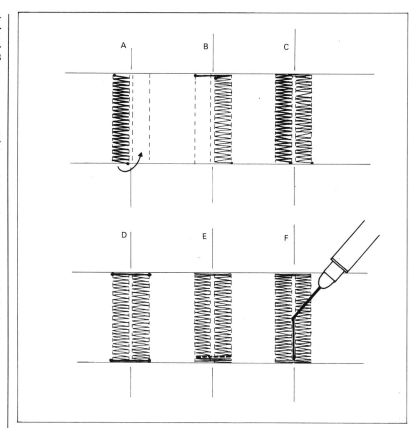

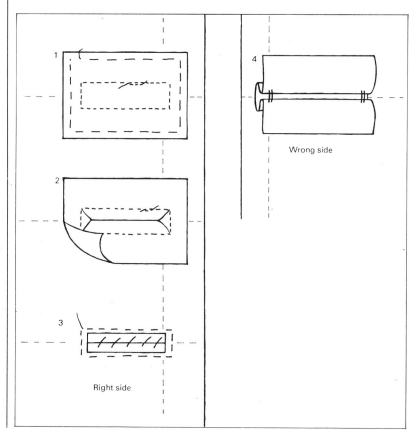

Buttonholes

Thread

Use machine embroidery thread, mercerized cotton, or fine 100% polyester.

Automatic machine

The control settings vary according to the machine. Follow the instruction book. The control is altered by the operator for each of the various steps.

Operator-controlled machines

Use a zig-zag machine. Mark the position of the buttonhole on the cloth, using a dressmaker's pencil. Set the machine to a close stitch-length and a width just under half-way. Set the needle to the left, and machine the left hand bar to the buttonhole length. Stop with the needle in the centre of the buttonhole, raise the foot and pivot the work to face the opposite way (fig. 10). Lower the foot, raise the needle, set the widest zig-zag width and sew five stitches to make a bar tack. Use the drop feed or hold back the cloth to sew in one place. Stop with the needle on the left, set the stitch width back to just under half way and sew the other buttonhole bar. Make a similar bar tack at the other end. Finish off with a few straight stitches, sewn on drop feed or across the bar tack.

Raised or corded buttonholes

Most buttonhole feet have a spur, or lug, at the back for holding in place the doubled cord to be buttonholed over. If there is no spur, hold the cord with a pin placed at right angles to the fabric edge, behind the foot. Use a thin crochet cord, or take a piece of the sewing thread, 40cm (16in) long. Fold this in half and then in half again. Use this four-strand thread as the filler cord. Hold the ends and then sew the buttonhole in the usual way. Pull up the ends afterwards and cut them off close or take them through to the wrong side.

Buttonholes on stretch fabrics

Sew round using a wide zig-zag or a stretch stitch. Work a satin stitch buttonhole on top.

Dressmaker's fabric-bound

1 Mark the buttonhole positions on to the right side of the fabric.
2 A rectangle of fabric, cut on the straight grain, measuring 2.5-3cm (1-1¼in) wider and longer than the buttonhole, is placed on the marked fabric, right sides together.
3 Machine an oblong the length of the buttonhole, and 3-4mm (⅛in), or three to four stitches, wide, depending on

10 (Top left) Six stages of making an operator-controlled buttonhole.
11 (Bottom left) Making a dressmaker's fabric-bound buttonhole.
12 (Below) Fabric-piped buttonhole.

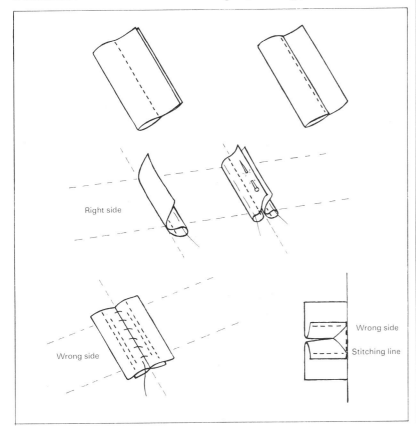

Right side

Wrong side

Wrong side

Stitching line

(Below) Detail of a cuff with fabric-bound buttonholes.

the thickness of the material A buttonhole attachment is available for the accurate sewing of these oblongs.

4   Cut along the centre line and snip into the corners.

5   Press well, easing the fabric rectangle towards the middle. Turn the edges through the slit to the wrong side. Pleat each long side of the rectangle to the middle and fold back on itself.

6   Tack the ends into position. These are later covered by the facing which is slit and turned in to reveal the buttonhole.

Dressmaker's fabric-piped

1   Mark the buttonhole positions on the right side of the fabric.

2   Cut a fabric strip, 3cm ($1\frac{1}{4}$in) wide, on the straight grain or on the cross.

3   Fold in half, lengthways, with the wrong sides facing. machine stitch 5mm ($\frac{3}{16}$in) from the folded edge for thick fabrics, and 3mm ($\frac{1}{8}$in) for lightweight ones.

4   For corded buttonholes, either thread a cord through with a bodkin or use a cording foot.

5   Cut off two strips for each buttonhole length, allowing 2cm ($\frac{3}{4}$in) extra.

6   Trim off one seam allowance to 1-2mm ($\frac{1}{16}$in). Lay the strip with the trimmed seam against the marked centre buttonhole line and tack into position. Tack the other strip facing the opposite way. Pin the large seam allowances together temporarily.

7   Machine the strips on to the fabric along the machine stitching lines first sewn on the strips.

8   Cut the marked centre-buttonhole line and into the corners, as for bound buttonholes. Pull these corner triangles out and machine at right angles flat on to the piping. Press well.

14 Casings – separate casing.

C

Casings

Used for threading elastic, cords, ribbon or tape.

Self hem

This can only be sewn on fabric

13 Casings – self hem.

that is cut to the straight grain. Plan the finished depth of the casing to be slightly wider than the elastic or cord to be inserted.

A hem allowance of 6-8mm ($\frac{1}{4}-\frac{3}{8}$in) is turned under and pressed. Turn the casing over on to the wrong side of the fabric, to the measured depth. Pin and machine baste in place. Machine the casing edge, leaving a space for inserting the elastic. This is sewn up afterwards. Make a buttonholed or faced slot for cords and ribbons.

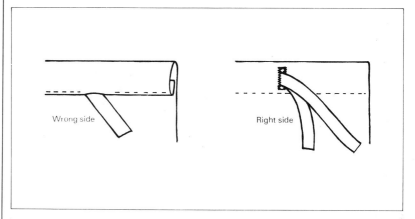

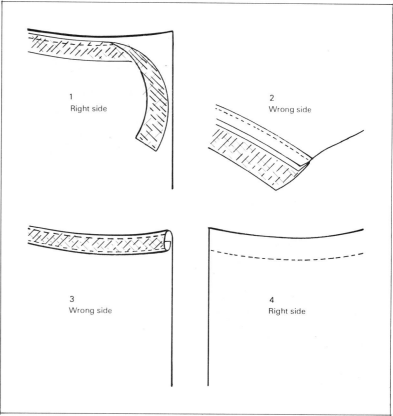

Separate casings

These can be cut from shaped fabric (for curves), crossway strips or purchased bias binding. Cut the strip the depth of the finished casing, plus two seam allowances. Join bias strips on the cross.

Place the fabric strip on top of the garment or article, right sides together, level with the fabric edges. Machine together, on the seam line. Press both seam allowances towards the casing, and stitch close to the seam line (see *Understitching*). Turn the casing over to the wrong side of the fabric, turn under the hem allowance, pin, hand tack and machine in position (fig. 14).

Circle stitching

Circle attachments

Various circle-sewing attachments are available for some makes of machine. They work on the principle of a spike set on to an adjustable scale, or movable bar. The fabric is either backed with typing copypaper, iron-on interfacing or stretched in an embroidery frame, before being centred on the spike. The fabric is rotated beneath the foot. Patterns are sewn with straight stitch or zigzag lines, automatic patterns or twin needlework. The distance between the central spike and the needle determines the radius of the circle. The minimum and maximum circle-size possible varies with the type of attachment used.

Sewing

Do not be tempted to pull or force the fabric round. The presser foot will move the fabric in conjunction with the feed teeth. It is only necessary to see that the material moves freely. Material in the frame has to be placed in position beneath the needle before the foot is put on. Use only those automatic patterns that are sewn in a forward direction. Try to join up a repeat by advancing or retarding the sewing and overlap satin stitching. Take the ends through to the back and tie off.

The circular embroidery frame

If your machine has no circle attachment, try sewing circles inside the circular embroidery frame. For framing the material, see *Darning*.

Place the frame beneath the needle first and screw the foot on afterwards. Set the machine for zig-zag or satin stitch. Place the foot right up against the right-hand inside of the frame. Sew, and guide the frame round, keeping it against the foot. A short quilting foot or appliqué foot is easier to hold in position. An unbound frame is less likely to catch on the foot edge. Try to guide round lightly, holding the frame at the rear to the right, and at the front to the left. For different-sized circles, use a different-sized frame. Use automatic patterns or twin needles. The simpler patterns are easier to control than the more complex ones.

Improvising

A second method is to hold a spiked pin or drawing pin on to the machine bed or extension table with sticky tape. Frame the fabric and centre on the spike. Place a cork on top of the spike and hold down lightly while the machine is sewing. Reposition the pin for different-sized circles.

Sewing over braid

Use a braiding foot with a hole

Decorative circles worked on a Bernina machine.

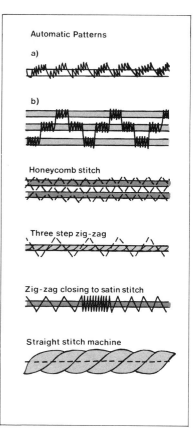

or slot to guide the thick thread beneath the needle Set the machine to a medium zig-zag stitch, or for a heavier effect a closer satin stitch. Stitch round, using any of the circle-stitching methods. To join up, stop when the beginning is reached, raise the foot and the take up lever to its highest point and pull the cord and sewing threads towards the back. Cut off and take all ends through to the wrong side, keeping the cords in line.

Making patterns

Sew circles of decreasing size, one inside the other. Alternate twin-needle sewing with automatic patterns and satin stitch lines. Overlap circles, either at random or to a repeat pattern, intersecting in the middles. Sew half circles, either within each other or facing in opposite directions. There are many possible variations. Mark circle centres on the fabric first.

Combining with other techniques

Sew circles on a double layer of organdie. Use twin needles and hemstitching needles to give various decorative effects.

(Above) Scalloped edge with eyelets worked on a Bernina.

Parts of the organdie can be cut away from behind to form a shadow work pattern. Combine circles or applied felt with heavier braid-stitched circles, some overlapping, to make a design for a wall panel.

Making scallops and festoons

Use the circle stitcher to sew a row of half circles to make a scalloped edge. First draw out the pattern, marking the centres of each circle. These are transferred to the fabric by using dressmakers' tracing paper or a tailor's tack. Work accurately for an even result. Allow for the width of the satin stitch or pattern along the sewing line. Use a shell or close automatic pattern stitch. Work on double fabric and cut away the surplus material close to the stitched edge.

Festoons are sewn by alternating half circles, first one way up, and then the other, along a clearly marked line. Mark out the pattern accurately to ensure the correct joining of the sewing line.

15 Cording secured by a variety of stitches including straight, three-step zig-zag and automatic stitch.

Cording
Straight-stitch machines

Sew fluffy threads in position under the presser foot. Anchor the end with a few stitches, then hold the thread fairly taut and up towards you. This gives greater control. Turn corners by pivoting on the lowered needle when the foot is raised. Guide the foot along the straight grain of the fabric. Take all ends through to the back and tie off.

Cable stitch
This stitch is sewn from the wrong side of the work. Wind a thick thread round the bobbin by hand. You may have to loosen the tiny screw on the tension blade. Hold a removable bobbin case over a box lid

and turn the screw one quarter turn only at a time. Some bobbin cases have a by-pass hole for thicker threads.

Sewing

Pull the thick thread up to the surface of the fabric by turning the balance wheel towards you by hand and holding on to the finer needle thread. Set a medium stitch-length and tighten the top tension slightly. The cord needs to lie flat with the finer thread drawing it into the fabric to give a rope-like or cable, appearance. The upper side is the right side.

The underbraider

This attachment for sewing braids on the straight stitch machine is both effective and easy to use. Pass the thread through a grooved metal plate fixed to the front of the needle-plate and work from the wrong side of the fabric.

Zig-zag machine

Hold cords or thick threads on to the surface of the material, using the wide-slot presser foot and the machine set for a wide zig-zag. The stitch should enclose the cord and not pierce it. Shorten the stitch length to satin stitch to cover the cord completely. The stitch-length control can be opened and closed alternately to expose more or less of the covered cord.

Cording or braiding foot

This has a groove or a hole into which the cord is threaded, to be held in position under the needle. A multiple cord foot has up to five holes to hold several threads at once. Use zig-zag stitch, satin stitch or a suitable automatic stitch. Try some of the patterns that move across from side to side. This will leave part of the cord exposed.

Turning corners

Lower the needle into the cloth on the inside swing. Pivot round when the foot is raised.

Corded pintucks   see *Twin needles.*

Corners
Straight-stitch sewing

To sew a square corner, machine down one side of the fabric, using a seam guide or a marked guide line. Stop with the needle down in the fabric at a distance from the end of the fabric equal to the seam width. Raise the foot, pivot the cloth on the needle at an angle of 90 degrees, lower the foot and sew down the new seam line (fig. 16).

Blunted corner

When sewing at an acute angle, stop just before the point is reached and sew two or three stitches across before continuing down the other side. This makes a better point for a collar when the fabric is turned to the right side (fig. 16).

Zig-zag stitch
Open corner

Mark the corner with dressmaker's pencil or a tacking stitch. Machine towards the

Turning corners with automatic stitches with lurex in the bobbin.

corner and stop one stitch-width away. Turn the balance wheel towards you by hand so that the needle pierces the corner mark on the inside swing. It may be necessary to adjust the cloth if the last stitch worked is too close or too far away. Raise the foot and pivot on the needle to face the new seam at right angles. Lower the foot and continue sewing.

Closed corner

Machine right up to the corner. Stop with the needle in the cloth on the outside swing. Pivot on the needle, lower the foot and continue sewing. The first stitch will overlap.

Satin stitch
Open corner

Work the same as for zig-zag open corner, stopping one stitch-width away from the corner. With the needle piercing the cloth on the left-hand swing, lift the foot and pivot on the needle at an angle of 90 degrees. Lower the foot and continue sewing.

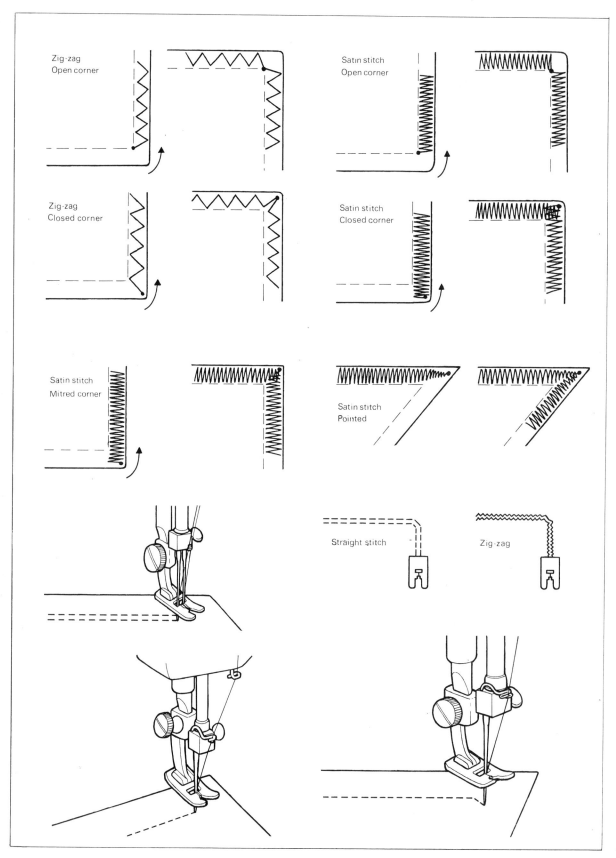

Zig-zag
Open corner

Satin stitch
Open corner

Zig-zag
Closed corner

Satin stitch
Closed corner

Satin stitch
Mitred corner

Satin stitch
Pointed

Straight stitch

Zig-zag

Closed corner

Machine right up to the corner. Stop with the needle at the right, raise the foot, pivot 90 degrees, lower the foot and continue sewing. The first few stitches will overlap.

Angled or mitred corner

Sew to the corner and stop with the needle in the cloth at the right-hand side. Lift the foot and pivot 90 degrees. Set the stitch-width control to 0, lower the foot and continue to sew slowly. Gradually open up the stitch-width control until the original width is reached (fig. 16). Continue sewing.

Pointed corner

Stop sewing about 5mm ($\frac{1}{8}$in) before you reach the corner. gradually close the stitch-width control while continuing to sew up to the corner point. Raise the foot, open up the stitch-width control to the original setting, pivot on the needle, lower the foot and continue to sew (fig. 16).

Blunt corner

Machine until you reach the middle of the corner and stop with the needle in the cloth, on the inside swing. Sew round the blunt angle, letting the needle pierce the same place each time on the inside swing. To do this, you will have to raise and lower the foot and adjust the cloth for each stitch.

Automatic pattern stitches

It is necessary to sew a trial strip of patterning in order to be able to plan the corner accurately. Use this strip to line up against the corner and mark off each pattern repeat (fig. 16). When sewing the actual pattern, the motifs may creep up on the marked lines. Retard or push forward the cloth so that the motifs meet perfectly at the corner. If a set number of motifs will not fit into the planned design, open up or close the stitch setting a little.

16 Turning corners by machine with straight stitch and zig-zag.

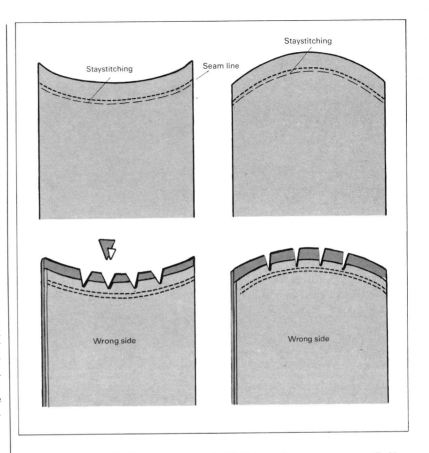

Twin and triple needles

It is not possible to pivot the cloth on multiple needles in one operation. Turn the corner in three stages. The needles are lowered so that they are only just in the cloth. Lift the presser foot and pivot the cloth on the inside needle far enough to make one stitch. Lower the foot and turn the balance wheel by hand to make the stitch. Repeat, keeping the inside needle as near as possible in the same place.

Zig-zag stitch

Stop within one stitch of the corner with the needles in the cloth on the right-hand swing. Have the needles just touching the fabric. Raise the foot and pivot to an angle of 45 degrees. Lower the foot and turn the balance wheel by hand to make one stitch into the corner on the left-hand swing. Take one more stitch to the right, pivoting and raising the foot (fig. 16). Carry on sewing.

17 Snipped, concave curve (left); slashed convex curve (right). In both cases a row of machine stay stitching along the inside of the seam line will prevent stretching.

Curves

Satin stitch curves

Mark the curve onto the fabric with dressmaker pencil, or a very hard lead pencil. It may help to sew the curve first with a straight stitch line. This is worked over. Machine in satin stitch until the curve is reached. Stop with the needle in the cloth at the inside of the curve. Raise the foot, move the cloth slightly, lower the foot and turn the balance wheel towards you by hand to make one stitch. Let the needle go back into its original position on the inner swing. Continue to sew, using this procedure to ease round the curve, the inner stitches sharing the same position every so often.

18 (Right) Automatic darning.
19 (Below right) The darning foot.
20 (Below right) Darning worked freely in a circular frame.

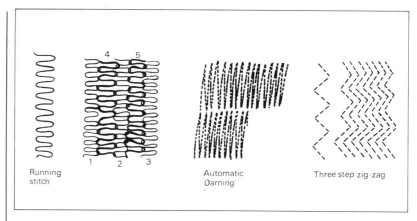

Running stitch   Automatic 'Darning'   Three step zig-zag

Slashed curves – straight-stitch seam

Before sewing two pieces of fabric together in a curved seam, machine a stay stitching line round the curve on each single piece of fabric, just outside the seam line. Pin and tack together before machining along the seam line. Sew slowly and guide the fabric lightly, holding it into the curve. For underarm seams, or crotch seams that are subject to strain or wear, use a triple seam stitch to prevent the curve from stretching. This stitch is very difficult to unpick. Fit the garment first, and machine baste before using the triple stitch.

Snipping

To make a curve lie flat, it is necessary to cut away some of the seam allowance. Trim one layer shorter than the other. On convex curves, for example, on a sleeve setting, snip down almost to the seam line, at 5mm ($\frac{1}{4}$in) intervals (fig. 17). On concave curves, for example, on a collar fitting, cut little V-shapes every 5mm ($\frac{1}{4}$in). Seams that are to be pressed out flat have equal seam allowances.

Decorative darning worked effectively on net.

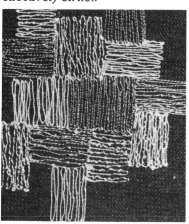

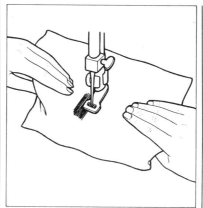

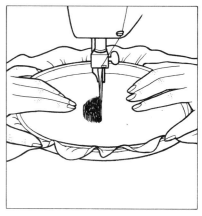

Cut and sew
see *Knitted garments*

D

Darning

Automatic darning stitch

This is available on some machines, either as a built-in utility stitch or as a drop-in pattern cam. The backwards and forwards movement is automatic. While the darning is in progress, pull the fabric slightly to the left. Use for reinforcing worn areas and fabric edges. Set the machine to straight stitch and loosen the top tension a little.

For other automatic stitches, see *Mending*.

The darning foot

These are available for most machines. Those sold in large drapery stores will fit several makes of machine. This foot is worked by a spring, sometimes activated by an arm which fits over the needlebar. As the needle rises, the foot lifts up and allows the fabric to be moved underneath. When the needle is in the cloth, the foot holds the fabric down. This gives continuous free movement in any direction.

Method
Set the machine to straight stitch. Put the feed teeth out of action. Consult your booklet under 'Darning'. The fabric to be darned is held firmly on either side, and moved backwards and forwards beneath the needle. If the fabric is fine, hold it stretched taut in the small darning hoop which may be provided with the machine.

Sewing

Use a toning thread, pull the under thread to the surface and make a few stitches to secure. Sew across the damaged area from side to side. Turn the fabric and sew across the other way (fig. 18).

Using thin wool

Wind thin wool matching the article round the bobbin. Loosen the bottom tension slightly. Use a matching unmercerized thread in the needle. Use this method on woollen cloth and fine knitwear.

Worn edges

Work in the normal way, but as soon as the edge is reached sew back quickly for a firmer edge.

Wool darning

This method is used on heavy knitwear. Some manufacturers provide a special wool darning foot. There is a slot in the foot that guides the wool automatically.
Method
Lay the wool in the slot, or thread it from the rear of the needle bar, through and down into the circular sewing area of the foot. This wool is secured with a few stitches on to the article to be mended. Lay the wool backwards and forwards closely across the hole by sewing with the foot (fig. 19). Start at the front of the hole and work towards the back. Cut off the wool. With toning thread, machine backwards and forwards in the opposite direction, to hold down the wool, using a zig-zag stitch. Hold the knitwear taut while you work.

Darning socks and sleeves

Use the free arm of the machine. Slide the outer darning ring into position under the foot. Pull the sock or sleeve area over the free arm and ring. Stretch and hold in place with the outer ring.

Working freely in a circular frame

Either use the small frame provided, or use a circular, wooden embroidery frame with a horizontally placed tightening screw. Frame the fabric by laying the wrong side of the area to be mended on top of the inner frame, placed on the table. Ease the outer frame over this, turn all over so that the fabric lies flat on the table. Pull taut and tighten the screw. Work into the frame this way up.

Setting the machine

Put the feed teeth out of action or use a cover plate. Set to straight stitch and slightly loosen the top tension. Remove the presser foot and insert the frame. Always remember to lower the presser foot lever, as this engages the tension. Bring the bottom thread to the surface of the fabric, hold the two ends and work a few stitches to secure them. Move the embroidery frame backwards and forwards beneath the needle to cover the damaged area. Keep your fingers well away, and hold the frame by the sides. Sew with an even speed. This method of free darning is used to work embroidery designs and monograms.

Decorative speed basting

The speed basting facility on some machines can be used to create a free long-and-short stitch type of embroidery. It is worked in the circular embroidery frame which is moved backwards or forwards while the needle hesitates ready for the next stitch. Remove the foot and set for darning.

Darts

This is a method of shaping and controlling fabric fullness in garment construction. The stitching line for the dart is marked on the fabric, which is then folded along the centre dart line, right sides together. Tack in position.

Sewing

Machine stitch from the wide end of the dart towards the point. Finish off by sewing a few stitches along the fold, and tie off the ends. Another method is to sew a few stitches in reverse, up the fold line (see fig. 21).

Double-ended darts

Start 1.5 cm ($\frac{1}{2}$ in) down from the top and reverse stitch up to the point. Continue as before.

Continuous thread darts

Some machines wind the bobbin through the needle which makes a continuous thread. Sew from the opposite way.

Method
Wind only a short length of thread on to the bobbin (see your machine instruction manual). With the bulk of the fabric to your left, place the fold up to the needle, at the point of the tacked dart. Lower the foot and machine to the wide end. Sew a few stitches in reverse. Rewind the bobbin for the next dart.

Decorative edges

Narrow corded edge

Mark a guide line for the finished edge and cut the fabric 2.5 cm (1 in) wider. Use a cording foot, or centre a fine cord in the middle of the presser foot. Set the machine to a medium satin stitch and a stitch-width that just encloses the cord. Machine down the seam line. Cut away the excess, close to the stitching. Set to a wider and closer satin stitch and sew over again (fig. 22).

Wide corded edge

Machine a line of wide satin stitches, leaving 2.5 cm (1 in)

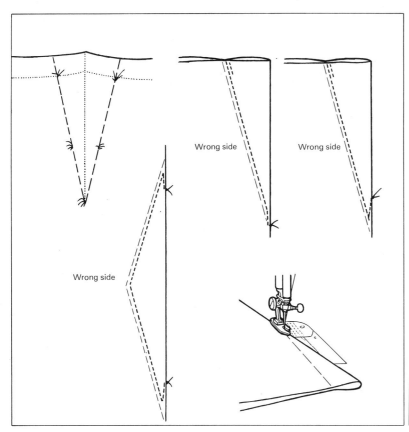

Wrong side

Wrong side

Wrong side

21 *Sewing darts by machine.*

excess fabric which is trimmed away. Lay a cord against the edge, on top of the satin stitch, held beneath the presser foot. Set to a medium width open satin stitch and sew over both the cord and the edge (fig. 22).

Corners

Stop just before the corner. Turn the balance wheel by hand to make a couple of stitches, ending with the needle down on the left hand swing. Lift the foot, pivot to 90 degrees, pulling the cord out into a little loop. Lower the foot and make another two stitches, turning the balance wheel by hand. Carry on sewing for 3-4cm (1-1½in). With the needle down, raise the foot and gently pull the cord into position (fig. 22).

22 (Below) Decorative edge stitching using a swing-needle.

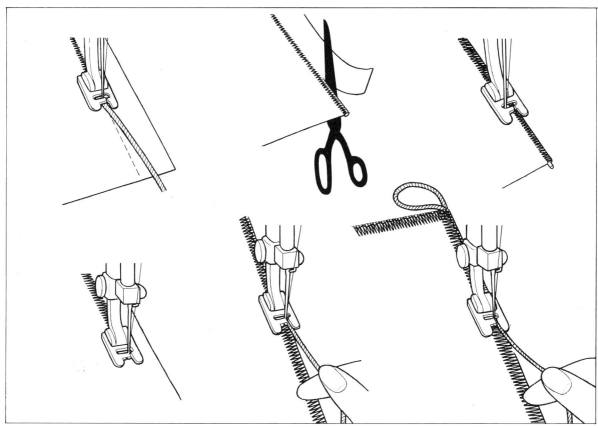

Edge stitches

Sew close satin-stitch automatic patterns on single material. The surplus fabric is cut away afterwards. The fabric must be firm or backed with iron-on interfacing. Use organdie double, with the two layers of fabric treated as one.

Utility stitches

These include the overlock, blind hem and elastic stitches. Fold under the hem and work the stitches right over on to the edge with the outward needle swing off the fabric.

Trimotion stitches

These make use of the automatic reverse feed. They look best worked just inside the edge of the turned-under hem (see *Stitches*).

Shell edges

The blind hem stitch

Use the ordinary zig-zag foot or a clear view embroidery foot. Fold under the fabric edge and place beneath the foot with the fold to the left. Machine blind stitch, so that the outer needle swing goes beyond the fabric edges. The fabric is drawn up into a shell shape. This works best on finer materials. Add a soft thread on the edge to reinforce and form a decorative contrast (fig. 22). Use elastic thread in the bobbin for a pronounced effect.

Using the roll or shell hemmer

Set the machine to a medium zig-zag. Turn the beginning of the hem under twice by hand and sew a few stitches before easing the fabric into the hemmer scroll. Keep the scroll full and continue to sew.

Decorative effects created using automatic patterns worked over braid in an attractive combination of different coloured threads including silver.

Decorative effects

Simple zig-zag machine

Using the foot

Work satin stitch lines in different widths. Alternate these lines with zig-zag stitch. Cross over the lines to form a grid. Open and close the stitch-length control while the machine is sewing. The satin stitch will open up to zig-zag and back again. These alterations are simple but by combining open and close, and wide and narrow, stitches a decorative texture can be built up.

Straight-stitch sewing

Alter the stitch-length control to make long or short stitches. Cross over lines to form a texture or combine with swing-needle sewing.

Thick threads in the bobbin

Use smooth, not too hard, threads – cotton perle, stranded embroidery thread, Gold-fingering, crochet threads or fine knitting threads. Wind the bobbin by hand and loosen the bottom tension (see Cable stitch under *Cording*). Work as a straight stitch line, zig-zag or open automatic pattern. Too close a stitch setting will cause the stitches to pile up. The wrong side of the work is the right side.

Metallic threads

Wind metallic cords round the bobbin by hand. Use the bobbin winding mechanism to wind flat lurex thread but do not pass it through the tension device. Slip a knitting needle through the reel, hold this in your hands and let it unwind without twisting the thread. Sew lurex and metallic cord on a more open satin stitch setting. Cords are better worked as straight stitch or zig-zag. Fine metallic cord is sewn from the top of the work through the needle.

Patterns over braid, ribbon or tape

This is an easy way of making your own decorative braid. It can be used for applying to fabric, binding edges or threaded through net. Choose a pattern that looks good on both sides if the ribbon is hanging free. Sew some patterns in lurex or rayon floss thread.

Shaded thread

Machine embroidery thread is available in shaded colours. Fine-shaded crochet cotton can be wound round the bobbin and worked from the wrong side. Sew automatic patterns or twin needle patterns, letting the colour changes flow in sequence. Lines of satin stitch can be worked, using the colour sequence change to form a new design. Always start with the lightest or darkest part of the thread. Alter the starting place each time to make a wave pattern or alternate blocks of light and dark.

E

Edges see *Decorative edges.*

Elastic

Sewing flat elastic on to fabric

Use a zig-zag foot or an even feed or walking foot. Either set the machine to stitch length 1.5 and the width to 3, or use the three-step zig-zag or one of the elastic stitches.

Method
Place the elastic on the fabric against the guide line. Machine without pulling; the elastic stitch will make it stretchy enough. Only stretch the elastic when you want a gathered effect (fig. 23).

Sewing on to stretch or jersey fabrics

Gather up to the required length, using long straight stitches. Pin the elastic on top and sew without stretching.

Flat elastic – covered edge

Sew the elastic flat, on to the wrong side of the fabric, 1 cm ($\frac{3}{8}$in) in from the edge, using a medium zig-zag stitch. Fold over the elastic once, flat, on to the wrong side of the fabric. Sew down on the right side with honeycomb or tricot stitch. Use for armholes, neck edges or shoulder straps of swim suits or stretchy sportswear (fig. 24).

Elastic thread

See *Shirring* under *Gathering.*

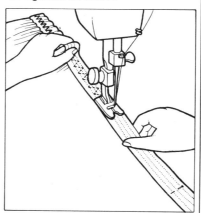

23 *Stretching elastic while sewing for a gathered effect.*

24 *(Below) Sewing flat elastic in position using a zig-zag stitch.*

Eyelets

These are used as an embroidered trimming on clothing or household linen, as a means of fastening an opening when threaded with cord, and as a form of decorative texture on embroidered panels.

Eyelet attachment

This is either fixed to, or takes the place of, the needle plate. A prong, to one side of the sewing slot, holds the fabric, which is stretched in the embroidery frame. The framed fabric, which is first pierced by an awl or cut into a triangle, is rotated on the prong, to form the eyelet.

Method
Put the feed out of action and set the stitch width according to eyelet size. Turn the frame evenly. Sew round small holes

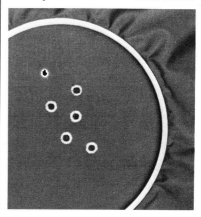

(Above) Eyelets worked on an Elna.

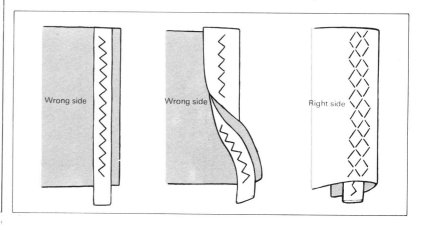

twice, and larger holes three times, finishing off with a few straight stitches to lock the thread.

Decorative eyelets

On certain machines the eyelet attachment can be used in conjunction with automatic pattern stitches. This produces circular flower designs.

Oval eyelets
Some automatic buttonhole attachments will make an oval eyelet. Cut the central fabric out afterwards.

F

Faggoting

A decorative stitch is used to hold two turned under pieces of fabric together with a small gap in-between. Fabrics with a tendency to fray are neatened along the seam edges first.

Stitches

Use wide trimotion stitches – three-step zig-zag, faggoting, feather, cross, honeycomb, lingerie or double-action stitch or a bridging stitch.

25 Faggoting.

Method
Either hold the fabric apart with the fingers, so that the needle catches on to the fabric at either side, or tack the turned-under fabric edges 2 mm ($\frac{1}{8}$ in) apart on to typing copy paper. Tear away gently afterwards, removing any awkward bits with tweezers. Use a transparent foot for easier sewing.

Fastenings – zig-zag machine

Buttons

Use a button sewing foot or the short quilting foot.

Method
Place the button in position on the cloth and centre under the button sewing foot. Turning the balance wheel by hand, let the left-hand swing of the needle slip into the left hand hole. Set the stitch width so that the needle slips into the right-hand hole on the right-hand swing. Lower the feed teeth or set the stitch length at 0. Make five or six stitches before setting the stitch width at 0 to make a few fastening-off stitches.

Four-hole button

Position and sew the rear set of holes first. Without cutting off the thread, raise the foot just enough to move the button towards the back, with the front holes aligned under the needle. Sew as before.

Shanked button

Some button sewing feet have a pin or adjustable flange to form the shank. To make a short shank, using a plain button sewing foot, place a needle on top of the button and sew over this. To make a large shank, place a matchstick beneath the button to raise it up. Leave long thread ends, cut off and thread these through a short hand-sewing needle. Wind round to make the shank, and fasten off by hand.

26 (Below) Sewing on a button by machine using a button sewing foot.

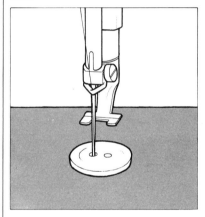

27 (Below) Raising the thread to make a shank.

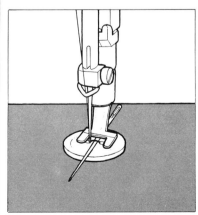

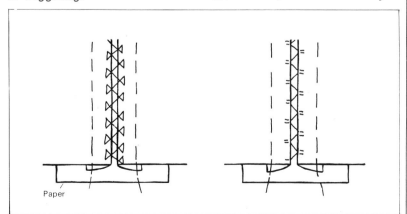

Paper

Hooks and eyes and snap fasteners

These are sewn on in the same way. Do not cut off threads until all the holes in one fastener are completed. Finish off with a few stitches at width-setting 0.

Feather stitching

A decorative stitch worked under the foot of a zig-zag machine, in conjunction with the embroidery frame.

Method
Frame the fabric (see *Darning*). Set the machine for satin stitch, and stitch-width from 2 to maximum. Have the feed teeth up. Remove the foot, place the framed fabric under the needle and replace the foot. Machine at an even speed, and at the same time turn the frame from side to side (like the steering wheel of a car). It may help to count up to three for each turn. Do not go over lines already sewn, but keep the feathery stitch open. Use a shaded, thread, or two colours in twin needles at maximum width setting 2.5 cm ($2\frac{1}{2}$ in).

Felling

Joining two pieces of fabric together with a flat seam, using the narrow hemmer or the felling foot, is also called lap hemming. Use on fine to medium woven fabrics.

Felling foot

Stage 1 Lay the fabric with the right sides together, the under layer protruding about 5mm ($\frac{1}{4}$ in) beyond the upper layer. Place the fabric in the felling foot so that only the bottom

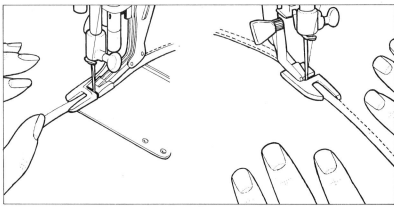

layer folds over, to form a ridged seam (fig. 28).
Stage 2 With the fabric opened out flat, insert the ridged seam into the felling foot, which turns it and sews into a narrow, flat seam. Hold the fabric out taut both sides.

Narrow hemmer foot

Stage 1 Place the two layers of fabric with the bottom layer protruding 5mm ($\frac{1}{4}$ in). Sew a narrow seam, using the inside of the scroll edge as a guide. If you prefer, sew this seam 6mm ($\frac{5}{16}$ in) from the top edge, using the straight stitch presser foot.
Stage 2 With the fabric opened out flat, turn under the seam allowance by hand, twice, to form a narrow hem. Place under the hemmer foot and sew a few stiches, stopping with the needle in the cloth. Raise the foot and ease the fabric into the narrow hemmer scroll. Lower the foot and sew, keeping the scroll full. Hold the fabric out taut while the seam is being sewn.

Felt

How to sew

A felted cloth is formed from compressed short fibre lengths. This will not stand up to washing. Use a longer stitch length, a wider stitch width and avoid sewing too close to edges. Use forward sewing

28 (Above) Two stages of machine sewing a felled seam with a felling foot. Bottom layer of fabric is folded over (left); and opened flat (right).

overlocking or edging stitches. Too much reverse sewing may destroy the felt.

Automatic patterns

Set on a not too close satin stitch and loosen the top tension. Alternatively, sew with thick threads in the bobbin and tighten the top tension. The under side will be the right side. Use rayon floss thread, crochet threads or flat lurex. Fine metallic cord tends to sink into the felt.

Fine fabrics

Natural woven

Cotton, linen, silk, fine wool.

Needles
Use a fine needle no. 70-80 (11-12), either a perfect stitch or a blue scarfed needle. These needles have a longer scarfe, or indentation on the needle eye, which gives a better stitch formation. Try using a fine ballpoint needle on a crêpe or fine seersucker weave.

Thread
Use a fine silk, mercerized cotton no. 50 or 60, or fine 100% polyester.

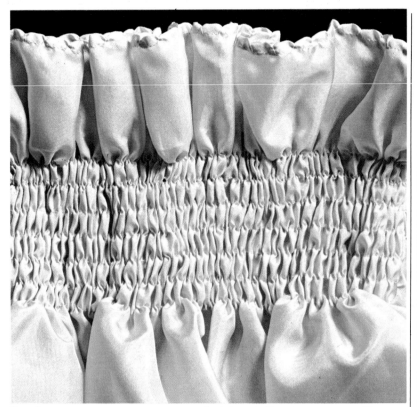

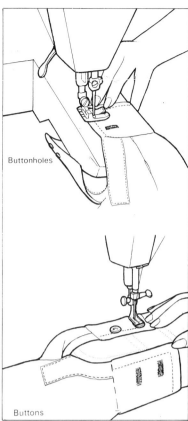

(Above) Shirring on pure silk.

Buttonholes

Buttons

29 Using a free-arm machine to work buttonholes (top) and buttons (above). A free arm allows you to sew sleeves and cuffs.

Sewing

The machine teeth may damage some fine fabrics. Place a piece of tissue paper beneath the fabric and the teeth. This tears away easily from the stitching line afterwards. The pressure adjustment on modern machines seldom needs alteration, but older machines may need some adjustment. If the cloth puckers, loosen the pressure. If it slips sideways, tighten it.

Use an even feed or a roller foot on slippery fabrics.

Stitching

Use a medium-to-short straight stitch for seams and loosen the top tension slightly. Use the straight stitch needleplate with the small round hole. Fine fabric could be forced down the wide zig-zag slot. Keep the feed teeth and needleplate free from fluff and be prepared to change the needle more often.

Use an overedge foot when sewing and neatening seam edges. This has a little bar which holds the fabric flat while the neatening stitch is sewn. A small space allows the com-pleted stitches to slide off. On sheer fabrics, turn up garment hems double and use a French seam to enclose all edges. See *Seams.*

Choose forward sewing overedge or overlock stitches, rather than those that use the reverse feed action.

Synthetics woven

Use a perfect stitch, or a fine ballpoint needle, and 100% polyester thread. A teflon-coated or glide foot may help on 'sticky' fabrics.

Free arm sewing

The free arm machine converts from flat bed sewing by re-moval of the extension table, the lowering of the flaps or by raising the machine above the sewing bed to reveal the narrow free arm. The width of the free arm varies from machine to machine.

Uses

The free arm is used for sewing in narrow or restricted places, for cuffs, sleeve openings, armholes, or trouser legs. The narrower the free arm, the better it is for this type of work, especially when sewing children's garments.

Applied work

Use the free arm for applying tapes, ribbons and sleeve badges and for sewing patches on to sleeve elbows, and trouser knees.

Bar tacks

These help to prevent strain on pocket tops, placket openings and belt bars.

Slip the made-up or purchased garment over the free arm and position for the bar tack. Set for darning or set the stitch length to 0. Set the stitch width from 3 to maximum and sew the bar tack in one place. A machine that has full needle penetration power will cope easily with thick fabrics and jeans. On other machines, turn the balance wheel by hand.

Buttons and buttonholes

Use the free arm to position narrow cuff openings. This is much easier than trying to sew flat.

Darning and mending

The free arm allows easy positioning of the worn area, especially inside narrow sleeves for elbow darns.

Edges

Use the free arm to sew elastic on to waistbands or pantie edges. Turn up sleeve hems and use for topstitching on set-in sleeves and cuffs.

French seams see
Seams.

Frills see *Gathering* and *Ruffles.*

Fringes

Fringing foot or tailor tacking foot

This foot can be used on a close setting for fringing, or on an open setting for tailor tacking (see *Tailor tacks*).

A small vertical blade, placed near the centre of the foot at right angles to the zig-zag slot, raises the stitch to form a loop. This loop can only be as tall as the blade is high, but the spacing of the loops is altered by increasing or decreasing the stitch length.

Method
Set the stitch width at 2 or just under. The needle must clear the blade both sides. Loosen the top tension or re-route the upper thread according to the machine instructions. Use a fine machine embroidery thread or mercerized cotton. Thread two colours into a larger needle and use as one, or work with shaded thread.

Decorative effect created by using shaded thread worked with a tailor tacking foot.

Straight line fringe

Set to a close satin stitch and machine the fringe against a guide line. To secure, lay the fringe to one side and hold down on the edge with a small straight stitch or a triple straight stitch. Leave the fringe looped or cut. Rows sewn 1 cm ($\frac{3}{8}$in) apart will form a pile fabric.

Circles

Mark out a circle on the fabric and sew the fringing, starting from the outside and spiralling inwards. The fringing can overlap the previous row for a close pile effect, or the rows may be

30 Decorative effects made by withdrawing threads from even-weave linen or linen-type fabric. Mark the straight of grain with tailor's chalk or withdraw a single thread to act as a marker before you begin stitching by machine.

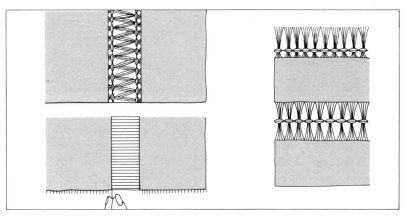

sewn apart. Back with iron-on interfacing to hold the loops in place.

Small decorative thread fringe

Set the machine to the widest stitch-width and loosen the top tension.
1   Machine a row of fairly close zig-zag stitches.
2   Sew a row of triple straight stitches down one edge to secure the stitches.
3   Turn to the wrong side and slit the stitches at the back with a seam-ripper or a pair of fine scissors. Pull out the cut threads.
4   The upper stitches are lifted up and drawn out into a fringe.

Sew on a satin stitch setting for a close fringe or sew some layers of zig-zag on top of each other. Use one of the close-setting automatic pattern stitches for a waved edge fringe of unequal length.

Loosen the top tension to make a longer fringe. Sew with thick threads in the bobbin. The wrong side of the work will be the right side, so tighten the top tension. Hold with the triple stitch as before.

Withdrawn thread fringe

This fringe is worked on even weave linen, or linen-type fabric, for table mats and coarse fringe edges on soft furnishings.

Method 1
Mark the fabric along the straight grain line with tailor's chalk or withdraw a single thread the depth of the finished fringe plus 1 cm ($\frac{3}{8}$in). Set the machine to a medium zig-zag width and machine along the marked line, keeping exactly to the straight grain of the fabric. Let the needle take in not less than three rows of fabric threads. Sew over a cord for a firmer line (fig. 30).

Withdrawing the threads
Start at the middle of a row, on the outside, and withdraw the threads one at a time until the zig-zag row is reached. Trim the finished fringe.

Method 2
Mark the fringe line as before. Withdraw the threads, leaving a few on the fabric edge. Set the machine for triple straight stitch, and sew along the fringe against the guide line. This stitch will draw the fringe threads into groups. Take out the remaining threads and trim the fringe (fig. 30).

Drawn thread work
Withdraw threads from within the fabric. Use the triple straight stitch to hold the threads in groups in the middle or on both sides (fig. 30).

Fur

Hand-sewn fur is held together with an oversewing stitch on the edges. This can be sewn by machine, but do not attempt to sew old or brittle fur.

Method
Use 100% polyester or silk thread. Choose a spear-pointed leather needle to suit the thickness of the backing skin, not the fur. Always cut fur from the skin side with a sharp blade, through the skin only, not through the fur. Place the fur

sides inwards and match the cut skin edges. Set the machine to a medium width and length zig-zag stitch and machine along the edge so that the left-hand needle swing pierces the skin, and the right-hand swing goes over and encloses the edge. Tie off the thread ends and open out flat. The oversewing stitch will lie straight across the fur and form a criss-cross on the back. Tease out the fur with a blunt needle and brush downwards.

Fur fabric

This is backed with a knitted type fabric, sometimes with a stiffening added.

Toys and patchwork

Mark pattern shapes on the back of the fabric. Cut out with sharp, pointed scissors, snipping into the backing only, not through the synthetic fur.

Sewing
Use a ball-pointed needle and 100% polyester thread. Place the cut edges together and oversew with a medium zig-zag stitch or use one of the overcasting or overedging stitches.

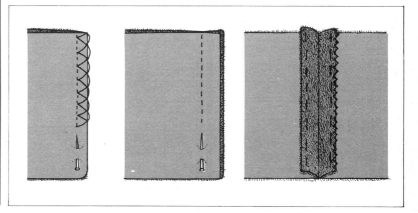

31 Seaming fur fabric with an overlocked edge (far left) or a straight stitch seam which is then neatened with zig-zag.

Many of these use the automatic reverse feed and will sew together and neaten at the same time.

Garment sewing

Cut out the marked pattern shapes with a pair of sharp scissors through the backing only. Leave the full 2cm ($\frac{7}{8}$in) seam allowance. Use a ball-pointed needle, size 90-100 (14-16) and 100% polyester thread. Use an even feed foot, walking foot, roller foot, or the zig-zag sewing foot.

Short pile fake fur

Use glass-headed pins to hold the seams together, not tacking stitches. Pin along the marked seam line and sew in the direction of the pile or nap. Use a medium to long straight stitch. Open out the seam on the wrong side and trim away the excess fur with sharp scissors. Neaten the seam edges with zig-zag

stitch or one of the overedging stitches. Tack the seam edges to the backing by hand or use the blind hemmer (see *Hems*).

Darts
Fold the half, right sides together. Machine the seam, slit down the fold, open out flat and neaten as above.

Long pile fake fur

Trim to a 5mm ($\frac{1}{4}$in) seam allowance. Do not pin, but hold together with paper-clips at right angles to the edges. Tuck in any stray fur fibres. Machine down the edge with a medium zig-zag stitch or one of the overedging stitches.

Darts
Mark the sewing lines on the back. Cut out the dart, leaving the 5mm ($\frac{1}{4}$in) seam allowance. Fold, fur sides facing and machine together, with zig-zag or overedge stitch.

G

Gathering

With a long straight stitch

Set to maximum length and loosen the top tension. Thread the machine with 100% polyester or mercerized cotton no. 40, with a contrasting colour in the bobbin. Sew 2mm ($\frac{1}{8}$in) above the marked gathering line, within the seam allowance. Sew a second row of stitches, starting from the same end, parallel with the first and 2mm ($\frac{1}{8}$in) below the marked gathering line. Leave long thread ends and knot them firmly (fig. 34).

Pulling up the threads

Pull up both of the contrasting colour bottom threads together. Do not pull the top threads – the stitches will lock and the threads may break. Ease the gathers along as you go, a little at a time. Divide a very long piece of gathering into separate sections. Place a pin at right angles to the gathers, at the row end, and wind the spare thread round this in a figure of eight, to secure while the gathering is adjusted.

Sewing gathered fabric on to a flat piece

Lay the sewn but ungathered fabric on top of the flat piece. Hold at either end with a pin placed at right angles to the seam. Match all pattern marks, fabric centres and any seam positions. Place a pin at right angles in each of these positions and at intervals in between (fig. 35). Pull up the gathers between the pins, easing gently along the threads. Tack in place, before machining between the two gathering lines with a medium length straight stitch. Machine slowly and adjust the gathers as they reach the foot. When all is finished, remove the gathering threads.

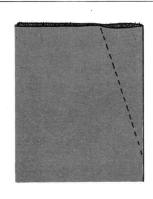
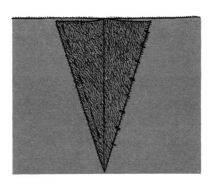

32 (Above) Stitching and neatening a dart sewn by machine on short-pile fur fabric.

33 (Below) Cutting out, then stitching and neatening a dart sewn on long-pile fur fabric.

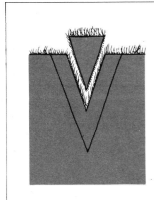

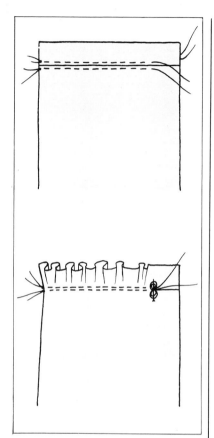

34 *Gathering with long straight stitch then pulling up threads and securing round a pin.*

Using the gathering foot

This short-fronted straight stitch foot allows the fabric to build up slightly beneath to form even gathers, which are locked in position. The amount of gathering is determined by the stitch-length. A long stitch will make tighter gathers, a smaller stitch will give less gathers. To increase the gathers slightly, increase the top tension.

Sewing

Make sure that the top thread is taken through the hole in the foot and that both threads are to the back of the machine. Make test samples on the fabric in use, to determine the best machine setting for the gathers and the amount of extra fabric needed to complete a measured piece. The finer the fabric, the more pronounced the gathers will be.

Measuring
Method 1

Cut a 10cm (4in) piece off the gathered test strip, keeping to the straight grain of the fabric. Measure the bottom, ungathered side. If this were 20cm (8in) you would need exactly twice the amount of fabric to make the gathers.

Method 2

Measure a length of ungathered fabric strip. Adjust the stitch length and tension controls to give the correct amount of gathers. Make a note of the gathered measurement and see how many times this goes into the length of the finished article.

Applying to fabric using the slotted gathering foot

Place the fabric to be gathered under the foot and feed the edge of the flat fabric into the slot. To keep the flat piece of fabric held in the slot, place the left hand beneath, to guide the gathered fabric, and the right hand on top to hold the flat fabric in towards the right. The

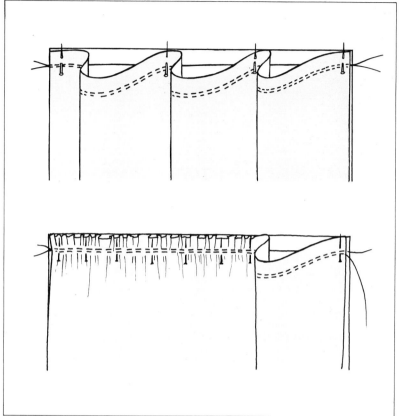

35 *Sewing gathered fabric on to a flat piece, securing with pins at regular intervals.*

upper piece of fabric can be pulled slightly to obtain tighter gathers.

Gathering with the ruffler attachment
see *Ruffles*

Gathering over perle thread

Use the zig-zag foot, braiding foot or the cording foot with a hole for the thread.

Method

Set the machine to zig-zag width, 2.5cm (2½in), and a medium stitch length. Loosen the top tension slightly. Use a thin cord, or perle thread no. 8. Now place the cord under the foot and secure with a few straight stitches before holding

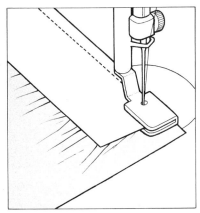

36 *Using a slotted gathering foot.*

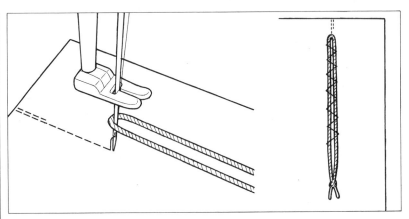

37 *Gathering over elastic thread.*

the cord on to the gathering line by enclosing with the zig-zag stitches. Sew two rows, 5mm (¼in) apart.

Braiding foot
The cord is placed in the braider slot, or threaded through the hole in the cording foot, and is brought to the back of the machine. Zig-zag over the cord.

Pulling up the threads
These are not pulled up until after the zig-zag stitches are completed. Hold both cords at once and gather up the material. These cords can be left in or removed after the gathering has been sewn into position. Snip the securing stitches and pull by holding the threads.

Gathering over elastic thread

Use the zig-zag foot or a braider foot with an open groove. The fine elastic thread is used double and is sewn on to the wrong side of the fabric.

Method 1
Sew a few straight stitches at the beginning of the marked seam. Stop with the needle in the cloth and raise the foot. Pass single elastic round the needle and hold the two long, double ends level. Knot them at the end (fig. 37). Lower the foot and sew a couple of stitches to secure the elastic before setting the ma-

chine to a medium zig-zag stitch. Lay the double elastic threads into the groove between the presser foot, or slip them under the braiding foot groove. Hold the elastic with a slight tension and zig-zag over. The stitches go either side and must not pierce the elastic. The elastic threads are pulled up afterwards to give the required amount of gathering. The loose ends are knotted and fastened off securely with hand stitches.

Method 2
Thread single elastic thread through the hole in the cording foot, or into the braiding foot groove. Pull to the back of the foot and knot the end and secure with a few straight stitches before setting to zig-zag and sewing as before.

Important Pull the fabric straight while you are sewing second and subsequent rows.

Decorative patterns over elastic threads
Use the double elastic thread method. It is essential that the elastic threads should lie exactly in the middle of the pattern, which is sewn over them. The stitches should not pierce the elastic. Sometimes a braiding foot will have the groove to one side of the central position. Use the presser foot instead.

Method
Sew from the wrong side of the fabric. Choose one of the open automatic reverse feed pattern

stitches, like cross-stitch or honeycomb. Set to the longest stitch-length and the widest width, after the initial straight stitches to secure the elastic.

Sewing
Hold the double thread with a slight tension. The elastic is pulled up afterwards to achieve the amount of gathering required. Pull the fabric straight while you are sewing the second or any subsequent rows. This method will need backing with similar fabric, sewn on by hand. This will prevent distortion of the decorative stitching, which will be on the right side. Use on pocket tops, gathered yokes or sleeve cuffs.

Elastic thread in the bobbin

The elastic thread is wound round the bobbin under a slight but constant tension. This is important for even results. It can be wound on by hand, or the machine bobbin winding mechanism may be used. Both work equally well. Loosen the bottom tension. If the bobbin case is removable, it is worth buying a separate one for working with thick threads of all kinds. The needle thread should match the fabric.

Sewing
The work is sewn from the right side. Set the machine to straight stitch. A longer stitch will make fuller gathers. Tighten the top tension for even closer gathers.

Always stretch the fabric when sewing the second or any subsequent rows. Knot all elastic ends together and fasten off with hand-sewn backstitches.

Decorative stitches

Use a zig-zag stitch, blind hem stitch or one of the other more open, decorative or utility stitches. Do not use those stitches that sew patterns in conjunction with the reverse feed. Set a medium to long stitch-length. Some line patterns distort when opened up, and are ineffective. Lines of wide zig-zag give a ribbed effect to the gathers. Blind hem stitch, worked in rows, produces a kind of shirred smocking. The decorative stitch method works best on finer fabrics and synthetic jersey.

Decorative shell edge

Use a fine, stretch jersey fabric. Turn under the edge and sew over with blind stitch, letting the outer needle swing go right over the folded edge. This gathers up to form a pronounced shell edge.

Gauging

This is a decorative method of controlling fabric fullness by sewing parallel rows of gathering stitch, using either the long straight stitch method, or zig-zag stitch over perle thread. The threads are all pulled up to an even length after the machining is completed. Tie off and secure all the thread ends with a few hand back-stitches. This method will need backing with lining or similar fabric since the gathers can move. The gauging can be caught to the backing at intervals if necessary (fig. 38).

Using the gathering foot

This works well on fine fabrics. Use the machine foot guide to

38 Gauging, a decorative method of controlling fabric fullness by sewing parallel rows of gathering using zig-zag over perle thread.

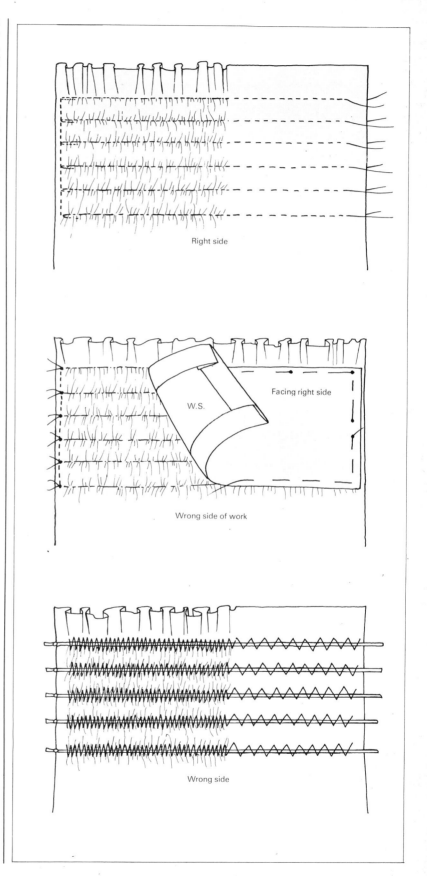

Right side

W.S.

Facing right side

Wrong side of work

Wrong side

A delicate piece of shirring worked on fine blue silk, this example on a Pfaff.

keep the rows parallel. The rows of stitching are firm and do not need backing.

Shirring

The fabric fullness is controlled by sewing parallel rows of stitching, using either of the elastic thread methods. The gathering stretches and is used on waistbands, necklines or cuffs.

Sewing
Use the presser foot as a guide for sewing the additional rows and stretch the fabric while sewing after the first row. Use straight stitch, zig-zag or blind hem stitch, or one of the decorative stitches sewn over the elastic thread. Tie off and fasten all ends securely. Hold the finished shirred fabric in steam from a boiling kettle for a brief period in order to shrink the elastic thread.

Waffling

Even rows of gauging or shirring are sewn at right angles to cross each other and form a grid or waffle pattern.

Waffled gauging

Use 100% polyester thread. Rule the pattern lines on the right side of the fabric with dressmaker's pencil, both ways. Draw the lines between 1-2cm apart ($\frac{3}{8}$-$\frac{1}{4}$in).

Straight-stitch method
Start 1cm ($\frac{3}{8}$in) in from the fabric edge and reverse stitch to secure the threads at the beginning. At the line end, leave long threads for pulling up the gathers. Sew all the rows of

Waffling worked with a quilting foot and guide on the Elna.

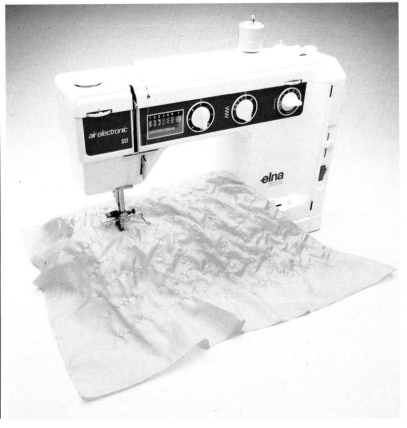

stitching one way first, always starting from the same end, and then sew the rows across the other way. Pull up all the bobbin threads one way first, easing the gathers along, and then pull them up the other way. Secure all ends.

Gathering foot
Work on fine fabric. This may be impossible to mark with guidelines, so use the presser foot width as a guide.

Zig-zag over perle thread
Work the lines further apart, on the wrong side of the fabric. Use this method for thicker fabrics, including velvet. Pull up the gathers afterwards.

Waffled shirring

Use the straight stitch method with the elastic thread wound round the bobbin. This is easier to work than the method sewn over elastic thread.

Sewing
Allow for wider spaces between the rows. The elastic threads make fuller gathers. Secure all threads at the beginning of the rows. Sew all lines one way, stretching the fabric for every row after the first. When sewing across the other way, it is necessary to stretch the fabric both ways at once. Sew slowly, a little at a time, and fasten off all the ends.

Steam the waffled fabric afterwards, to shrink the elastic threads. Always make up a waffled fabric first and lay the paper pattern for the article in question on top. Put a weight in the middle, pin the edges and cut out.

Elastic thread – sewing in circles

Wind the elastic thread round the bobbin. Place the material in a circular embroidery frame and set for darning (see Darning). The upper side of the fabric is the right side. Pull the bottom elastic thread through to the surface, lower the needle and the presser foot lever and sew round in circles, keeping an even speed. If the fabric is not tightly framed, the stitches may not catch.

Darning foot
This can be used on its own on thicker fabrics, or in conjunction with the embroidery frame to make a better stitch. Do not sew the circles too small. The fabric will gather up strongly when it is released. Sew as a continuous line of overlapping loops.

H

Headings for curtains

Plain

Mark the fold line at the curtain top. Cut a piece of iron-on interfacing 5 cm (2 in) wide and line up against the fold line on the wrong side of the fabric. Iron in position. Turn over the top and machine in place. Add curtain rings (fig. 39).

Gathered

Turn over the top. Sew two rows of machine gathering stitches one above, and one below, the turned-over edge. Pull up the gathers and lay the flat tape centrally over the join. Pin, tack and machine in place. The gathering threads are removed afterwards (fig. 39).

Plain pleated

Mark the pleat positions. Machine together at right angles to the hem on the right side. Either press flat or leave as cartridge pleats.

Rufflette tape

Cut the tape 8 cm (3¼ in) longer than the curtain width. Release one pair of cord ends and tie them into a knot. Turn over the curtain fabric top, and centre the tape over the cut edge. Turn the tape ends under, pin in position and machine along top, bottom and side edges, without catching the cord ends. These are pulled up and knotted afterwards.

Stand-up heading – pencil pleats

Turn over the curtain top 2.5 cm (1 in). Tack in position. Place the special tape almost up to the top with the slots for the long pleat hooks at the bottom. If the tape has three cords, knot all three together at one end. Turn under the tape ends and machine close to all edges.

Hems

Plain hems

Turn the fabric under twice, hand tack and pin baste, or machine baste, before sewing down with straight stitches or zig-zag stitch. For accurate sewing use a seam guide, held or clipped on to the machine bed.

Edge stitcher
A single turned under hem is held into one of the guide slots in this straight stitch machine attachment.

The adjustable hemmer
This is another straight stitch machine attachment. Use for straight hems on household linen. The fabric is inserted into the adjustable slide, which keeps it folded to the correct width.

The narrow hemmer
This works best on fine fabrics.

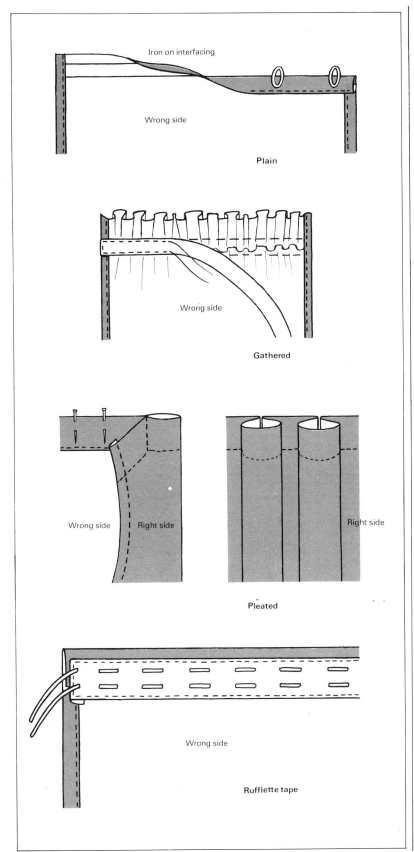

Iron on interfacing

Wrong side

Plain

Wrong side

Gathered

Wrong side   Right side

Right side

Pleated

Wrong side

Rufflette tape

39 Four methods of sewing headings for curtains.

Fold under twice by hand to make a narrow 3mm ($\frac{1}{8}$in) hem. Set the machine to straight stitch and sew a few stitches, stopping with the needle in the hem. Raise the foot and slide the hem edge into the scroll. Lower the foot and sew, holding the fabric into the scroll. A wide-slot narrow hemmer is available for zig-zag machines.

Alternative method
Clip off the corner of the fabric. Pass a double thread through the top edge and hold this, to slip the fabric into the scroll from left to right. Hold taut and ease the fabric backwards until it is in position. Lower the foot, and turn the balance wheel by hand for the first few stitches.

Narrow hemmer corner
Trim the 3mm ($\frac{1}{8}$in) seam allowance off the corner. Hem the first side to the end. Place a double thread in the corner and use this to slide the fabric through the scroll ready to hem the second side (fig. 40).

Blind hemmer – zig-zag machine

The blind hemmer guide is incorporated with the blind hemmer foot, or a separate

(Below) Sample showing hemstitching with a decorative scalloped edge.

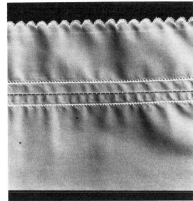

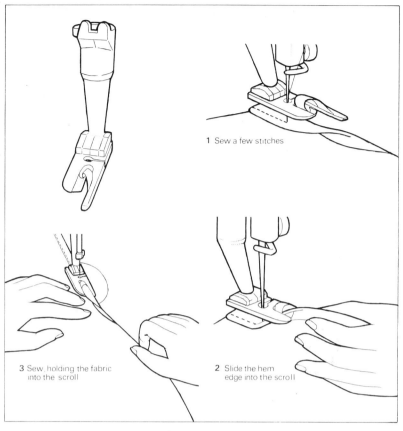

40 *Using the narrow hemmer foot on the machine.*

guide is used with the zig-zag presser foot. If the machine does not have a blind hem stitch, which sews several straight stitches followed by a wide zig-zag, use a wide zig-zag on a long stitch setting.

Sewing

Prepare the hem by neatening the raw edges on thick fabrics, or by turning under 1 cm ($\frac{3}{8}$ in) on finer fabrics. Turn the hem up and tack 1 cm ($\frac{3}{8}$ in) from the top edge on thick fabrics and 5 mm ($\frac{1}{4}$ in) on finer fabrics (fig. 41). With the bulk of the fabric to the left, place under the foot so that the tacked fold fits into the guide and the needle only just pierces the fabric on the left-hand swing.

Stretch fabrics

There is a special blind hem stitch which uses small zig-zag stitches alternated with the large one.

Curved hems

With slight fullness

Turn up the hem to the measured length. Tack along this line by hand. Trim the hem allowance to the correct width and machine two rows of long gathering stitches along the upper edge. Pull up the threads to the correct length, easing the gathers along.

Shaped hems

Cut a second strip of fabric to the hem shape. Lay the right sides together, matching edges and seam along the bottom. Clip the curves, turn up and slip stitch in place by hand.

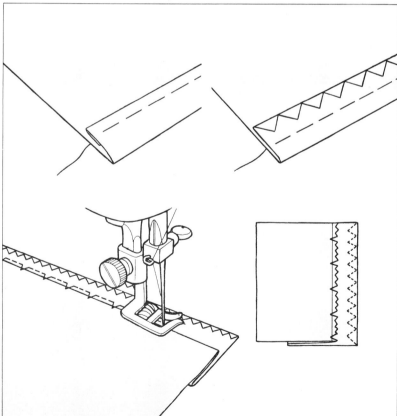

41 *Sewing and finishing hems with the blind hemmer foot.*

A lettuce hem being stitched on the Elna with a wide zig-zag on very fine, sheer fabric.

Narrow hemmer

Machine a line of straight stitches 3mm ($\frac{1}{8}$in) from the fabric edge first, before using the hemmer foot.

Lettuce hem

This method works best on fine, stretch jersey fabrics – natural or synthetic – or on fine knitteds

Method

Use 100% polyester thread and set the machine to a wide zig-zag stitch. Alternatively, use one of the overedging stitches and the overedging foot. Allow for a 5mm ($\frac{1}{4}$in) hem, which is turned up and sewn as you go. With the wrong side of the fabric facing, fold up the hem once. Place under the foot and sew a few stitches, turning the balance wheel by hand. Let the needle pierce both layers of fabric on the left-hand swing, and into, or just over, the fold (if you use the overedge foot), on the right-hand swing. Hold the fabric taut with one hand behind, and one hand in front of, the presser foot. The more the fabric is stretched, the greater the rippled effect.

Fine Fabrics. Narrow decorative hem

Turn under a single 1cm ($\frac{3}{8}$in) hem on to the wrong side. Set the machine to zig-zag 1.5-2cm ($\frac{5}{8}-\frac{3}{4}$in), and stitch-length less than 1cm ($\frac{3}{8}$in). Sew zig-zag stitch over the edge. Trim the surplus hem from the back, using the tips of the scissors only.

Hem finishes

Bound see *Bias binding.*

Overlocked see *Overcasting.*

Shell edges see *Decorative edges.*

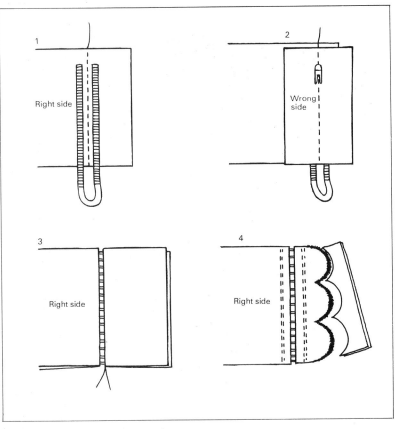

Hemstitcher

This is a flat metal fork used for making a decorative hemstitch to join together two separate folds of fabric.

Decorative hem

Cut the main fabric to the correct length. Crease a guide line 5cm (2in) from the lower edge. Cut a strip of similar fabric, 10cm (4in) wide. Fold in half lengthways and make a crease line down the middle.

Method

Place the main fabric, right side up, under the machine presser foot, lining it up with the guide line. Place the hemstitcher fork on top of the guide line, open ends towards the needle. Position the fabric strip on top, wrong side up, lining up the crease with the gap in the middle of the hemstitcher. Do this by feel, using a thumbnail or a screwdriver. Set the machine for the longest straight-stitch.

Sewing

Machine slowly down the hem-stitcher through both layers. Withdraw and realign the hem-stitcher for longer seams. When finished, remove from the machine, withdraw the hem-stitcher and fold both fabric pieces back on themselves. Pull apart to set the hemstitches. Press and topstitch a presser-foot width away from the join, on both sides. Trim underneath on the main fabric. Finish off the bottom of the double layer cloth with a decorative edge stitch or machine a satin stitch pattern and trim away the surplus (see *Scalloping*).

Hemstitching see *Wing needles.*

42 (Left) Using the metal hemstitcher fork to make a decorative stitch joining two folds of fabric.

(Right) Attaching interlining with a decorative trimotion stitch.

I
Interfacing
Attaching

This method works best on thicker fabrics. Use the blind hemmer foot and guide and set to blind hem stitch. Lay the interfacing in position on the wrong side of the fabric. Tack 5mm ($\frac{1}{4}$in) from the interfacing edge. Turn back the fabric to the right side and turn the unfaced portion back on itself at the tacking line. Machine down the 5mm ($\frac{1}{2}$in) allowance on the interfacing, catching on to the garment fabric with the blind hem stitch.

Interlining and linings
Attach to a facing with a decorative stitch

Turn under the seam allowance and press. Place on top of the facing, with the fold against the stitching line. Centre the machine foot on the stitching line and hold in place with one of the bridging stitches, cross-stitch, honeycomb or faggoting.

43 (Below) Attaching interfacing to wrong side of fabric (left); and with a blind hem stitch (right).

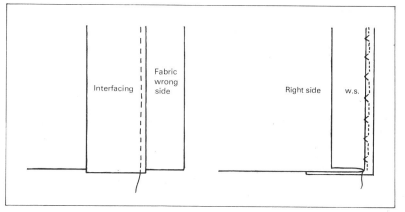

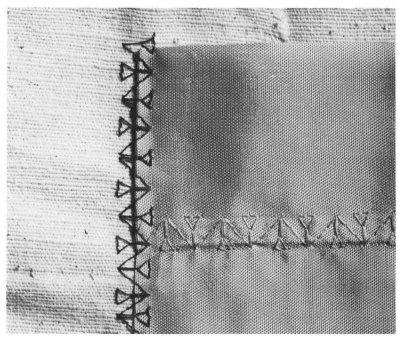

J

Jersey and stretch fabrics

This includes all jersey knit and stretch fabrics, both natural and synthetic.

Threads

100% polyester thread can be used for all jersey and stretch fabrics, either natural or synthetic. Silk thread can be used on silk and wool jersey. It is not advisable to use mercerized cotton on synthetics.

Needles

Use a ball-pointed needle on all natural and most synthetic jersey. The round point slips in between, and does not pierce, the knitted loops. Sometimes a perfect stitch or scarfed needle will work best on fine synthetic knits, such as nylon tricot.

Machine feet

Use the normal zig-zag presser foot, or a stretch stitch foot, for most close knitted jersey. Use the dual feed, even feed, roller foot or walking foot on thicker knits, synthetics or difficult stretch fabrics.

Tension

Loosen the top tension slightly.

Foot pressure

Decrease the pressure for soft or stretchy knits. Increase the pressure for ciré, nylon tricot or firm-surfaced synthetic knits. Use a normal pressure when using any of the even feed devices.

Sewing plain seams

Set the machine to a medium stitch-length and very narrow zig-zag. This looks like a normal seam in wear. Open out flat and neaten with one of the overlock stitches. On straight-stitch machines, use a slightly longer stitch.

To prevent stretching

Sew the zig-zag stitch over a thin cord. The seam is pressed before the cord is removed. Press wool jersey under a damp cloth; press synthetic under a dry cloth. For a firm edge, such as a jersey hem, leave the cord in.

Non-stretch seams

Use triple straight-stitch for seams under strain, such as armhole and crotch seams. This stitch has many names, including straight stretch stitch and triple seam stitch. It is a tri-motion stitch that sews back on itself to produce three parallel rows of stitching. It is very firm and almost impossible to un-pick on some fabrics. Sew the seam with a normal, long, straight-stitch for fitting. Sew the triple straight-stitch on top. Open the seam out flat. Double stitch seams if there is no triple straight-stitch.

Maximum stretch seams

Either shorten the narrow zig-zag stitch-length or use one of the elastic stretch stitches. Try three-step or triple zig-zag on a narrow-width setting, or stretch blind stitch on a narrower setting. This combines small

44 Stitching jersey and stretch fabrics: 1 Narrow zig-zag; 2 Zig-zag over cord; 3 Triple straight stitch; 4 Three-step zig-zag; 5 Stretch blind stitch; 6 Neatening and sewing in one operation; 7 Lapped seam in serpentine stitch.

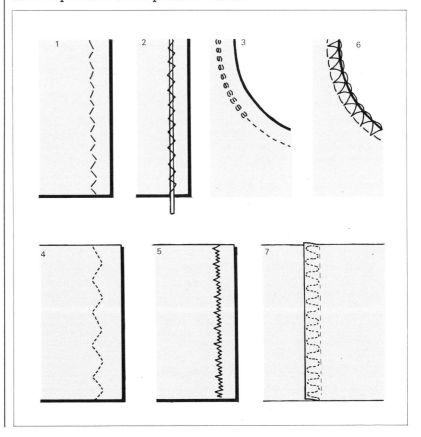

and large zig-zags. If the stitches are too wide, the opened-out seams will not lie flat. Use on garments that require a great deal of stretch, such as ski clothes, sportswear and swim suits.

Stretch seams

Neatening and sewing in one operation
Allow 5mm ($\frac{1}{4}$ in) seam allowance. Machine so that the right hand swing of the needle goes over the fabric edges. Use pullover or jersey stitch, or stretch overlock. Use this method to attach and neaten collars at the same time. This seam can be bound or turned down. Also use for binding armholes and necklines with split tubing or tubular bands.

Super stretch and elastic fabrics

Flat, overlapped seams
Use one of the serpentine stitches, universal stitch, double action, multistretch or three-step zig-zag. This prevents puckering.

Butt joining
Turn under the seam allowances. Use a bridging or feather stitch to join the two pieces of fabric together on the right side. Use for girdles and swim suits.

Turned-down hems
For a decorative finish use super stretch, honeycomb or cross stitch. These stitches are also used for sewing braids or borders on to stretch armholes and neckbands for sportswear and swim suits.

Elastic blind hem
Use elastic blind hem stitch (see *Hems*).

Jersey fabrics

Lapped seams
Use a double overlock stitch to hold the lapped fabric in position. Let the right hand needle swing enclose the cut right hand edge. Trim the surplus from the under left hand edge afterwards.

K

Knitted garments

Needles and threads
Use a ball-pointed needle, size 70-80 (11-12) for medium weight knits, or 80-90 (12-14) for double knits. Use 100% polyester thread for all types fo knitwear. This will not break and has built-in stretch. It is also possible to use a very thin wool wound round the bobbin to combine with the upper polyester thread. Loosen the bottom tension.

Machine feet
The zig-zag presser foot can be used on all fine and ·medium knits. A roller foot, or an even feed device, may help on thicker or *bouclé* knits. There is also a 'no-snag' foot available for sewing very loopy knits.

Stitches
Sew seams with a very narrow zig-zag, three-step zig-zag or one of the special stretch stitches. Neaten edges with one of the stretch overlock stitches (see *Stitches*).

Cut and sew method

This can be worked using the domestic overlock machine.

Using the zig-zag machine

This method can be used for making alterations on existing knitwear, or for cutting and sewing up knitted fabric made on the knitting machine. It is not recommended for hand knitwear.

Method
Prepare the knitted fabric according to type, either by washing and pressing, or steaming, or dry pressing.

Choose a simple shaped paper pattern and lay this on to the wrong side of the knitted fabric, which is placed flat on the table. Hold the pattern down with weights. Now mark round the outside with a tacking stitch in contrasting wool, or place berry pins round the edge. This will be the cutting line. Lift off the paper pattern. Machine round the marked line, using a medium length zig-zag stitch. Do not pull the fabric. If it is very loose and stretchy, hold just outside the cutting line with transparent sticky tape. Do not sew over this (fig. 45).

Method 2
Lay narrow strips of iron-on interfacing over the tacked cutting line. Zig-zag stitch through this on the line. Trim the interfacing, close to the stitching.

Cutting out
Cut up to the zig-zag line without snipping the stitches. Use one of the overlock or overedge stitches to sew all the way round again.

Sewing up
Use any of the methods described under *Jersey and stretch fabrics*. If your machine has a chain stitching device, try using this. Tie off the chain ends.

Sewing on bands and facings
Double over flat bands and enclose the overlocked garment edge between. Tack into position, using thin knit thread. The band is sewn on from the top in one operation, so make the under half of the band slightly wider (fig. 45).

Ribbed neckbands
Machine the ribbed band into a

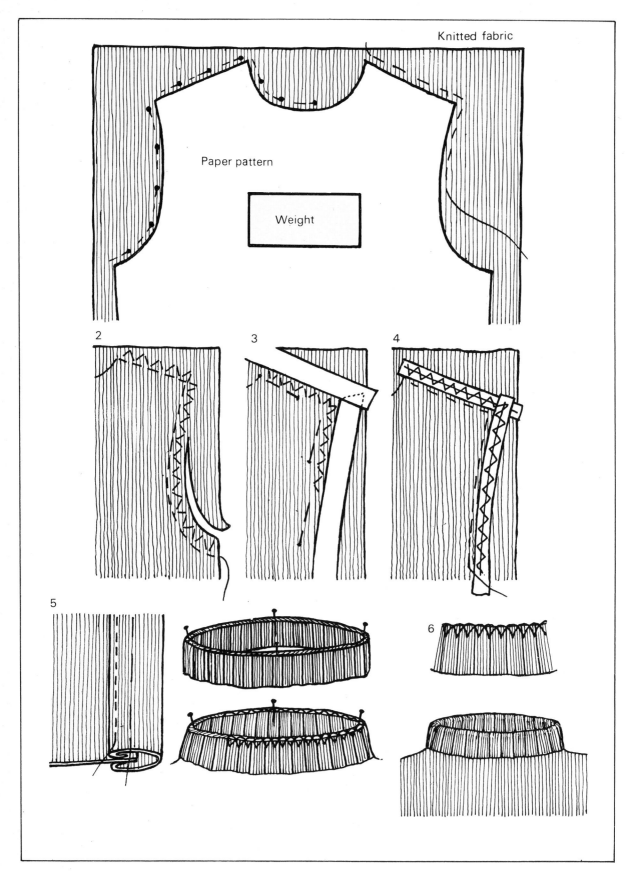

Knitted fabric

Paper pattern

Weight

2

3

4

5

6

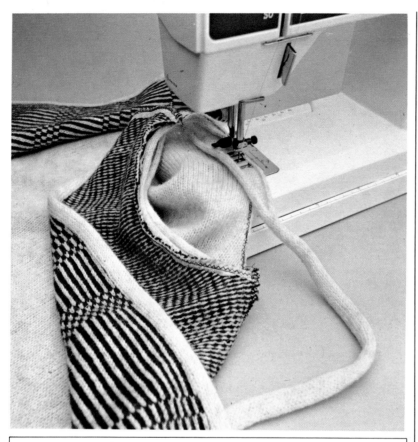

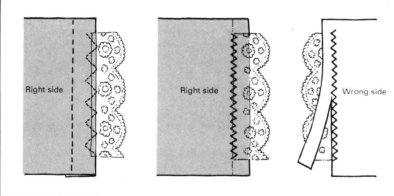

46 (Above) Attaching lace to a hemmed edge (left) and to a raw edge (centre). Cut away excess fabric along stitching line (right).

45 (Left) Cut-and-sew method of making up and finishing knitted garments: 1 Marking out pattern; 2 Zig-zag outline stitched; 3 Transparent tape used on stretchy knits; 4 Zig-zag through strips of iron-on interfacing; 5 Raw edge encased in double band of knitting; 6 Ribbed neckband.

Cut-and-sew method for assembling a waistcoat using a narrow zig-zag.

Method
The underneath is the right side of the work. Lay a wool or knit thread along the right hand fabric edge and machine over with a wide zig-zag stitch. This will make a firmer edge.

Narrow hem
Fold the knit material up once and machine with an overlock stitch to catch over the fabric edge. Trim off the surplus fabric close to the stitching (fig. 45).

L

Lace

Attaching

To a hemmed edge
Hold the lace up to the hemmed edge and machine together by butt-joining. Use bridging stitch, faggoting stitch or three-step zig-zag.

To a raw edge
Mark a guide line 2 cm ($\frac{5}{8}$ in) in from the edge, and lay the straight lace edge up against it. Centre the presser foot over the lace edge and sew down using zig-zag stitch, or a straight-stitch close to the edge. The excess fabric can be turned back underneath, afterwards, and neatened or hemmed. Alternatively, cut off the excess, close to the stitching. Cover the original stitch line with wider satin stitch (fig. 46).

Fine fabric should be backed with thin paper.

To cover the hem line

Apply a ribbon or braid over both the lace edge and the hem stitching line, or stitch over the hem with a decorative pattern stitch.

ring. Fold over double with the two edges level. Mark the centre, front and back, and the two sides with berry pins. Place in position, right sides facing, with the edges against the neck edge. Machine together using stretch overlock stitch (fig. 45).

Neatening edges
Wind matching fine wool or knit thread on to the bobbin. Loosen the bottom tension. Use a matching polyester thread in the needle and tighten the top tension.

Inserting lace

Pin the lace in position on to the right side of the material. Centre the presser foot over the lace edge on the left hand side and machine with a zig-zag stitch. Make a similar seam down the right hand side. Cut the underneath fabric down the middle, without cutting the lace. Turn back and trim or hem the edges. Cover the original stitches with satin stitch.

Using the edge stitcher

This straight-stitch machine foot has a series of staggered slots on both sides, and a fine adjuster to centre it beneath the needle. it is an excellent method of sewing on lace. The fabric is hemmed, or folded under, and fed into one slot while the lace is fed into another so that it is sewn either on top or underneath. The edge stitcher can be used for sewing in-

sertions, in two separate stages, or for joining two pieces of lace together, edge to edge.

Using the narrow hemmer with a slot

Turn the fabric under twice by hand and machine a few stitches. With the foot down on the hem raise the needle to its highest point and pass the lace through the slot, momentarily easing the pressure on the hem, but not enough to displace it. The needle stitches through both the narrow hem and the lace – this should be held well into the slot while sewing.

Joining lace

Join patterned lace by overlapping the pattern repeat. Machine a straight-stitch line round the pattern outline. Sew a second line and cut away the surplus from underneath (fig. 46).

Decorative pieces of applied lace and lace edging.

Stretch lace   see *Elastic*

Leather and suede

Needles
For all thick or tough leathers, use a wedge-pointed leather needle. Most light leather and suede can be sewn with a normal machine needle, size 90-100 (14-16).

Threads
Use 100% polyester or mercerized cotton to match the weight of leather.

Machine feet
Use the normal presser foot, a roller foot or a teflon-coated or glide foot. It is possible to get a stick-on teflon sole for some

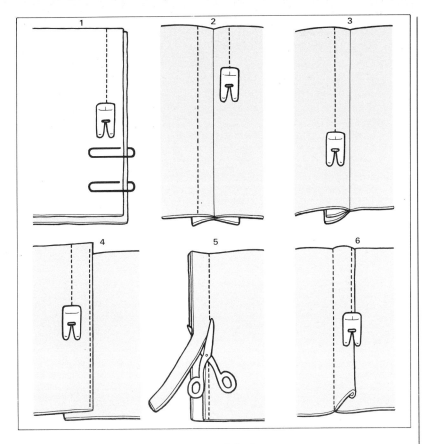

47 Sewing leather and suede: 1 & 2 Plain seam top stitched; 3 Single seam top stitched; 4 Lapped seam top stitched; 5 & 6 Flat felled seam top stitched.

presser feet. The glide foot is useful for sewing over any fabric or leather that sticks. The roller foot can be used on most leathers, but may mark suede.

Cutting out
Cut leather with a leather-knife or sharp scissors. Use pinking shears on lighter leather for decorative seams and patches.

Working methods
Do not baste or tack seams. Pin within the seam allowance or hold together with paper clips at right angles to the seam. Hold down opened-out seam allowances with rubber adhesive. Use iron-on interfacing. Thick seam allowances will need skiving with a special tool, to reduce the bulk on the edges. To flatten seams, tap them lightly with a wooden mallet.

Stitches
Avoid those that sew in reverse – too many needle holes will mark and damage the skin. Set a slightly longer stitch-length than normal.

Seams
Butt joining
This method is used for patchwork. Hold the cut-out patches together on the wrong side, and at intervals, with sticky tape. Join with zig-zag stitch, three-step zig-zag or any of the forward-sewing bridging stitches.

Plain seam top stitched
With right sides facing, machine a straight-stitch seam. Turn the seam allowances one to each side and glue in position. Press down well. Turn to the right side. Top stitch both sides one presser-foot width away from the seam.

Single seam – top stitched
Light leather
Both seam allowances are turned over to the same side and held in position with rubber adhesive. Turn the work to the right side and top stitch one presser-foot width away from the seam line, through all layers.

Heavy leather
Reduce one seam allowance by trimming close to the stitching. Turn the larger allowance over this edge and hold down with rubber adhesive. Turn to the right side and top stitch through the double layer.

Lapped seam
Place one lapped edge over the other on the right side and hold with rubber adhesive. Top stitch close to the cut edge, and again, one presser-foot width further in.

Flat felled seam
Machine together, wrong sides facing. Trim off the surplus right hand seam allowance. Turn over the wide seam allowance and top stitch in place, turning under as you sew.

Darts
Mark the sewing lines and the centre line on the wrong side. Cut down the centre line almost to the point. Fold, right sides together, hold with paper clips, to match the seam lines, and machine together. Press out the seam allowances and glue to either side.

M

Matching stripes and checks

Normal sewing foot
Place pins at right angles to the seam, matching the checks, with the points just touching the seam line. Machine with the pins in position, or tack first and remove the pins. Loosen the foot pressure slightly.

Even feed method

Line up the matching checks at the start of the seam. Hold with a pin at right angles to the seam, 3-4 cm ($1\frac{1}{2}$ in) down from the top. Fit the dual-feed device, even feed foot, roller foot or walking foot. Pull the threads towards the back and start 5mm ($\frac{1}{4}$ in) in from the top.

Sewing

Remove the pin when a few stitches are sewn. Guide the fabric lightly beneath the foot. Do not pull or stretch.

Mending

Tears and rips

Some machines have an automatic mending or running stitch. Alternatively, use an open zig-zag of the three-step zig-zag stitch.

Method
Back the torn or frayed area with a slightly larger piece of thin fabric. Sew zig-zag or three-step zig-zag in close parallel rows, overlapping. Cut away any spare fabric from behind, afterwards.

Tears in thicker fabric or jersey

Use a mending, running or three-step zig-zag stitch to hold together the two sides of the tear, centred beneath the presser foot.

Use maximum width and a closer stitch-length than normal. Sew shorter stitches at the beginning and end of the tear.

Millinery

Stitched brims

Parallel bands of stitching are used both to decorate and to reinforce brims on dressmaker and felt hats.

Hat with machine-stitched brim and neatly stitched join.

Dressmaker hats

Interline the two brim pieces with woven inferfacing. This has more 'give' and can be shaped and steam-set. Sew up the back seams and machine the two brim sections together. Turn to the right side and press the seam well, under a cloth.

Sewing

Have a perfectly even tension, top and bottom. Machine one presser foot width away from the brim edge, all the way round, and join up with the beginning for a few stitches. Gradually open out the stitching line to sew parallel with the first one. Continue round in a spiral, using the presser foot width as a guide, until the entire brim is sewn. You may find it easier to use the free arm. Try not to stop in the middle; continuous sewing will make for an even result.

Felt brims

These can first be bound with a ribbon on the edge. Tack in place, then sew the first round of stitching to catch in the ribbon. Continue as before.

Stitched crowns

Shaped crown pieces may be top stitched to outline seams, or segments may be sewn round in a spiral from the outside to the centre. Lower the needle in the cloth at any sharp corner, raise the foot and pivot round before lowering the foot to carry on.

Trimmings

Use very close rows of stitching, following the outline shape. This will help to stiffen the fabric. Experiment with automatic pattern stitches for decorative effect. For heavier stitching, use the triple straight-stitch or triple zig-zag (also called ric-rac stitch).

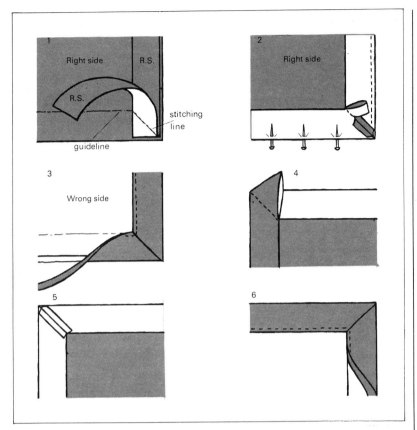

48 Mitred corners made with an applied facing (1, 2 & 3), or with a self-facing (4, 5 & 6).

Coloured net being gathered on the Elna using a roller foot.

Mitred corners

Applied facing

Cut a facing strip the finished width plus two seams allowances. Cut the length to the finished measurement of the fabric edges plus one strip width. Have the right side uppermost and lay the strip on top of the fabric, down one edge. At the corner, fold the strip up level with the bottom edge and then fold it back on itself, level with the edge (fig. 48). Crease, to mark the diagonal fold, pin and tack together. Do the same at the other corners. Pick up the facing and machine each mitred corner. Trim the seams and press out flat.

Sewing together

Pin the facing to the fabric, matching the corners, and machine all round the outer edge. For a facing, have the pieces right sides together, turn the facing to the wrong side and hem or machine in place. For a border, machine with the wrong sides together, turn the border to the right side and machine with the hem turned under, or use a satin stitch.

Self facing

Cut the fabric to the required measurement, plus one facing width and one seam allowance on each fabric edge. Mark the fold line and machine diagonally up each mitred corner (fig. 48). Trim and press the seam out flat. Machine in place on the wrong side of the fabric. Finally, machine an edge stitch on to the outer fabric edge.

N
Net

Threads
Sew cotton net with mercerized cotton no. 60, and synthetic net with 100% polyester fine thread.

Machine feet
Large meshed net can catch on the ordinary presser foot. Use a roller foot or a no-snag foot.

Net curtains

Side hems
Match up the meshes of the net. Sew a straight-stitch seam and hold the meshes level at the back and front of the sewing area. Lengthen the stitch and loosen the top tension if necessary.

Joining
Match the meshes or the pattern. Pin or tack a seam about

1 cm ($\frac{3}{8}$ in) wide. Use zig-zag, three-step zig-zag or one of the serpentine stretch stitches. Trim the seam close to the stitches.

Hems

Turn up the hem twice, with the inner edge to the bottom of the fold. Zig-zag into position.

Dress net

This is used for bridal wear, ballet and evening dresses. machine together with a straight-stitch, the length of stitch being determined by the size of the mesh. Experiment on a scrap piece first. There is no need to neaten the seams. For easier control of extra fullness, box pleat the fabric first, then gather in the normal way. Tie off all thread ends very securely.

O

Overcasting

Neatening seam edges pressed open

Softer fabrics

Sew just inside the edge, using zig-zag stitch, or preferably three-step zig-zag. Trim the fabric up to the stitches, but do not cut them.

Firmer fabrics

Machine so that the zig-zag or overlock stitch encloses the fabric with the right hand needle swing over the edge. An overedge presser foot will hold the fabric flat.

Seams pressed to one side

Use a wide zig-zag or three-step zig-zag, the blind hemmer stitch or an overlock stitch.

Overcasting and sewing in one operation

It is necessary to use one of the overlock stitches. These can be worked on to the fabric and the surplus trimmed away afterwards. Alternatively, the two edges can be placed right sides together and sewn with the needle passing right over the outer edges. It is possible to use a double row of zig-zag, or the blind hem stitch if the machine has no overlock stitches.

Use single overlock and double overlock for woven fabrics. Use stretch overlock or overedge stretch stitch for stretch fabrics (fig. 49).

49 Overcasting: 1 Zig-zag seam neatening; 2 Overedge or blind hem stitch; 3 Three-step zig-zag; 4 Overcast and sewn in one; 5(a) Single, (b) double and (c) stretch overlock; 6 Oversewn patchwork.

Operator-controlled patterns

The stitch-width control on the simple type zig-zag machine is moved while the machine is sewing, to produce decorative patterns.

Method
Back the fabric with iron-on interfacing or typing copy paper. Use a transparent embroidery foot. Set to satin stitch and loosen the top tension slightly. Use machine embroidery thread or mercerized cotton, top and bottom.

1 With the needle in the centre position, machine with an even speed and open and close the width control gradually. Try to keep an even rhythm – count, if it helps.

2 Alternate wide blocks with intervals of straight-stitch in between.

3 Work as for (1) but alter the needle position to the left or to the right. This will give a pattern with one straight side.

4 Set the width to halfway and slowly alter the needle position from left to centre, or from right to centre. This will give scallops.

5 Set the width control between halfway and maximum. Alter the needle position to form blocks of stitching that change position. Make wider block patterns by starting at the right on maximum width. Finish the block on the left. Lift the

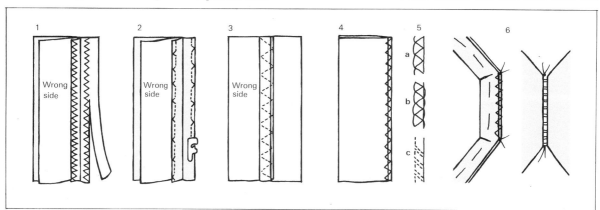

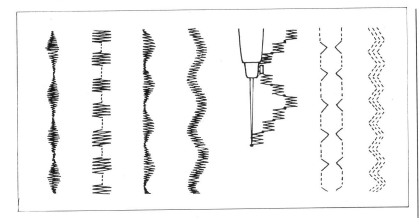

50 Operator-controlled patterns worked on a swing-needle machine adjusting the width lever.

presser foot, set to 0 width, and sew one stitch. Lift the foot again and set to maximum to work the next block. The blocks can move across the fabric in steps. Now work back the other way, this time stopping on the right of the block.

These patterns can be sewn in rows opposite each other. They combine with rows of satin stitch, zig-zag, or blind hem stitch. Rows of three-step zig-zag sewn close make an all-over pattern.

P

Pads
Shoulder pads

Shaped
Draw round a saucer or a small

plate and use as a pattern to cut three circles from the garment fabric. Fold two of the circles in half and cut down the fold line. Trim the curved edge on these four pieces, each one smaller than the last. Lay them in order, with the straight edges level, against the centre of the large circle. Fold over to enclose the layers (fig. 51).

Sewing
Tack together through all layers. Starting on the long edge, machine round one presser foot width away. Continue to sew round in a spiral until the centre is reached. Overlock-stitch the raw edges, or cut with pinking shears.

Roll pad

Cut out one circle shape. Fold in half and cut along the fold line. Machine together round the semicircular outline. Turn to

51 Shoulder pads.

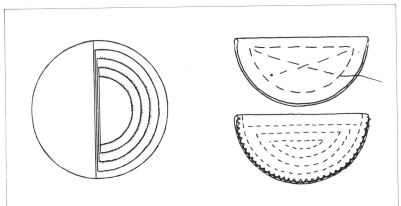

the right side. Stuff with terylene wadding along the seam edge. Machine a crescent-shaped line to hold the padding. Trim the seam allowance to width 2.5cm (1 in) and neaten the edge.

Square pad

Cut an oblong of fabric, 13cm (5in) by 15cm (6in). Fold in half lengthways. Machine the two side seams. Turn to the right side. Pad the end with terylene wadding, and machine across to hold this in place. Trim to 2.5cm (1in) and neaten the edges.

Patching
Woven fabrics

Cut a square or oblong patch to cover the damaged area and pin in position. On simple zig-zag machines, hold down with zig-zag stitches sewn with the right hand needle swing enclosing the raw edge. Sew another row of zig-zag stitches inside this. Cut away the worn fabric from behind, close to the zig-zag stitches.

Utility stitches
Machine round the edge, using the three-step zig-zag or one of the serpentine running or mending stitches. Sew zig-zag stitches round first for a firmer edge on fabrics that fray. Machine a line of straight stitches on to the inner stitch edge. This will make the trimming of the damaged fabric easier.

Jersey fabrics

Cut the patch round or oval. Match the nap of the fabric and avoid stretching. Now tack into position. On zig-zag machines, sew over the outer edge first with one row of zig-zag. For very stretchy fabrics, sew over a fine cord or wool thread. Machine another row of zig-zag, a presser foot width away, inside the seam. Trim the damaged area away from behind.

Utility stitches
Use the three-step zig-zag, on a short stitch length but wide width setting. You can also use cross stitch or a serpentine running stitch.

Pile fabrics

Corduroy, needlecord, suede cloth, velveteen, velour

Needles
Use as fine a needle as the fabric will allow, from 70-90 (11-14), preferably a ball-point, or perfect stitch.

Thread
Use a fine 100% polyester, silk or machine embroidery thread.

Sewing
Machine in the direction of the nap. Avoid all top stitching and choose simple seams. Seam edges can be overcast or bound to prevent fraying. Use the zig-zag foot for overcasting, and a roller foot, even feed foot or dual feed device, for sewing long seams.

Stitches
Use a medium-length straight-stitch for seams. For overcasting use a medium zig-zag on extra fraying fabrics, cross stitch or honeycomb stitch.

Deep pile fabrics see *Fur fabrics.*

Napped fabrics

Camel hair, cashmere, mohair
Machine in the direction of the nap, using the presser foot, a roller foot or even feed foot. Set to a medium, or long, straight-stitch and use 100% polyester

thread. Hold all seams and edges flat with topstitching.

Towelling

Woven
This is also called Terry cloth. Use a medium-to-large needle and 100% polyester thread or strong mercerized cotton. For sewing straight seams, use a longer stitch-length. A roller foot or a no-snag foot will prevent the loops from catching.

Seams
Sew a straight-stitch seam and trim the allowance to 1.5cm ($\frac{3}{4}$in). Press the seams out flat and hold the edges down with zig-zag or an overlock stitch.

Stretch towelling
This fabric can be very stretchy. Use a very narrow, long zig-zag for plain seams. Open out flat and hold down with three-step zig-zag or a multi-stretch stitch. To prevent garment seams from stretching out of shape, place an elastic thread along a double fabric edge and machine all together with a stretch overlock seam. Use this technique on cuffs and neck openings.

Pin tucks

These narrow tucks are sewn using twin-needles and the machine set for straight-stitch,

52 Working pintucks on the machine.

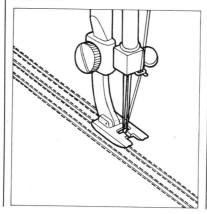

three-step zig-zag, or outline scallop. Two top threads, one for each needle, share one bobbin thread (see *Twin needles*).

Use a fine machine embroidery thread or mercerized cotton. For plain pin tucks, use a wide-spaced embroidery foot. This central space will help to push up the pin tuck fabric. Use a shorter stitch-length. A tighter top tension will make a more pronounced pin tuck.

Stitch on the straight grain and always work the tucks from the same direction. Machine a tucked fabric and cut out afterwards.

Corded pin tucks

These are sometimes referred to as cording. The twin needles enclose a thin cord, held beneath the fabric. Some machines have a hole in the needleplate. The cord is threaded up through this and is held beneath the foot.

Other types of machine have a cording, or braiding, guide that fits on the needleplate. A slotted groove allows the thread to be passed through. An improvized guide can be made from a 2cm ($\frac{3}{4}$in) long piece of plastic sleeving, cut from an electric flex. Hold in front of the feed teeth with transparent sticky tape.

Pin tuck feet
These machine feet have grooves underneath to help line up the pin tucks in rows. For wider spaced tucks, sew one presser foot width apart.

Filler cord
Use buttonhole thread or perle cotton with lightweight fabrics. A fine cord can be used on heavyweight materials.

Corners
Let the needle points just pierce the fabric. Raise the presser foot and turn the fabric slightly. Lower the foot and make one stitch, and lift and turn once more. Continue sewing with straight stitches as before.

Piping

Piped cord seam

Use a one-sided zipper or piping foot, or – preferably – the adjustable two-sided zipper foot, which allows the seam to be sewn on either side.

Piping cord
This comes in different thicknesses. Always pre-shrink cotton cord before use. Join cord by splicing or cut the ends straight and stitch or glue them.

Bias strips
Cut wide enough to cover the cord, plus 2.5 cm (1 in) for seam allowance. Allow extra for thicker fabrics. For joining see *Bias binding*.

Method
Piped edge
Fold the strip to enclose the piping cord, right sides outside, raw edges even, and tack in place. Lay the piping strip against the raw edge of the main

fabric on the right side, all raw edges even (fig. 53). Pin and machine baste in position with a long straight-stitch, fairly close to the piping. If possible, have the cord to the left of the foot.

Machine a second line of medium length straight-stitches, right up to the piping. Adjust the foot so that the needle sews close up to the piping but is still protected. Hold the cord up towards the needle. Turn the seam allowances back.

Piped seam
Lay a facing strip, or second fabric piece, on top of the piped edge, wrong side uppermost, raw edge against the piped edges. Tack or machine baste. Machine a straight-stitch line close up against the piping edge. Turn the hem to the back to enclose all raw edges.

53 Inserting piping: 1, 2, 3 & 4 Making a piped cord seam; 5 & 6 Making a decorative piped edge.

Plain piped edge or seam

The bias strip is used without a filler cord. Machine with the fabric seam on the right, using the presser foot as a guide.

Piped shell edge

Use a soft, fine fabric for the piping. Fold in half, lengthways, and place beneath the main fabric so that the protruding edge is the correct width to be oversewn with the blind hem stitch. Machine a line of straight-stitches close to the fold, to hold the piping.

Piped shell tuck

Proceed as for the shell edging, but trim the piped seam allowance close to the seam. Fold over on to the main fabric and hold down by machining close to the folded edge.

Plastic-coated fabrics
PVC

This stands for polyvinyl chloride, and is coated on to a woven or knitted background fabric.

Polyurethane-coated fabrics

A thinly coated film is porous; thicker coatings are waterproof, but do not breathe. The coating can be clear, or printed in solid colour patterns. Use for making aprons, rainwear and sports clothes.

Vinyl-coated fabrics

This coating is non-porous and the finish ranges from dull to lustrous. It comes in clear or solid colours, and patterns may

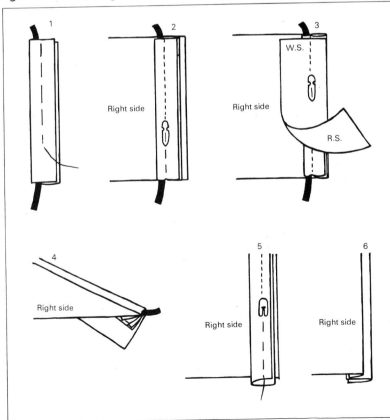

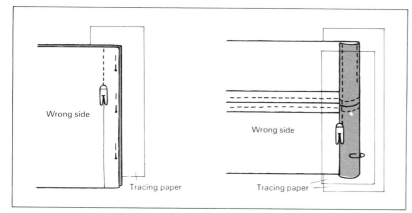

54 Sewing seams (left) and hems (right) with plastic-coated fabrics.

be embossed or printed on to the applied surface. This is a heavier fabric and is used in upholstery and for making belts and bags.

Needles
Use a sharp or a wedge-point leather needle, size 90-100 (14-16), or a ball-point needle on some finely coated knit-back fabrics.

Thread
Thread the machine with 100% polyester or mercerized cotton, top and bottom. It is also possible to use nylon monofilament thread.

Sewing
Set a longer stitch-length, from 10-12 stitches per 2.5cm (1in). This fabric is easier to sew on the wrong knit or woven-backed side. The plastic surface sticks under the machine foot. Either apply a few drops of machine oil, talcum powder or French chalk, in front of the presser foot, or use a teflon-coated or glide foot. A roller foot or an even feed foot may help. Alternatively, place a piece of tracing paper between the plastic fabric and the foot.

Seams

Sewn, right sides together
Sandwich a piece of tracing paper between the layers. Line up the fabric edges. Pin the fabric and tracing paper together, far enough within the seam allowance to permit the foot to pass (fig. 54). Machine and tear away the paper.

Top stitching
If the fabric is porous, sew through tracing paper. For non-porous fabrics, apply a drop of machine oil in front of the foot while you sew.

Hems
Hold hems in position with paper clips at right angles to the hem. If the fabric sticks to the machine bed, place tracing paper underneath, and on top as well. Machine again, close to the fold.

Darts

Light fabrics
Fold and machine the dart along the seam line. Cut along the fold and turn back the seam allowances. Press down with the fingers, or glue into position. Always test glue on fabrics first, in case it should mark.

Heavy fabrics
Slit down the centre fold line, nearly to the point. Trim the seam allowances and machine along the seam lines. Press down or glue.

Plastic fabrics for embroidery

Work with the roller foot or a glide foot, or smear machine oil or talcum powder on to the fabric to prevent sticking. Set satin stitch on maximum width and not too close. The needle holes may tear the fabric.

Transparent PVC
This lends itself to embroidery designs constructed in see-through layers. Sew ribbon or tape, or embroider satin stitch strips. Cut these out and interlace them through the ground film.

Polythene
Strong polythene can enclose thick threads, sequins or fabric shapes machined round the edges. Incorporate this technique with others.

Transparent plastic film
Embroidered motifs on fine fabric or net are imprisoned between two layers of sticky-backed transparent film. This is particularly useful for making window blinds or shower curtains.

Pleats

Dressmaker pleats

These are tacked in position first. If they are all facing the same way, machine in the same direction, in order to let the pleats lie flat. When machining over a box pleat, stop just before the start of the pleat and raise the presser foot slightly to ease the fabric into position ready to carry on sewing.

Pleating with the ruffler attachment
This is a complicated-looking, but easy-to-use, machine attachment. A lever is connected to the needlebar to work the mechanism which activates the ruffler blades. The blades can be set to make one gather, or pleat, at every stitch, one at every 5th or 6th stitch and one at every 12th stitch. Different makes vary slightly. A screw adjuster allows the depth of the pleat to be altered.

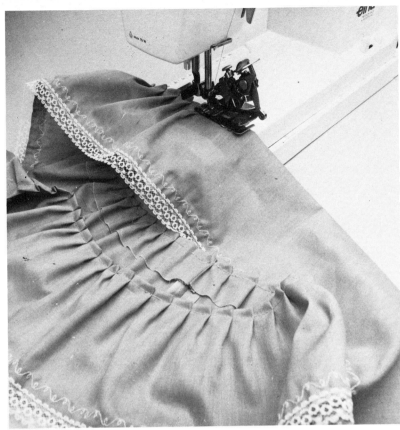

A sample of ruffling being worked on the Elna with the ruffler attachment. The lace was applied using the edge stitcher then decorative automatic patterns were added.

Q

Quilting

A layer of padding is sandwiched between a light backing cloth and the upper fabric. Careful tacking will help to produce even results.

Wadding
Use terylene wadding – thick for quilted bedcovers and tea cosies, medium and lightweight for quilted garments. A well washed piece of old blanket, or several layers of soft, thick cloth can be used instead.

Tacking
Tack through all layers at regular intervals, from the middle outwards, top to bottom and side to side.

Needles and thread
These should suit the fabric. Machine embroidery thread is more lustrous. Lurex and metallic threads wound round the bobbin can be used to quilt from the wrong side (fig. 55).

Tension
Tighten the top tension and use a longer stitch.

Foot
Use a quilting foot and guide. This is a short foot with a turned-up edge to go over the thick fabric. Sometimes the longer, zipper foot can do double duty as a quilter foot. The metal guide fits through a transverse slot and can be adjusted to the required width between rows.

Sewing
The two layers of fabric and the wadding can creep under the machine foot. There are several ways of dealing with this problem.

1 Always start from the top of the fabric, in the centre, and work rows to either side in turn.

2 Start in the centre but machine rows in alternate directions.

3 Always start from the middle of the fabric and work

Needle and thread
Use needle size no. 90 (14) and mercerized cotton.

Method
Pass the material to be pleated under the front guide prong and between the blued metal blades, until it is just past the needle. Always pass the fabric from front to back. Re-insert it if it is wrong; do not pull backwards. Never operate the ruffler unless there is fabric in-between the blades. Lower the foot ready to sew.

5 or 6 stitch pleat
Set in the correct slot according to the instruction booklet. The blade will push the fabric forward at every 5th or 6th stitch. Lower the adjuster screw to make a deeper pleat.

Pleated frills
These can be sewn on their own with the top hem turned under, or attached to the main fabric at the same time. Place the fabric underneath the ruffler, and the frill strip between the blades. The frill can be sewn between two pieces of fabric by laying the upper piece above the blades.

Pleated ruffles
Pass wide ribbon or lace through the guide prong and sew it on to the surface of the fabric.

Pleated trimming
Pass narrow ribbon, braid or lace through the small upper guide slots of the ruffler attachment.

Gathering with the ruffler
Set the ruffler to make one small pleat, or gather, for every stitch. To make finer gathers, shorten the stitch and also shorten the blade stroke by raising the adjuster screw on the ruffler attachment.

the rows outwards. When one half of the quilting is completed, it is turned round and sewn the other way.

Method

Machine the first, middle line. Set the guide to the pattern width and machine the second row with the guide in the first line, like a plough in a furrow.

Patterns

Machine squares or diamonds with the fabric grain, or on the diagonal. Work zig-zag stitch, or a row of twin-needle stitching, instead of the normal straight-stitch. Some automatic pattern stitches are suitable for decorative quilting. Experiment on spare pieces of fabric first to see which will look the best.

Printed fabrics

Machine-quilt striped or checked fabric, using the print lines as a guide. Embroider lines of pattern stitches in between, before quilting.

Line patterns

Make up patterns based on right angles and curves. Sew them in mirror image on alternate rows. Lift the foot and pivot on the needle at sharp corners.

Quilted knitting or jersey fabric

Use a roller foot or an even feed foot. Do not pull or stretch the fabric, but let the foot do the work.

Making up

Work quilting before cutting out since the stitching will shrink the fabric. Trim excess wadding from the seams after they have been stitched. Neaten inside seams by trimming in layers and hemming one lining seam allowance over the raw edges.

A beautiful quilted evening bag with whipped stitch embroidery by machine and hand-sewn beading.

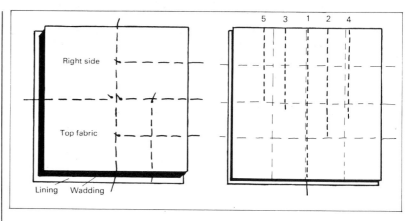

55 Tacking and sewing quilting.

R

Reinforcements

Additional stitches are used both to decorate and to give strength to areas liable to strain – jean seams, pockets, waistbands, knee, shoulder and elbow pads in suede or leather and on children's clothes.

Stitches

Sew zig-zag or triple straight-stitch on waistbands, side seams or pockets. Work ric-rac stitch or single or double overlock, on pockets, side seams and patches for extra strength.

Sewing

Machine ric-rac or overlock stitch with the needle in the main fabric to the right. Stitch the reinforcement on the left-hand swing of the machine needle and proceed to the end.

Rouleau loops

Narrow fabric tubes are used to make tie-ends for garment closures or for drawstrings on necklines, wasitbands and cuffs. They are also used for loop closures, belt carriers and trimmings. Woven fabric is cut on the bias or the true cross, and jersey fabrics are cut on the straight.

Method
Cut strips four times the finished width. With right sides together, fold in half lengthways. Stretch to reduce the 'give'. Pin and machine down the middle, using a medium length straight-stitch, or a very narrow zig-zag on jersey fabrics. Trim a little of the seam if necessary. Leave long thread ends, fasten them securely and tie into a bodkin eye. Pass this through the tube and draw the fabric to the right side. A latchet-hook turning tool is very useful.

Rouleau loops are used to fasten lapped and edge-to-edge openings.

Single loops
The loops should be long enough to go round the button plus two of the project seam allowances.

1 Use a card template to mark the loop positions on the right side of the fabric.

2 Lay each cut loop in place against the marks, the ends level with the main fabric edge. Tack down along the seam line.

3 Lay the facing strip on top and machine through all layers along the seam line. Turn all to the right side. Secure by understitching, on to the facing, or topstitching along the fabric edge (fig. 57).

Continuous loops
These are made from a continuous strip, which is wound backwards and forwards across the guide lines. Mark the

57 (Right) Attaching rouleau: 1 & 2 in single loops; 3 in continuous loops; 4 adding facing strip.

seam line and the width of the loops. Tack the strip on to both lines and snip the curves within the seam allowance. Face and finish as for single loops. (fig. 57).

Trimmings
Stiffen rouleau strips by inserting a piping cord. Use these to make knots, bows or belt carriers.

56 Making rouleau strips for use as loops for fastening.

Rufflette tape
see *Headings.*

S

Scalloping
Embroidered scallops

Method 1
Automatic scallop stitch
Back fine fabrics with iron-on

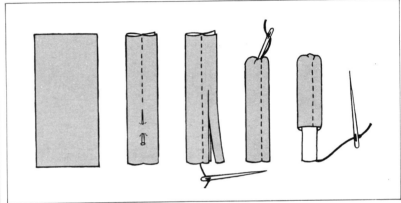

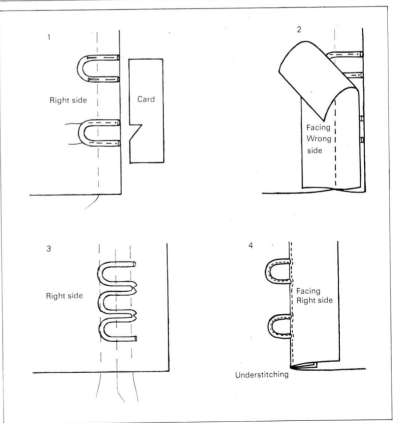

interfacing, which is trimmed away afterwards, or back with typing copy paper or work on double fabric. The surplus fabric is cut away close to the stitching line after the sewing is completed. This method is not suitable for fabrics that fray.

Method 2
Trace around a manufacturer's scallop pattern guide. An edge template can be made by drawing circles round an egg cup on to card or by using a pair of compasses.

Sewing
Fit the transparent embroidery foot and machine a straight-stitch outline. Then sew round in satin stitch, moving the width lever from 0 at the indentations to maximum width on the outer curve. This requires practice, but makes an excellent edging for table linen or pillowcases. Lower the needle at the narrow point, raise the foot and pivot round ready for the next scallop.

Cut round the scallops close to the stitching. Set the machine to a narrow satin stitch, and machine over the outline to enclose the cut edge. A thin cord can be applied to the edge, using the cording foot.

Open scallops

These are sewn over typing paper which is torn away afterwards. Sew with machine embroidery thread and use a fine perle cord for the filler thread. Fit the transparent embroidery foot.

Method
Double over the typing paper to make it thicker and place it under the machine foot. Lay the fabric on top, with the hem turned under. Centre the fabric so that the fold line is in the middle of the foot and the typing paper protrudes 3-4 cm (1-1½in) beyond the fold. The filler cord is laid loosely beneath the foot (fig. 58).

Sewing
Set to automatic scallop stitch.

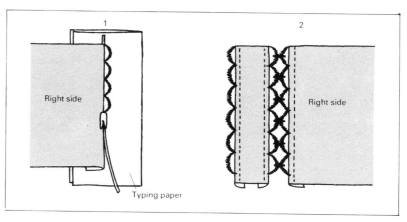

58 1 Open scalloped seam.
2 Scalloped shaped hem.

Scalloped shaped hem

Experiment with the width control as machines vary. Use a medium-length stitch to start with and then reduce to satin stitch as the cord catches in. The needle should pierce the cloth fold when the point of the scallop is reached.

Two rows of open scallops can be placed opposite one another and held down with a wide zig-zag stitch on drop feed or 0 setting. Sew a few straight-stitches to secure the back tack (fig. 58).

Scalloped edge worked on the Pfaff.

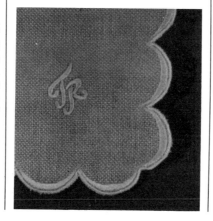

Small scallops
1 Fold up a 4 cm (1½in) hem, right sides facing. Set the machine to an automatic scallop line stitch. Use a pattern elongator, or lengthen the stitch to increase the scallop length.
2 Machine the scallop line, one presser-foot width from the fold edge. Trim away the seam allowance to 3mm (⅛in) and clip into the corners. Snip the seam allowance at intervals. Turn to the right side, push out the scallops and press well.

Large scallops
Draw round a template on to the double hem and machine the outline in straight-stitch. Clip and turn as for the small scallop hem.

Shadow work scallops

Work with twin needles on the right side of double organdie. Use an automatic outline stitch, or sew over template lines. Thread coloured wool into the twin-needle channel, then cut away the surplus fabric. Alternatively, sew with a thick coloured thread in the bobbin.

Marking and cutting scalloped hem.

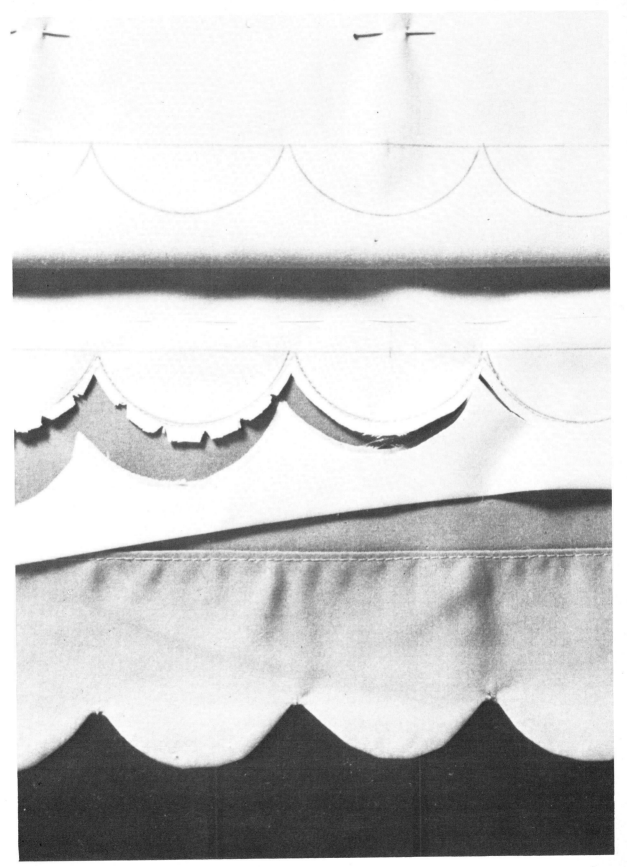

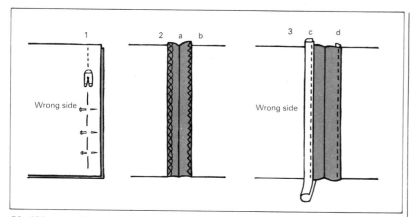

59 (Above) Plain seam: 1 Straight stitched; 2(a) Neatened with overlock, (b) with zig-zag; 3(c) bound, (d) turned and hemmed.

Seams

Dressmaker or plain seams

Sewn on both straight and curved edges. Do not use on fine or sheer fabrics, or those that are liable to strain.

Place the fabric right sides together and tack or pin baste. Machine with straight-stitch along the stitching line. Press out flat and neaten the edges by turning under and straight-stitching, binding, or oversewing (fig. 59).

French seam

This is neat seam, used on sheer fabrics or those that fray badly. Place the fabric pieces wrong sides together. Sew a narrow seam 1 cm ($\frac{3}{8}$ in) from the raw edges. Trim to 3 mm ($\frac{1}{8}$ in), open out and press the seam edges to one side. Fold the fabric with the right sides together and press the seam again, easing over the seam fabric with the fingers. Tack and machine again, 6 mm ($\frac{1}{4}$ in) in from the enclosed seam edge (fig. 60).

Lapped seam

Place the fabric pieces right sides together. Tack or machine baste along the seam line. Open out flat on to the right side, with the seam allowances both lying the same way. Press and tack together. Top stitch by machine through all layers, 2 mm ($\frac{1}{16}$ in) from the folded edge. Remove the tacking.

Tucked seam

Proceed as for a lapped seam, but sew a wider-spaced top stitching line. This is only suitable for straight seams that are not under strain.

Machine fell seam or double-stitched seam

Used on heavier but not bulky fabrics. Excellent for sewing jeans and shirts.

Place the wrong sides of the fabric together and machine as for a plain seam. Press the seam allowances open. Trim one edge to 5 mm ($\frac{3}{16}$ in). Turn the other seam edge over twice to enclose the trimmed edge. Press flat, pin and tack. Machine on the right side close to the edge. The stitches can be worked in a contrasting colour on denim or sports clothes.

Welt seam

This is often worked on heavier fabrics, such as tweed or camel hair.

Machine together, right sides facing. Trim away 5 mm ($\frac{3}{16}$ in) from one seam allowance. Turn the other edge over flat and tack. Top stitch 6 mm ($\frac{1}{4}$ in) away from the seam join on the right.

Piped and corded seam   see Piping.

Shell edging

On the straight   see Decorative edges.
On the cross   see Tucks.

Shirring see Shirring under Gathering.

60 French seam.

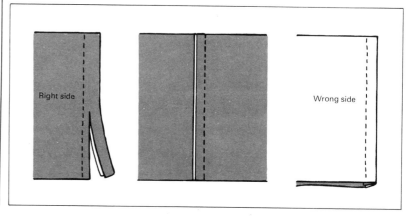

Shoulder pads see *Pads*.

Smocking

Fine woven fabric

Method 1
Prepare the ground fabric by machining rows of gathering threads 6-15mm ($\frac{1}{4}$–$\frac{5}{8}$in) apart, using the long stitch technique (see *Gathering*). Work with a tighter top tension and pull up the bottom threads. Secure all ends and even out the gathers. These threads can be left in after the embroidery is finished. As the fabric will not be stable, back the smocked area with a piece of material. If the threads are removed the smocking will stretch, so allow for this when choosing the stitches.

Method 2
Make the gathers by sewing over a thin cord with a zig-zag stitch using a thread to tone with the background fabric. Sew from the wrong side. Draw up the cords and secure firmly at the ends. Leave the cords in, to make a firmer type of smocking.

Method 3
Work with elastic thread, either zig-zagged over or sewn with thin elastic thread wound round the bobbin.

Embroidering
Make a test sample to find out which of your automatic patterns work best. Try cross stitch, honeycomb or ric rac. Close satin stitch patterns can be opened out by lengthening the stitch or using a pattern elongator. If your machine has few pattern stitches, use blind hem stitch worked first one way, then the other. Three-step zig-zag can be alternated with lines of zig-zag.

Threads
Use machine embroidery thread, or fine mercerized cotton. Thick 100% polyester will give some of the patterns a bolder look. Rayon floss thread wound round the bobbin is sewn from the wrong side of the work. This would be suitable for zig-zag or blind stitch sewing.

Ric-rac or narrow braid

Slightly thicker fabrics, such as wool and cotton mix or fine jersey fabrics, need a bolder approach. Make the gathering rows 1.5-2cm ($\frac{1}{2}$–$\frac{3}{4}$in) apart.

Method
Machine ric-rac or narrow braid on top of the gathered area, using a straight stitch. Cross over in lattice patterns, working across first one way, in a zig-zag, then crossing over the lines on the way back.

Smocking worked with trimotion stitches and three colours of coarse thread through the needle.

Machine grounds for hand smocking

Sew rows of narrow pin tucks, using the twin needles. These tucks are caught together with hand smocking stitches as if they were the hand stitched reeds. This is particularly effective on jersey fabrics. On a larger scale, tucks are sewn on to small areas of knitwear, smocked together with wool.

Stay stitching

A line of straight machine stitches is sewn just outside the stitching line, within the seam allowance, to prevent stretching and to strengthen fabric prior to seaming.

Curves
Stay stitch round the neckline and underarm curves. Sew round any curved line or seam that is to be nicked or slashed. Use this technique on turned scallop hems.

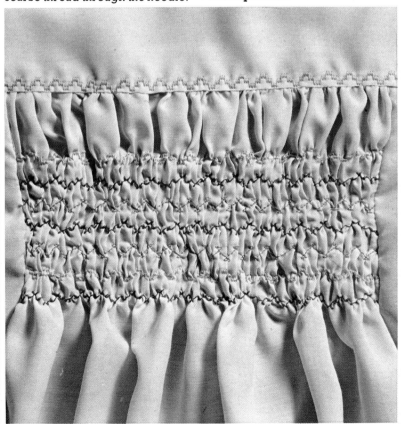

Points

Use stay stitching to double up on acute angles. Sew round collar points, or slashed openings before they are cut.

Stretch fabrics

Stay stitch extra stretchy fabrics such as stretch towelling with triple straight-stitch.

Stitches

The following stitches are listed by their most common names:

Stitches and their uses

Straight-stitch

Garment construction. Top stitching. Stay stitching. Under stitching. Twin- and triple-needle sewing. Quilting. Embroidery and darning. Sewing with elastic thread.

Long straight-stitch

Basting. Gathering.

Zig-zag

Neatening hems and edges. Top stitching. Narrow zig-zag seams on jersey. Quilting. Oversewing patchwork, fur fabric and leather. Attaching tape, braid, lace or elastic. Applying thick threads or cord elastic. Decorative stitching. Buttonholes and button sewing. Twin- and triple-needle sewing.

Blind hem

Blind hemming. Neatening edges. Attaching interfacing. Decorative stitching. Shell edges on fine fabrics.

Overcasting stitches

Neatening edges. Neatening and sewing together in one operation. Sewing on patches and elastic. Decorative sewing.

Stretch stitches
Three-step zig-zag

Seams on very stretchy or elastic fabrics. Sewing lingerie and fine fabrics. Neatening edges. Attaching stretch lace and elastic. Top stitching stretch hems. Decorative stitching. Smocking. Mending.

Elastic blind stitch

Sewing stretch hems. Overcasting.

Triple straight-stitch

Preventing seams from stretching on stretch fabrics. Top stitching. Reinforcing.

T Stitch

Attaching elastic and elastic lace. Sewing blanket hems. Decorative top stitching and edges on stretch fabrics. Drawn thread work. Hemstitching. Applying fabric and patches.

Serpentine stitches: stretch stitch, running stitch, multistretch stitch, lingerie stitch

Attaching elastic, elastic lace and braid. Sewing seams on super-stretch or elastic fabrics. Mending, patching and darning. Sewing fine fabrics and lingerie. Sewing stretch towelling. Sewing knitting.

Stretch overcasting stitches
Stretch overlock

Joining stretch, jersey and knitted fabrics. Neatening edges on stretch fabrics.

Overedge stitch

Sewing and neatening loosely woven or knitted fabrics.

Pullover stitch

Edge sewing stitch for knitted and stretch fabrics.

Bridging stitches

Used for butt joining two seams together. Sewing two seams together held apart with a gap in the middle. Sewing stretch fabrics. Top stitching. Decoration. Smocking.

Decorative and utility stitches
Cross stitch. Honeycomb stitch

Decoration. Sewing down single stretch hems. Sewing on elastic. Sewing over elastic shirring thread. Smocking. Neatening fabrics that fray.

Feather stitch

Decorative and smocking.

Ric-rac

Reversible top stitching. Reinforcing for pockets and seams. Heavy-duty sewing. Decorative.

Arrowhead

Patching. Decorative. Top stitching. Butt joining.

Suede see Leather.

Suede cloth see Pile fabrics.

T

Tacking see Basting.

Tailor tacks

Tailor tacking, fringing or loop foot

Thread loops are sewn over a raised flange on the foot (see under *Fringing*). These thread loops are used for both marking lines on single fabric and making tailor tacks on double fabric.

Method
First mark all the outlines on to the fabric with tailor's chalk. If seam lines are to be marked, pin them together first, then sew double. Thread the machine according to the instruction book and fit the foot with the needle at its highest position. Set stitch-length up to maximum, stitch-width at 2.

Threads

For thicker tufts, thread two fine embroidery or cotton tacking

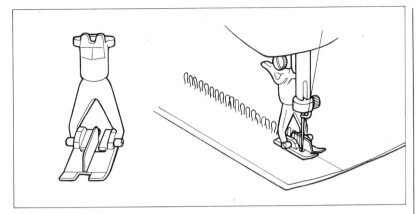

61 Tailor tacking foot.

threads through the needle. Always use a contrasting colour. For thinner fabrics use a single thread with a finer needle. Draw two pieces of fabric apart after sewing and cut between the threads.

Chain stitching

This withdraws easily and is good for marking on single fabric. It can be used on double material, and the chain stitches snipped in between, but is not as effective as the tailor tacks.

Thick fabrics

Woven wool fabric

This can be bulky, and yet remain soft. Use needle size 80-100 (12-16), according to the fabric density; and silk, polyester or mercerized cotton.

Sewing

Set a longer stitch and loosen the top tension slightly. If necessary, loosen the foot pressure, but most machines with universal pressure will cope. Tack or machine baste all seams first, or use an even feed foot. Use welt or top stitched seams on very thick fabrics.

Strong woven cottons

Denim, sailcloth, ticking, upholstery fabrics

Use a large size needle, 100-120 (16-18), and strong mercerized cotton or heavy duty polyester. Set the stitch-length from 8-10 stitches per 2.5cm (1in) and loosen the top tension a little. Reduce the foot pressure if necessary. If your machine has an electronic foot control with full needle penetration power, there should be no trouble in sewing over thick seam joins. Machine fell, or double stitched seams, used on jeans and sportswear, make a very bulky area on the join. Sew slowly, or turn the balance wheel by hand to help the machine over the join. Raise the presser foot lever slightly or adjust the pressure control. Some machines have a double lift for the presser foot, which makes it easier to insert and deal with thick fabric layers.

Laminated fabrics

A woven or knitted fabric is bonded to a backing of synthetic-knit construction. Thicker bonded fabrics have polyurethane foam in between the layers, and all are bonded together. Some thicker woven fabrics have a foam backing only.

Use needle size 90-100 (14-16), ball-point to match a knitted backing, or sharp for foam-backed woven fabrics. Use a long straight-stitch and a lighter top tension.

Sewing

A roller foot, even feed or walking foot, will help when sewing the knit-back fabrics. A roller foot, or a teflon-coated or glide foot, prevents sticking when working over foam. Alternatively, place tissue paper both on top and beneath the foam-backed fabric.

Trim the foam or backing from the seams and use flat fell or welt seams, or double top stitched seams. Reinforce underneath buttonholes, and button positions.

Machine darts together, slit the centre seam, trim the foam and hold back with slip stitches. Stay stitch all bias seams to prevent stretching.

Blankets

Hems

Wind a thicker, contrast thread in the bobbin. Thread the needle with 100% polyester. Use double overlock stitch, T stitch, right hand overlock or plain zig-zag. Tighten the top tension and loosen the bottom tension.

Place the fabric with the wrong side uppermost. Turn over a narrow hem and stitch so that the right hand needle swing goes right over to enclose the fabric edge. If the tension is correct, only the thicker thread will show.

Top stitching

This is machine stitching worked on the right side of the fabric both to decorate and to reinforce seams. Use a slightly longer stitch than for normal sewing. Loosen the top tension enough to make the stitch look rounded.

Threads

For a thinner line use the garment sewing thread or machine embroidery thread no. 50; for a stronger line, machine embroidery no. 30, heavy silk thread, heavy-duty mercerized cotton or 100% polyester.

Bold top stitching

Use a buttonhole twist in the needle, or a fine perle cotton in

Sample showing various top stitches including straight top stitching in a coarse thread. Between the rows of straight stitching is a row of ric-rac in finer thread.

the bobbin which is sewn from the wrong side.

Double thread method

Place two reels of heavy-duty polyester on to the top of the machine and wind the two threads as a single one on to the bobbin, using the bobbin winding mechanism. Work with the double thread in the bottom, stitching from the wrong side of the work. This makes a double, professional type of stitch

Automatic patterns

Try out the patterns on to the project material first. Use zigzag or overcasting stitches as well as the decorative ones. Ric rac stitch is especially suitable, since this is reversible for seams that show on both sides. Try some of the trimotion or reverse stitch patterns on a very narrow setting, or T stitch or one of the overedging stitches.

Twin needles

These will sew a double line, which looks well on smooth fabrics.

Jersey and stretch fabrics

Use one of the trimotion pattern stitches (cross stitch or honeycomb), double overlock or one of the serpentine stitches such as super stretch, running or three-step zig-zag.

Towelling see *Pile fabrics.*
Tracing and marking

Dressmaker's pencil

This is a white marking pencil that does not give a fine line. It is similar to tailor's chalk.

Hard pencil

A hard pencil should be used sparingly as the lead tends to smudge. It can be useful where other methods are inapplicable.

Machining through tracing paper

Lay the design on to the fabric and machine through, using the foot for straight lines, and holding all in an embroidery frame and sewing freely for curved designs. Tear away afterwards.

Pressure or needlemarking

This works well on cotton fabrics. The design is marked with the eye end of a large needle, either directly on to the cloth or through tracing paper.

Prick and pounce

A traditional but very effective marking method. Draw the design outline on typing top paper. Place on to an old blanket or thick cloth. Prick through all lines all the way round with close dots. Use a rolled-up piece of felt to rub talcum powder or chalk through the pricked paper on to dark fabrics, or powdered charcoal on to light fabrics. Lift the paper and join up the dotted lines with a fine brush and water-colour paint.

Tacking

Either tack the design directly, or tack through an outline marked on to tissue paper. This is torn away afterwards. If tracing paper is used, then slit the design line with a sharp needle point. This will prevent the stitches from dragging.

Tucks

Tucks are used to control fullness in garment construction and to form a decorative surface.

Plain tucks

Mark the fabric on the straight grain, fold the right sides together, lay to the right up against a seam guide and sew with a straight-stitch.

Narrow tucks with the edge stitcher

Adjust the foot so that the fabric fold can be fed into one of the slots, to be sewn to the required width. Mark the positions for all the tucks beforehand.

The tuckmarker

This is a straight-stitch machine attachment. It can only be used successfully on cotton fabrics since synthetics will not hold the pressure mark. The first tuck is folded by hand and placed into the tuckmarker guide. This is set to mark the crease line for the next tuck automatically.

Crossed tuck rows

All these methods will produce tucks sewn in parallel rows. The fabric can be creased and tucked the opposite way, with the tuck rows crossing at right angles to one another. Either press the first set of tucks all one way, or sew the first row pushed to the right, the second

Clever use of tucks on gingham.

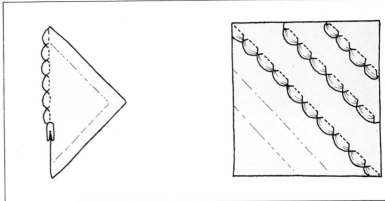

62 Shell tucks on sheer fabric.

to the left. A complete area of alternated rows will produce a ripple effect. This can be worked evenly, or altered to create areas of ridged texture for embroidery. A further design element can be added by working this method on striped or checked fabric such as gingham.

Shell-tucked fabric

This works best on fine or sheer knit synthetics. Fold the fabric on the diagonal, wrong sides together. Set the machine for blind hem stitch and use the zig-zag foot (fig. 62).

Place the fold beneath the foot, with the fabric to the right. Let the left hand needle swing over and enclose the fold with the blind hem stitch. This forms a shell pattern when opened out flat. Sew diagonal rows parallel to one another.

Twin needles

Two needles share a single shank and are set from 1.5 mm ($\frac{1}{16}$ in) to 4 mm ($\frac{1}{8}$ in) apart.

Threading

Two separate top threads are guided as one to the tension discs, where they are separated. The threads pass through the take-up lever and are separated again at the needle-thread guides. If there is only one guide, pass the left hand thread through and have the right hand thread outside before threading the needles. These two top threads share one bobbin thread.

Uses

Twin needles are used for sewing a double straight-stitch line for top stitching, pin tucks, quilting or decorative sewing.

With automatic patterns
Working with the circle stitcher, flower stitcher, spiral stitcher.

For doubling up on suitable patterns see the machine instruction book.

Threads
Use machine embroidery thread No. 50 or No. 30, mercerized cotton No. 60 or No. 40. Alternatively, use fine metallic cord in one needle and plain thread in the other, or thread with two separate shades or use shaded machine embroidery thread.

Sewing
Set a maximum width of 2-2½. Bring the bottom thread to the surface of the fabric by holding on to both needle threads. Sew as for a single thread.

Shadow work
Wind a thick, darker, contrasting colour thread on to the bobbin. Work on organdie or sheer fabric. The thick thread will show through as a pale colour.

Triple needles

Let the middle needle thread pass through the inner tension disc, and the outer needle threads through the outer tension disc. Two threads share one needle thread guide. Set the maximum width at 1½, and no more.

Corners
For turning corners, see *Corners*.

Twin-wing needles see *Wing Needles*.

U
Understitching

This is a line of stitching which secures a facing to the seam allowances and helps to make it lie flat.

Method
Open out the seam and press both seam allowances to the facing side, rolling the seam line over towards the facing.

Tack this into position and machine a line of straight stitches close to the seam join, through the facing and seam allowances only.

Unpicking

Straight seams

Slide a pin under one stitch and pull up a loop of thread. Cut further along and pull out the thread. Turn to the under side and pull out the bottom thread. Cotton will break, but polyester thread must be cut. It is easier to tackle short lengths. This method is safer than using a seam-ripper.

Zig-zag

Draw up the underneath stitch-line, cut and pull out.

Satin stitch or automatic pattern stitches.

Turn to the wrong side. Slit up the underneath stitches with a quick-unpicker or a pair of sharp scissors.

Sewing
Start again a few stitches back, easing the needle into the same holes by turning the balance wheel by hand.

V

Vanishing muslin

This is a special woven backing tacked to the wrong side of fabric to give support for embroidery. It is used as an alternative to working in the

Flowers worked on vanishing muslin.

embroidery frame. The vanishing muslin is melted away afterwards by means of a hot iron. It shrivels first, then disintegrates. Do not use the heat method on synthetics, but tear away the muslin afterwards.

Lace work

Use a cotton thread only and machine directly on to the vanishing muslin. Work a criss-cross pattern of threads that all join on to each other. Iron away the muslin to leave the thread pattern.

This method can be used to make small lace motifs, such as flower petals, leaves or a butterfly. Apply to clothing or use for a three-dimensional effect on embroidered pictures.

Velcro

This is a closure made from two strips of synthetic tape, one with a soft pile surface, the other with a series of tiny hooks. When these are placed with the surfaces facing, the hooks catch on to the pile.

Method
Turn under a single or double fabric hem, slightly wider than the tape. Pin into position and machine stitch all round on the narrow plain edges. Sew the pile side tape first, line up the hooked side and sew on to the matching fabric hem.

W

Wing needles

Wing needles are also called hemstitching needles. They are used to make a decorative hemstitch on fine fabrics, especially organdies, A wing, or spear-shaped flange on either one or both sides of the needle pierces a pattern of holes. The fabric needs to be firm and crisp since the holes close up on soft or synthetic fabric.

Thread
Use machine embroidery thread or mercerized cotton.

Method
Fit the transparent embroidery foot and set the machine for a medium-width short zig-zag.

Single hemstitch rows

Holes will alternate from side-to-side of the zig-zag stitch line. Sew in spaced rows on single layer organdie.

Chess board pattern
Work through two layers of contrasting colour sheer fabric. Machine a square grid pattern with the lines not less than 2 cm ($\frac{3}{4}$ in) apart. Cut away alternate squares from behind.

Waved outline
Decorative outline stitches are sewn in a grid pattern, in double rows with the pattern shapes opposite one another. Cut away the contrast fabric behind.

Multiple hemstitch rows

Work on single fabric. Sew zig-zag stitches to the end of the row. Leave the tip of the needle in the cloth and turn the work. As the second row is sewn, the needle should slip into the same holes. Guide the fabric lightly.

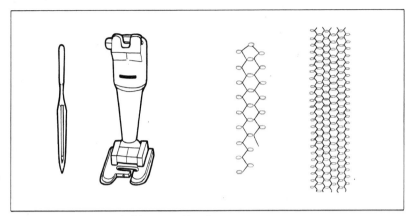

63 A wing or hemstitching needle with vertical flanges which pierce the fabric, making decorative holes where they enter the fabric.

Appliqué

Cover a piece of fabric with this 'trellis' pattern. Cut out leaf or small pattern shapes and apply to a similar fabric. Outline the shape with cord or stitching and cut away the plain fabric from behind.

Twin-wing needle or double hemstitch needle

One plain and one wing needle share the same shank. For threading, see *Twin-needles*. A double stitch line is formed, one plain and one with holes.

64 Twin-wing needle and stitches:
1 Straight stitch; 2 Zig-zag stitch;
3 Blind hem stitch.

Straight sewing

Set the machine to a straight-stitch length of $1\frac{1}{2}$-2. When the first row has been sewn, raise both the needle and the foot and then turn the work. Put the wing needle into the last hole of the row just sewn, lower the foot and sew back, letting the wing needle share the holes of the previous row.

Zig-zag

Set stitch-width 1-2 and stitch-length 1-2 and sew the first row. Let the needle just pierce the cloth on the final left hand stitch. Turn back the balance wheel by hand and lift the presser foot. Turn the fabric round with the wing needle still in the same hole. Sew the second row, sharing the holes.

Decorative stitches

Use the blind hem stitch, three-step zig-zag or any of the forward-sewing, open-line stitches.

Z

Zip fasteners

Alternative machine methods

Centrally placed

Fit the zipper or piping foot.

1 Stitch the seam to just above the zipper opening mark. Reverse a few stitches to secure.

2 Stitch the remainder of the seam, using a long straight-stitch. Neaten the seam edges and press out flat.

3 Place the opened zip, right sides downwards and with the teeth centrally on the seam line on the wrong side of the seam. Have the zipper stops 7mm ($\frac{3}{8}$in) below the top fabric seam line (fig. 65).

4 Pin the right hand tape to the opened out, right hand seam allowance only. Machine down from top to bottom, using the woven tape line as a guide.

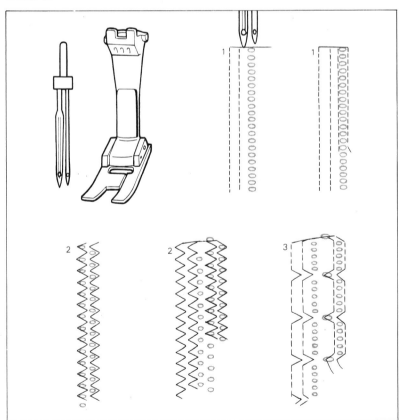

5 Fold out the left-hand seam allowance and stitch the other open zip side in a similar manner.

6 Close the zip and turn to the right side. Press and tack across the bottom of the zip and 6mm ($\frac{1}{4}$in) parallel with the seam line on either side (fig. 65).

7 Top stitch just outside the tacking line on all three sides. Remove all tacking threads and the machine basting from the zipper seam.

In a side seam – lapped method

Allow 4mm ($\frac{3}{16}$in) wider seam allowances.

1 Machine baste the seam opening for the zip.

2 With the top of the seam towards you, open out the right hand seam allowance. Lay the open zip on top, wrong side uppermost, teeth along the central seam line. Have the zipper stops 7mm ($\frac{3}{8}$in) below the top fabric seam line.

3 Stitch along the tape guide line from bottom to top, through the seam allowance only.

4 Close the zip and fold over to the right. Top stitch the seam allowance close to the tape edge.

5 Turn all to the right side. Flatten the zip on to the unsewn seam allowance. Tack through all layers, along the bottom and 1 cm ($\frac{3}{8}$in) parallel with the seam line to the top. Top stitch just outside this line, across the bottom and up to the top. Remove all tacking threads.

Conspicuous

Cut out a slot in the fabric for the zip. Cut a facing to match, and machine in place. Snip corners, turn and press. Centre over the zip, tack in place and machine round close to the faced edges.

Invisible zip using the special foot

These zips do not have teeth, but coils which mesh together. A special foot, designed for this make of zip, slots over the coils to sew the correct distance away. Leave the seam completely open but mark the stitching line.

1 Open the zip. Press the tapes on the wrong side, lifting the coils up and towards the centre.

2 Place one fabric piece right sides up. Lay the zip on top, right sides down, so that the tape is on the seam allowance and the coils centre on the seam line (fig. 66).

3 Position the zip top 7mm ($\frac{3}{8}$in) below the top fabric seam line and hold with a pin.

4 Fit the zipper under the foot to align the inner channel over the coil and the needle hole above the tape.

5 Machine down to the bottom as far as the puller tab. Secure the threads by backstitching and tie the top threads.

6 Sew down the other zipper side the same way, with the right sides of zip and fabric together.

7 Fasten off and close the zip. Tack across the bottom through seam allowances only.

8 Position the needle to the right of the zipper foot and stitch the main seam together, starting just above the zip end and sewing to the bottom of the seam.

Normal zipper foot

Use the same construction. Stitch the tape to the seam allowance with the stitching as close as possible and the chain mesh pushed up.

65 (Below) Machining a centrally-placed zip fastener in position beginning on right side of the turning with the garment wrong side up. The zip tape is then top stitched in place from the right side of the garment with straight stitch.
66 (Bottom) Inserting an invisible zip fastener using a zipper foot.

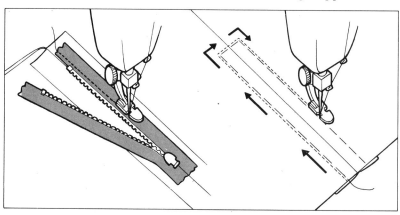

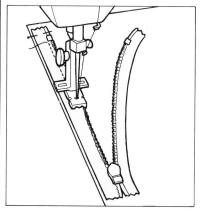

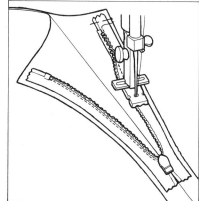

Sewing Machines
Glossary

adjustable hemmer attachment with slotted guide to indicate correct hem width.

alphabet stitcher special attachment on some machines which enables letters of the alphabet to be embroidered.

appliqué pieces of fabric or thick thread applied to a background fabric for decorative purposes.

appliqué perse motifs cut from printed patterned fabric and applied to a background.

automatic machine machine which will stitch automatic non-turn buttonholes and some automatic and utility stitches.

automatic pattern embroidery pattern either built into the machine or worked by an auxiliary cam.

automatic stitch one which can either be dialed or made by inserting a cam in the machine.

balance wheel wheel at the right-hand end of the machine which can be rotated by hand to raise or lower the needle.

ball-pointed needle needle with a blunt, ball-pointed tip for stitching loose-weave fabrics.

basting see tacking.

basting needle needle with a raised eye used with zig-zag stitch setting to work long rows of tacking stitch.

binder foot for applying bias binding to a fabric edge.

blind hemmer foot and guide positions folded fabric edge correctly to be caught by the needle.

bobbin circular spool on which the bottom machine thread is wound.

bobbin case container into which the bobbin is inserted.

broderie anglaise whitework embroidery with holes punched with a stiletto and neatened round the edges with satin or buttonhole stitch.

butt joining two pieces of fabric held close together by a pattern or zig-zag stitch.

buttonholer attachment which can be adjusted to sew buttonholes of different sizes.

carrick-ma-cross Irish technique whereby a design is embroidered on to a layer of muslin on top of net then the surplus fabric is cut away to reveal the net.

chain stitcher substitute for the bobbin case on some machines for sewing chain stitch.

chemical lace specially-treated net which can be worked with decorative stitching then made to disintegrate by applying a hot iron.

circular stitcher device screwed on to the machine bed which acts as a guide for sewing circles.

corded quilting narrow channels of double stitching threaded with cord or thick thread from behind.

coverplate smooth metal plate covering the feed teeth of the machine allowing free movement of the fabric under the sewing foot.

cut-and-sew original method of assembling knitwear using the domestic overlock.

cutwork design on plain fabric in satin or buttonhole stitch in which holes are then cut.

darning addition of thread stitchery to reinforce a worn area of fabric.

drawn thread work threads withdrawn one way from the fabric, while the remaining ones are stitched together to form a pattern.

dual feed built-in even feed device on the Pfaff machine.

electronic machine one in which stitch patterns and various functions are controlled by non-mechanical electric circuitry.

even feed device which allows double fabric to pass under the foot at an even rate without slipping.

eyelet stitcher small plate either added to or

exchanged for the feed teeth for sewing eyelets.

faggoting joining two pieces of neatened fabric together with a decorative stitch.

feather stitch automatic pattern stitch using the reverse feed.

feed teeth rows of metal teeth set into the needleplate below the needle which control the stitch length and the movement of the fabric.

flat bed machine without a free arm.

flower stitcher attachment used in conjunction with automatic patterns to form small flower-like designs.

free arm machine with space beneath the base to allow items such as sleeves and cuffs to be slipped over the needleplate for ease of working.

free embroidery machine embroidery worked without the foot, usually in a frame.

fringe foot tailor tacking foot.

gathering method of reducing fabric fullness by drawing up rows of straight stitch.

guipure embroidered lace with a raised appearance worked by machine nowadays with surplus fabric cut away or dissolved by chemical means.

hemstitching needle machine needle with one or two wings or flanges which pierce the fabric as it sews (see also *wing* and *twin-wing needles*).

Italian quilting see *corded quilting*.

interfacing layer of woven or non-woven fabric inserted between top fabric and facing to give extra body.

interlining lining sandwiched between top fabric and outer lining to give extra weight or warmth.

lettuce hem hem rolled and stitched on the bias with zig-zag on sheer fabrics to give a slightly frilly, decorative edge.

lock stitch straight stitch on conventional domestic sewing machines.

log cabin traditional American patchwork construction.

looping foot see *fringe foot*.

Lurex decorative metallic thread in gold or silver, either flat or as a covering for thin cord.

mitred corner angled seam for reducing excess fabric on a corner.

monogram stitcher guide attachment for working decorative initials by machine.

needleplate flat metal plate through which the machine needle passes and which encloses the feed teeth.

no-snag foot for use with fine, sheer fabrics and those easily caught or snagged by an ordinary machine foot.

open needle needle with an open eye for ease of threading.

overcasting stitching worked along the raw edge of the fabric to neaten it and prevent fraying.

overlock reverse feed or trimotion stitch which encloses and neatens a raw edge.

padded quilting quilting where wadding or padding is inserted into small stitched areas.

patchwork fabric pieces sewn together to form a regular or geometric pattern.

perfect stitch needle needle with a long scarfe or indentation to the eye to aid stitch formation.

pillow quilting small fabric bags, stuffed and sewn up then joined together to form a whole.

pintuck very narrow tuck worked either with a twin needle or an edge stitcher.

piping cord, usually covered by a casing of bias strip, used as a decorative finish to seams and edges.

presser bar device which controls the pressure of the presser foot.

PVC polyvinyl chloride, a synthetic plastic-like material with a high-sheen surface.

quilting process of joining two or more layers of fabric together with decorative stitching (see also *corded*, *padded*, *pillow* and *shadow quilting*).

reverse appliqué patterns cut out through several layers of fabric held together by decorative stitching.

ric-rac manufactured woven flat tape with a serpentine shape.

roller foot machine foot with one or more rollers set ahead of the needle to guide difficult and slippery fabrics evenly on to the feed teeth.

rouleau loops loops made from tubes of bias strip used as decorative fastenings on clothing.

ruffler attachment for straight-stitch

machines with twin blades which form pleats or gathers of various widths.

rufflette tape for attaching to curtain headings.

rug fork long two-pronged fork around which yarn is wrapped for stitching by machine.

satin stitch closed zig-zag stitch.

scalloping method of finishing hems with a decorative shell-shape edge.

Seminole type of patchwork named after the Indians who created it.

shadow quilting double layer of quilted fabric with padding showing through in a contrasting colour.

shirring decorative method of reducing fabric fullness with spaced rows of gathering.

shuttle mechanism stitch-forming mechanism which surrounds the bobbin or shuttle which holds the thread beneath the needleplate.

smocking stitch patterning worked on a section of gathered fabric to form a decoration.

stay stitching line of straight stitch worked round edges such as armholes to prevent fabric stretching and losing shape.

stretch stitch special elongated zig-zag for stitching stretch fabrics such as jerseys and knits.

strip patchwork patchwork made up of long strips, each made up of small pieces which have first been machined together.

swing needle machine machine which can sew zig-zags as well as straight stitch.

tacking long, loose stitches worked as a temporary method of marking a seam or holding two or more layers of fabric together.

tailor tacks small tufts of thread used as markers when matching two or more layers of fabric, particularly in dressmaking.

take-up lever lever with an eye through which the machine thread passes from the tension discs to the needle.

Teflon foot ordinary straight-stitch machine foot coated with durable black Teflon for smooth action and longer wear.

tension discs flat metal discs controlled by springs through which the top thread passes, the grip of the discs controlling the flow of the thread and the tension under which it reaches the needle.

top stitching straight stitch worked along seam edges such as collars and cuffs, sometimes to hold flat but often for purely decorative purposes.

tricot foot foot to aid the sewing of very fine jersey fabrics.

trimotion stitch automatic pattern stitch formed by a side-by-side motion with reverse feed.

triple needle machine needle with three points on a single shank.

tuckmarker attachment which measures the correct width of each tuck as it is sewn.

tufting machine commercial machine used for making tufted lines such as those on a candlewick bedspread.

twin needle machine needle with two points on a single shank.

twin-wing needle machine needle with flanges on each side which pierce the fabric leaving small holes.

underbraider plate with a groove through which cord or braid can be fed while stitching.

vanishing muslin fabric used as a backing and which can either be torn away or ironed away afterwards.

vari-overlock foot foot with a small bar to keep fabric flat and prevent stitches puckering while overlocking fabric edge.

Velcro manufactured fastening strip which holds fast when two layers are put together.

wadded quilting worked through three layers including a top fabric, wadding and lining, this quilting is sometimes called 'English'.

waffling parallel rows of shirring forming a grid pattern.

walking foot silimar to an even feed foot for sewing double layers of fabric likely to creep.

weaver's reed see *rug fork*.

whipped stitch looped stitch formed by tightening the top tension and loosening the bottom tension.

wing needle another name for a hemstitching needle.

zig-zagger attachment for sewing zig-zag on a straight-stitch machine.

Sewing Machines
Index